POWER
and the
Corporate Mind

Abraham Zaleznik

Manfred F. R. Kets de Vries

Chicago, 1985

ISBN: 0-933893-05-1
Library of Congress: 85-71835

Bonus Books, Inc.
160 East Illinois Street
Chicago, IL 60611

The author is grateful for permission to quote from the follow-
ing published sources:
The Diaries of Harold Nicolson: The War Years, edited by
Nigel Nicolson. Copyright © 1967 by William Collins Sons and
Co., Ltd. Reprinted by permission of Atheneum Publishers.
Making It by Norman Podhoretz. Copyright © 1967 by Norman
Podhoretz. Reprinted by permission of Random House, Inc.
Presidential Power by Richard M. Neustadt. Copyright © 1960
by John Wiley & Sons, Inc. Reprinted by permission of John
Wiley & Sons, Inc.
The Ordeal of Power by Emmet John Hughes. Copyright ©
1962, 1963 by Emmet John Hughes. Reprinted by permission
of Atheneum Publishers.

Contents

Foreword   *v*

Foreword — Second Edition   *xi*

1. Introduction   *1*

2. Leadership and Executive Action   *11*

3. Power and Motivation   *39*

4. Power and Human Development   *60*

5. Power and the Fragmented Self   *85*

6. Power and Politics in Organizations   *109*

7. Subordinacy   *144*

8. Superordinacy   *168*

9. Disappointment   *196*

10. Myth and Reality of Entrepreneurship   *215*

11. Minimum Man and Maximum Man   *230*

12. Philosophers and Kings   *257*

Notes   *269*

Index   *281*

Foreword

In 1966, I wrote a book entitled *Human Dilemmas of Leadership** as a preliminary statement on the applications of Freudian psychoanalysis to leadership and organization theory. While writing that book I was just beginning my work in clinical psychoanalysis, although I had been a candidate at the Boston Psychoanalytic Institute since 1960. As a member of the faculty of the Harvard Business School I had had many occasions to conduct research studies in organizations and to consult with companies and government agencies on problems of organization structure, executive relationships, and management succession. Actively involved as a consultant in organizations, securely established in a fine university and professional school, I hardly expected major changes in my outlook and capacities. To my surprise and pleasure, however, my work with patients and my growing appreciation of the complexities and subtleties of psychoanalytic theory served both to sharpen my ability to observe and to focus my interests on power as a practical problem in corporate life and as a theoretical issue in the psychology of leadership.

The clinical perspective of psychoanalysis is the base upon which *Power and the Corporate Mind* stands. This book, written with my coauthor and friend, Professor Manfred F. R. Kets de Vries, continues the work I began with earlier publications

* New York: Harper & Row Publishers.

and, I hope, leads the way to further communications on the psychodynamics of leadership and organizations. While the issues involved in the analysis of leadership have attained particular prominence during the past years, understanding how leaders accumulate and use power is a special and continuing requirement of a democratic society.

Power and the Corporate Mind is not a prescription for solving leadership problems. The way unconscious motivation determines how leaders act can be observed and interpreted for purposes of understanding. The question of how this understanding can be used, apart from insight, really calls upon the intellectual and moral standards of people for whom understanding is often not enough.

In one of his case studies, Freud remarked how easily one can mistake a patient's efforts at self-cure for the illness itself.* In paranoia, for example, the delusional ideas appear to be the sickness, but in the dynamics of the mind they are defensive weapons that ward off depression and the destruction of the self. Leaders also erect defenses and one can easily confuse the world view, when it is based on mistrust, as the pathology of leadership instead of the efforts of a beleaguered power figure to protect himself from self-generated fears and anxieties. In its most pathological form, power acts like perversions and addictions: one can never get enough of what has symbolically become a necessity of existence, and one must forever be on guard against the dangers of losing control of the life-giving substance. The result of this pathological extreme is defense. For society, however, the cost is not simply personal suffering on the part of individuals. The suffering goes beyond one individual's claim for survival. Leaders willy-nilly project their world view onto others. They draw people into coalitions designed to protect the power reservoir and to reinforce their world view. So what appears to be defensive and pathological for an individual weakens the institution and its capacity to act collectively in the interests of human growth and regulation.

It is almost too trite to propose a universal contradiction: the

---

* See the case of Schreber in S. Freud, *The Standard Edition of the Complete Psychological Works of Sigmund Freud,* Vol. XII, London, The Hogarth Press, 1958, pp. 3–82.

power chief executives wield vis à vis the fragility of their subjective hold of power. Expounding a world view, expressing
the habitual optimism of a "doer," a man of action, only reas-
sures momentarily, especially in the presence of an audience
that voices reassurance out of loyalty. But what happens when
the need or urge to reassure disappears, when followers lose
their attachment to leaders and the legitimacy of their power?

The loss of confidence in American leadership in the 1960's
and 1970's, culminating in the resignation of a President under
the shadow of grave misconduct in office, came about not because of structural failures, but as a consequence of personal
tragedy: the incapacity to make human the power available
through the office. This incapacity has reached epidemic proportions and no institution escapes its effects. People who
aspire to power frequently operate on a borrowed ego, a corporate mind in place of a cohesive self and an awareness of who
one is in the flow of history and time. Busily reaching for
power, the individual attempts to cast off unacceptable self-
images and remains divided and ill at ease. The orientation to
power then becomes defensive, as a means for uniting a divided
self and as a substitute for a sustaining ego ideal. Society usually responds to the personal tragedy of its leaders by introduc-
ing additional structural controls so that when power again
corrupts, countermeasures are already in place. But structural
measures can incapacitate a society further since they are coun-
terdefensive. While controls may prevent the disasters that
stem from the abuses of power, they sap energy for the positive
uses of power, for engaging critical issues, formulating strategies, and mobilizing support for actions. There is no substitute
for the confidence leaders engender in their office by personi-
fying widely shared ideals and hopes. If all that comes of the
recent upheavals in authority relations is further mistrust of
leadership, we will have destroyed the basis for action and reinforced the maladies of a bureaucratic society.

The psychoanalytic study of neurotic suffering and the origins of psychic wounds reveals the defensive uses of power. It
also offers insight into the nature of healing. Psychoanalysis
heals through change in psychological structure and, consequently, in the world view individuals use in their orientations

to power and human relationships. But perhaps more challenging is the question of how healing occurs apart from psychoanalysis. Gifted people invariably require some mode of self-healing either through their work, their idealizations, or their intimate relationships. Whatever the means, self-healing implies a capacity to take oneself as an object of personal awareness. Too often, education forces a separation of the person and the roles he is expected to play in society. What then emerges, particularly for executives and public officials, is a split between the private and public self. The private self claims attention usually under the stress of adverse experience and the self-scrutiny that occurs is painful and possibly debasing.

The ancient question "What is the ideal way to educate and train leaders?" has been renewed in the great universities because of obvious deficiencies in the behavior of professionally-trained individuals — lawyers as well as businessmen. Philip B. Kurland, writing in the *New York Times* about proposals to remedy the defects in legal education stated, "the fact of the matter is that law school education — and the fashionable, tax-deductible, post-admission education programs frequently held in plush places — cannot teach wisdom, or experience, or judgment, or dedication, or even morality. And it is essentially from deficiencies in these areas that the profession suffers."* Change law school to business school or a school of public administration and the same statement can be made; we would only add to Professor Kurland's observation the point that what schools cannot, or seem unwilling, to teach is a form of psychological intelligence in which new levels of self-awareness can deepen understanding of historical forces.

Professor Kets de Vries and I have benefited from our association with the Harvard Business School, whose Dean, Lawrence E. Fouraker, provided a great deal of help in freeing time for writing this book. Professor Kets de Vries is also grateful for the assistance provided during his tenure on the Faculty of INSEAD, a management education center in Fontainebleau, France.

I thank my colleagues in the Boston Psychoanalytic Society

* Op. Ed. Page, April 24, 1975.

and Institute and the Group for Applied Psychoanalysis, especially Professor Bruce Mazlish for many valuable hours of discussion. The American Psychoanalytic Association provided an exciting forum in arranging for the discussion group on "Psychodynamic Problems in Organizations." My colleagues and friends in Group VIII of the Center for Advanced Psychoanalytic Studies in Princeton have my special thanks for their contributions to my understanding of psychoanalysis.

My son, Ira Zaleznik, gave me a great deal of help as research assistant and I am especially grateful to him. The list is long of people who helped in typing and editing the manuscript. I want to offer my special appreciation to Richard McAdoo and Grant Ujifusa of Houghton Mifflin Company and Frances L. Apt for their suggestions for improving the various drafts of this book.

Finally, I want to thank publicly my coauthor, Professor Kets de Vries, presently on the Faculty of Management at McGill University. He sustained, with infinite patience and good cheer, what must have been a nerve-wracking experience in the changes we brought about before completing this book. I believe our respective egos are none the worse for wear, and we look forward to continued friendship.

ABRAHAM ZALEZNIK

April 26, 1975
Lexington, Massachusetts

Foreword — Second Edition

Power and the Corporate Mind first appeared under the terrible shadow of two critical events in our national consciousness — the Vietnam tragedy and the disgrace of President Nixon. The outcome of American involvement in Southeast Asia shocked us into the realization that military might alone is a poor resource in struggles involving people committed to ideas as well as land and material riches. The trauma of Watergate forced us to relearn a lesson as familiar to the ancients as it is to us now, a lesson well narrated in literature, from the Greek tragedies to contemporary works. This lesson, simply put, is that human beings determine whether the power they acquire and wield is used for good or evil. In the encounter between man and organizations, the individual is far more potent a force than most of us now believe.

President Nixon's abuse of power, position and trust reminded us that people can use offices they hold as a stage for acting out their personal conflicts and insecurities. These personal conflicts can have severe public consequences such as the decline and fall of major corporations or the erosion of trust in people who hold authority. We wrote *Power and the Corporate Mind* in order to bring man back to center stage in the drama of organizational life. Vietnam, Watergate, and many other terrible events of the last decade have confirmed our intention. Organizational theorists can no longer claim that what happens in public and private organizations and institutions is the net effect of a calculus of rewards and costs.

Power in organizations has two faces. One face looks outward, assessing the external sources of power in the structure of organizations, the allocation of roles, and the definition of responsibilities and rights. The other face looks inward, examining what goes on inside the power holder. The two faces are linked. Psychoanalysis reveals that the events in the external world that are significant to the power holder are mirrored within. People are products of experiences they have never relinquished. Personal history will always make its claim even though it operates silently and, paradoxically, usually beyond the individual's awareness.

Leadership revolves around these inward representations within powerholders and within the people over whom they exercise power. The mutual expectations of leader and the led are a product of past experiences manifesting themselves in the present. Leaders receive attachments from those who surround them which are a legacy of their past experience. And a leader is caught up by his or her own past and the past of the organization over which he or she presides.

In cases where power acts as a pathogen, careful scrutiny suggests that unconscious motives which originated in the person's past have come to dominate perceptions of the value, meaning, and uses of power. In some cases the need for power leads to perverse mental activity. A perversion is the inability to satisfy an appetite, whether for food, sex, or some substance that is symbolically overloaded in its meaning for the individual. Power is susceptible to this overloading and, consequently, the individual cannot get enough of it. Psychoanalytic investigation reveals that people who engage in perversions embed idealizations of their own selves and other important figures from their past histories in symbols of power, money, sex, and food. These idealizations cannot tolerate the realities of living people, the nature of life and the limits to individual and collective power. This confrontation between what is ideal to the individual and real in the world as we know it can drive some people mad with frustration and anger.

Even those leaders who escape the ravages of power as a perversion are engaged in personal conflicts that arise from their past histories. It is plainly false to assert that leaders who are effective are "normal," while those who are ineffective are "neurotic." Creative individuals, and we would define leadership as a form of creativity, are engaged simultaneously in working out their internal problems as well as problems that exist in the external world. What distinguishes effective from ineffective leaders is not the presence or absence of neurosis, but the ability of the individual to take himself or herself as an object of study in isolation or in interaction with others. To reflect on one's self while transacting business with others of lesser power, is one way of fulfilling Socrates' admonition to "know thyself."

Power is the potential one individual has to change the thinking and behavior of other people. Executives who activate this potential influence the perceptions, attitudes, and values of the people who ultimately will accept, reject, or modify executive aims and directives. As a precondition for acting on other people, the would-be leader must engage in self-reflection in order to heal the rifts within the psyche, tame the urges of power and aggression, and discover and utilize talents. Only thus can power enrich other people's lives.

In *Power and the Corporate Mind* we move beyond the perspective of clinical interpretations of power and pathology in organizations, for it is clear to us that the problems of power and leadership involve more than the playing out of neurotic impulses in executive roles.

A wider view of power involves looking at contemporary attitudes toward achievement and progress. Although scientists and business managers hold widely different world views, most of them share the belief that there is no limit to achievement. Scientific and technological revolutions unleashed the age-old fantasy that man can conquer nature. In business management, this belief has taken the form of believing that no goal is beyond the reach of people who work hard and cooperate.

This belief in the possibility of unlimited achievement has created a climate of optimism. The optimism of science is well-founded. The last century has seen monumental advances in the physical and biological sciences which have enabled people to enjoy improved standards of living and physical health. And there is no evidence of a slow-down in the rate of scientific advancement. In the information sciences, biology, physics, and chemistry researchers are at work uncovering new knowledge. The results from laboratories are just as rapidly applied to such diverse fields as computer engineering, medicine, and technology. The factory of today has gone far beyond the knowledge that led to the assembly line and mass production during the first half of the twentieth century. Today, we are in the midst of a technical revolution in which information and communication capabilities are altering fundamentally the relationship between man and machine.

Among managers optimism contains cross currents. On the one hand, it leads to the quick embrace of novel material. No technique escapes management attention provided it promises progress. On the other hand, this same optimism can lead to smugness, complacency, and an ostrich-like attitude toward any information that threatens the manager's sense of control. This current of optimism has led to the conviction that good managers can manage anything (without previous experience or knowledge of what they are managing). This disregard of limits to managerial power, incidentally, corresponds to the way politicians often think about America's political power. Vietnam should have taught us a different lesson just as the current wave of divestiture should teach us that a corporate umbrella sheltering a conglomeration of unrelated businesses will collapse under the burden of a special form of misuse of authority and power.

This misuse of power occurs when corporate staffs beholden to the office of the chief executive overextend their reach in the control of operations. Very bright but inexperienced people often use power in the name of the chief executive's office to initiate thought and action. Surprisingly, this incongruity in power is often carried out in the name of a decentralization which represents a victory of form over substance. Watergate forewarned us of this problem. For the corruption of power in that case lay not only in the insecurity and anxiety of the President, but also in the distortions that arose from the power position of his White House staff. Young people with heady staff assignments saw that their careers hinged on acting single-mindedly on behalf of the personal interests of the chief executive. They lacked the perspectives on power that come only with maturity. Consequently, they overreached their intelligence and forced the blunders that ultimately led to Watergate. This cause of failure in the Nixon White

House also exists in those American corporations that believe a manager can manage anything and that process is the ultimate lever that allows people to transcend the limits to power.

The main theme of *Power and the Corporate Mind* is that, in spite of centuries of economic modernization and technological progress, the fundamental biological and psychological structure of man has not changed. The evolution of personality continues to be the slow movement from dependency to independence and competency. Above all, people have not outgrown their need for attachment.

This last quarter of the twentieth century has been characterized as an age of narcissism. The imperial self in the United States has displaced the ideal of self in the expression of talents, intimacy of relationships and achievement of an ethical standard in which giving is favored over getting.

In understanding this age of narcissism, we should take care not to mistake symptom for illness. The narcissistic personality is less an adaptation than a symptom of the stresses of living in an age where material progress continues to outstrip people's capacities for self-understanding and control. There is no greater need for self-understanding today than in the people who achieve positions of power.

Power and the Corporate Mind is a contribution to this search for self-understanding. It is no less vital a search today than it was ten years ago when the book first appeared. In presenting psychoanalytic knowledge to the modern manager, we ask our audience to put aside the impulse to find the quick cure, the simple message, and the easy lessons of how to go about running a business. Instead, we ask our readers to go on a journey during which reflection will be more important than action, and paying heed to one's own experience will be infinitely more valuable than grasping for answers.

May, 1985

Abraham Zaleznik
Konosuke Matsushita
  Professor of Leadership
Harvard Business School
Cambridge, Massachusetts

Manfred F.R. Kets de Vries
Professor of Organizational
  Behavior and Management
  Policy
European Institute of Business
Administration (INSEAD)
Paris, France

CHAPTER 1

Introduction

GENERAL DWIGHT DAVID EISENHOWER had to make a decision during the 1952 presidential campaign. Senator Joseph McCarthy of Wisconsin had attacked the loyalty and integrity of General of the Army George C. Marshall, Eisenhower's friend and former superior. As the campaign train approached Milwaukee, where Senator McCarthy would join Eisenhower on the platform, the presidential aspirant had a prepared text that read:

> To defend freedom . . . is to respect freedom. This respect demands, in turn, respect for the integrity of fellow citizens who enjoy their right to disagree. The right to question a man's judgment carries with it no automatic right to question his honor.
> Let me be quite specific. I know that charges of disloyalty have, in the past, been leveled against General George C. Marshall. I have been privileged for thirty-five years to know General Marshall personally. I know him as a man and a soldier, to be dedicated with singular selflessness and the profoundest patriotism to the service of America. And this episode is a sobering lesson in the way freedom must not defend itself.[1]

Despite the conviction that produced these lofty thoughts, Eisenhower, at the last moment, submitted to political pressure and struck the defense of Marshall from his text. He allowed himself to appear with McCarthy and remained mute following a vicious attack on an honorable statesman and friend. The doubts about Eisenhower's capacity to move from the military to the White House began to harden.

Emmet John Hughes, who wrote the words Eisenhower could not bring himself to read, suggested that the dilemma for Eisenhower was personal as well as practical, and that the decision was the result of competing claims on Eisenhower's self-image and personality.

> . . . the event gave warning that certain qualities in the man, even virtues in themselves, could be wrenched in the play of politics and made to seem misshapen. Clearly there was in him a profound humility — a refusal to *use* the full force of his personal authority or political position against a critical consensus. He saw himself realistically as a man of military affairs, a stranger to political affairs, surrounded by Republican leaders who — by their own testimony, at least — were political "experts." He would have abhorred any image of himself as a man-on-horseback, crudely importing military discipline into a civil arena. Hence, even if the self-denying constraint drove him close to a teeth-grinding anger, he must shun the merest suggestion of martial arrogance. He must show and prove himself, in short, a modest enough member of "the team." He would use this phrase through the years, long after it grew stale, to describe or to commend all his political associates be they his cabinet or his White House staff, his Administration or his party. I am sure that the word "team" genuinely expressed for him a set of virtues transferred from the military life: coordination and cooperation, service and selflessness. Yet I often wondered if the simple, terse exhortation were not addressed, perhaps only half-consciously, as much to himself as to others.[2]

One question begets another. If Eisenhower exhorted his staff to act like members of a "team," to cooperate and subordinate the self in the name of higher interests and ideals, and if, in exhorting others, Eisenhower sought *unconsciously* to force himself to curb his own aggression, what explains his continuing self-restraint in the face of unprecedented power and prestige? Undoubtedly, shifting one's leadership and power from the military arena to civilian government (and politics) could create anxiety. There is a need to absorb and to react to new responsibilities and uncertain standards of conduct. But Eisenhower was not a stranger to responsibility or to the world of politics, especially after his successful tenure as Supreme Allied Commander. Perhaps the uncertainty and the exhortation were intended to restrain his own ambition and prevent him from committing tactical errors while he strengthened his base of power. But the evidence suggests that, for Eisenhower, personal ambition and the desire for power meant far less, at least consciously, than loyalty and the sense of duty. The primacy of the team over the man, of loyalty to others over self-interest, inhibit ambition and subordinate one's own desires to the wider interest. So long as interest in power can remain attached to universal ideals, the risks of abusing power diminish.

Humility in a chief executive officer is often seen as a virtue, not a vice. However, humility can stem from the fear of exercising power and the anxieties of command as much as from ideals of teamwork and cooperation. If humility is a reaction to self-doubts and to a sense of illegitimate power, then sins of omission will be the consequences. Though no one questions Eisenhower's integrity (in fact, his simplicity and good will accounted for much of his appeal), controversy about his leadership centered on his reluctance to assert himself and to assume the initiative when he was President.

Power is an ugly word. It connotes dominance and submission, control and acquiescence, one man's will at the expense of another man's self-esteem. The word also evokes images of a human disorder, in which pride and ambition disturb perception. Power can obscure vision, distorting it by manipulation and intrigue. Yet it is power, the ability to control and influence others, that provides the basis for the direction of organizations and for the attainment of social goals. Leadership is the exercise of power.

If there were complete equality among men, power would be absent from their interaction. Individual self-interest would necessarily give way to cooperation. But the moments when personal interests overlap rather than conflict are rare. As society and its institutions become more complex, divisions of function and status define special loyalties and preferences. The aim of particular groups has often been the preservation of power and advantage against encroachments from competing interest groups.

Men engaged in cooperative activity must, for the sake of a shared purpose, make an alliance among their individual wills; and purpose requires a common effort, which can be thwarted when there is mistrust of those in power. Mistrust, either of the person or of the position, can block decision-making. But some resolutions to the conflict between power and purpose do exist.

One solution is ideology — a vision of an ideal state in which the exercise of power is accepted in the service of belief. But when beliefs take hold strongly, ideology can become a dogma that violates humanity and dignity. New conflicts then arise between personal conscience and collective ideals.

Another traditional solution to the conflicts created by power is charismatic leadership. The magnetic pull of a charismatic leader engages personal loyalty, assuring acceptance of goals and decisions. But what prevents such leaders from becoming tyrants? Plato spoke of philosophers and kings. He envisioned a society in which leaders would possess the gift bestowed by reflection and the perspective gleaned from education. An educated mind has the capacity for both imagination and self-control. According to Plato's view, the taming of power depends partly upon the personal qualities of leaders, their psychological make-up as well as their schooling. But the Platonic leader, or any charismatic leader, does not possess much attraction for contemporary society. Recent history has shown, tragically, that such leaders are often destructive and primitive in their actions and ideals. So most societies have established a rule of law and not of men. Trust, therefore, resides in institutions and not in personalities.

Vesting power in institutions, a third solution to the problem of control, poses its own problems. As power is distributed among office holders in institutions, the determination of goals and the allocation of resources become complicated. Moreover, the leaders who move to the top of an organization are not necessarily the most capable or imaginative. Too often the mantle falls to the survivors of organizational politics: those who reflect the characteristics of the corporate mind, a mind trained to calculate but not feel, to value means over ends, and, above all, to preserve power even at the expense of policy and initiative.

Traditional solutions aimed at controlling abuses of power ignore personality. Psychoanalysis, the science of the unconscious developed by Sigmund Freud, now makes it possible to understand how the personalities of leaders ultimately determine power conflicts. Because the emphasis is on the life cycle, attention shifts to the origins of the need for power early in life and the roots of anxiety and defensiveness in the adult who seeks and holds corporate office. The adult who assumes leadership in organizations brings to his job an orientation to power that is built partly on fantasy derived from the past and partly on an objective assessment of situations and realities. When, as they frequently do, elements of fantasy and reality intermingle, one cannot easily distinguish the forces acting upon leaders. These forces are not simply realities that people can assess, measure, and validate in consultations with associates. There are strong subjective elements — the creative projection of an idea in the mind of a leader, or irrational fear, or distrust, all of which can dominate the realities of objective situations.

People generally trust leaders. The sign on the barroom door cautions patrons, "Don't shoot the piano player, he's the only one we've got"; similarly, the threat of a chaotic, leaderless organization is often more disturbing than continuing acquiescence to mediocre or impulsive executives. After one has initially extended trust to a leader, the idea of disturbance in his personality will be hard to accept. And yet if he abuses power or becomes reckless, his private sources of motivation must be called into question. What is it that drives a leader into irrational decisions? What causes him to make impossible demands on the institution?

In 1968, a symposium of the American Psychiatric Association on "Private Conflicts with Public Consequences" considered whether political leaders are more vulnerable than ordinary people to mental illness and other stress reactions. The argument presenting the psychological dangers of power and position stated that the power held by executives impedes their capacity to protect themselves against their own excesses. The pressure of decisions requires some defense against being overwhelmed by information and the complexity of problems. Executives, therefore, often insulate themselves against reality with staffs whose loyalty is primarily to them. The leader who engages loyalty in the broad sense has only a short way to go before he requires strict protection of his prerogatives and unwavering endorsement of his monolithic power. Since his staff depends upon him, its members are likely to sift out unpleasant information, supplying only the good news he expects.

Abuses of power in organizations are both subtle and cruel. It is no longer a simple matter of dominance by leaders and submission by subordinates. For example, the failure to act when one should causes trouble for those dependent upon executives, and when the leader takes no visible action, subordinates find it difficult to express their anger. Consequently, the pain must be endured silently, further depersonalizing the superior-subordinate relationship.

The use of scapegoats (or so-called "lightning rods") to draw controversy away from the chief executive is another form of cruelty. Its political justification is the preservation of a range of options for the executive. Using people for ulterior motives, however, often creates in him a guarded atmosphere, even a kind of paranoid wariness. In time, as events run counter to expectation, the executive becomes vulnerable to rage and depression. The usual antidote to depressive reactions, probably the most serious indication of impending psychological chaos, is the emergence of the grandiose self-image within the psyche — an internal pattern that is often reinforced by a misguided staff.

The ancient Greeks warned of hubris, the sin of pride that refuses to set or acknowledge the limits of power. Psychoanalysis explains hubris as the failure of an individual to modify or relinquish a grandiose self-image. In its extreme form, grandiosity becomes megalomania. The wise use of power requires a sense of time and progression. Grandiosity knows nothing of time, since all problems appear in the present; any delay between intention and action frustrates the victim of hubris. Where overweening pride exists, perspective about the self in relation to others and about the consequences of individual action is lost.

Grandiosity and the resultant distortions of one's sense of power are not confined to "great men," whose self-esteem is independent of a position held within an organization. The most vulnerable leaders are those who view themselves as "self-made" men even in the face of their dependence on position and power. These men reject their past, because the unconscious hostilities toward themselves and other people derive from ambivalent attitudes toward parents and siblings, and therefore function with a poor sense of time and of human relations.

Paradoxically, unconscious anger often supports achievement and the rise to power in corporate life; it can produce a certain blandness in character, an outward compliance to the forms and conventions of corporate activity. The same aggression prevents the individual from developing attachments and commitments and sustains, in the compliant leader, a morally neutral attitude, reducing guilt or qualms about actions that would bother more sensitive people. For the self-made man, the danger of unconscious hostility is that, once in power, he may find his characteristic forms of control inadequate; grandiosity and hubris may then make themselves evident.

There is a certain wisdom in corporate affairs that safeguards the institution against grandiosity, both latent and overt, in its leaders. Today the safeguarding takes the form of coalitions and consensus leadership. Corporate giants like General Motors do not appoint one man as the head of the organization. Instead, there is a troika or some other constellation of people with corporate roles, and the mechanisms for making decisions require consensus in the executive coalition. Since each executive in the group has a constituency, direct or implicit, genuine consensus requires a flow of communication. In one sense, the communication assures wider participation than one customarily expects of corporate structure, but it does not necessarily insure high quality in the decisions made or the feeling of participation. In consensus politics, interchanges and decisions are visible; they take place on the surface of events, reflecting the need for acquiescence and participation. At the same time, an interchange proceeds behind the scenes, requiring adroitness, control of emotion, and a certain toughness of character to support the calculation of interests and outcomes for all the groups involved.

Our system of education for leadership fails to allow for the influence of personal forces on political events. A successful career depends on the accord of personal character with the social realities of an organization. Although formal training for a career emphasizes the content of work and profession, it does not prepare a person for the human problems he will face in coming to terms with corporate life. Politics is a people-oriented activity, and large-scale organizations are inherently political in their reliance on power to make things happen. If executives learn to play the game of power without first resolving their unhappy attachment to other people, the stage is set for destructive or ineffective leadership.

On June 19, 1973, Dan Rather, interviewing Barry Goldwater for CBS News, elicited a direct comment on the importance of personality and leadership style. Responding to Rather's question on the causes of Watergate, Goldwater stated that he thought Watergate had occurred because of Nixon's being a "loner," a "man who never lets his hair down in front of others." Consequently, Goldwater suggested, President Nixon's personality fostered an atmosphere in which subordinates ran wild.[3]

Goldwater was correct in attributing the atmosphere of an executive structure to the personality of its chief, but his statement did not explain the origins of this atmosphere and its significance in the lives of those who worked in it. People often reveal themselves to others without knowing it. They express needs, reflect fears, and even expose their vulnerabilities, all the rituals and role-playing in corporate life notwithstanding. Signals appear despite conscious control by leaders of an organization; they are received subliminally; people respond to them in ways that create a consistent and recognizable group atmosphere.

The rationalizations for policies and decisions in an executive apparatus also tellingly reflect the character of the group atmosphere. Is it only to preserve power? If so, the language of decision will portray a world of the defenders of power whose bastion is stormed by enemies, both the infidels and the ignorant. Is it to heal divisions and to create reconciliations? If that, then the language of decisions will speak in softer terms, evoking the drama of suffering and its amelioration.

All of these projections of leadership and power reflect the personality of its central figure, the chief executive. In spite of attempts to detach leadership and atmosphere of the group from the heavy influence of personality, that influence still prevails, even in coalition structures. Its prevalence stems from the power of human emotions, from the extraordinary way people take in and retain another person's view of himself (even beyond his own will to control it).

Psychoanalysis, especially when applied to political theory and action, often oversimplifies. There is never a single cause of a complex situation and it would be absurd to reduce corporate problems to the personality of one man. Yet to exclude the effects of personality and the drive for power on institutions is another kind of oversimplification. Social and political analysis can be well served by a combination of both institutional and psychological realities.

Another danger in using psychoanalysis in political studies is the distortions that can occur when one uses emotional illness to explain behavior. It is true that psychoanalysis began with Freud's heroic effort to cure mental illness. But the therapeutic procedure of psychoanalysis is also a method of investigating the psyche. When investigation is combined with a search for a cure in which the patient participates fully, easy distinctions between sickness and health fall by the wayside. Behavior that appears normal on the surface can later be shown to contain serious mental conflicts. Similarly, the symptoms of mental illness may reflect the best solution available to a person in his efforts to protect his sense of self-worth.

The striving for, and the expression of, power frequently involves forces that make men sick. The demagogue in politics, the manipulator in business, the megalomaniac in science, and the depressive in literature struggle to demarcate illness from creativity and to maintain this demarcation at whatever the personal cost. In psychoanalysis, one becomes aware how subtle is the distinction between sickness and health, as one perceives the fine line between defense and adaptation, between regression and progression. Above all, we owe to psychoanalysis the notion that, however bizarre and meaningless behavior may appear, significance and order exist if one can exercise the tools of perception and empathy to discover patterns in thought and action.

The traditional modes of analyzing power and decision have been exhausted. Technical models of rational behavior, of organizational behavior, and of bureaucratic imperatives can no longer instruct us. It is, therefore, timely to reconstruct how man orients himself to power and how he expresses this orientation in leadership capabilities and in political behavior.

In the chapters that follow, we range from corporate behavior as a form of political expression to the psychology of power in the preservation of self and identity. These two themes merge in our concern for the attachment of superior and subordinate in struggles over dependency and control, and in the search for self-esteem. The central psychological theme is the shifting anxieties associated with human development. The stability and equilibrium of one age form the ground upon which the conflicts of another are fought and the compromises of character are decided. The problem of loss of self-esteem and the search for restitution of some idealized past move counter to the forces that push the individual to repress and circumvent painful experience.

Throughout these psychoanalytic interpretations runs concern for the meaning of power and the nature of the corporate mind. For the person seeking a career of leadership, fitting into and becoming fit for various kinds of organizations frequently involve a certain reduction of self-esteem. The costs need accounting in the emotional economics of corporate relations.

CHAPTER 2

Leadership and Executive Action

A man who wishes to make a profession of goodness in everything must necessarily come to grief among so many who are
not good. Therefore, it is necessary for a prince, who wishes
to maintain himself, to learn how not to be good, and to use
this knowledge and not use it, according to the necessity of
the case . . .[1]

—*Machiavelli*

MACHIAVELLI'S ADVICE to leaders can be taken in two ways: either to become amoral, manipulative, expedient without regard
for ethical concerns, or to become thinkers closely attuned to
the distinction of one situation from another, much like the
physician who is careful to diagnose before he prescribes. When
Machiavelli says to the prince "learn how not to be good," one
should not assume he is advocating immoral and unethical
leadership. After all, the definitions of being good are all too
often couched in the language of self-interest and conventional
wisdom. If being good is limited to simple acceptability, there
is no real need for *leadership,* for change in the face of new
problems and new human concerns.

The critical ingredient of Machiavelli's prescription for
leadership is the discernment of the "necessity of the case."
What complicates matters is the fact that the case cannot be
isolated from the character of the leader. Inevitably, his vision
or blind spots determine the limits of his actions. So the proper
object of the study of leadership is the individual in a situation — the "case," so to speak. The case also includes the people
close to the leader, people who offer or withhold advice based
on their position and personality. In the words of George

Homans, the need in the analysis of organizations is "to bring man back in."[2] Man has been left out in the interests of clarifying structure and process, which attributes more to the powers of rationality than experience permits.

An analysis of leadership must concern itself more with individual action in human situations than with structure in relation to impersonal forces. It is true that there are impersonal factors that seem to put pressure on people to act in selected ways. But if the key to initiatives lies in the experience of forces outside persons, that judgment is sustained by insight. Insight blends the external and objective with self-knowledge, so the personal strengths and weaknesses of the leader enter the case realistically.

There are three problems, common to all organizations, that test definitions of what is impersonal and personal in executive action. The first is the decision to organize, which establishes the formal structure and distributes authority. The second is control, the regulation of behavior and the willingness of people to meet expectations. The third is action itself — the crucial meeting of man and situation where, for whatever reasons, leaders decide to commit themselves to certain alternatives and exclude others. These problems appear and reappear in organizations, reflecting the tensions between individual interests and the needs and demands of other people and the organization. Machiavelli's "necessity of the case" governs when executives face issues of organizing, controlling the actions of others, and becoming personally involved in weighing options and making decisions.

The Distribution of Authority

Directing an organization means that one must arrive at some basis for allocating authority so that relative power is proportional to responsibility and competence. Any allocation must meet two criteria: first, the allocation must be rational, and second, the allocation must be just. Rationality means that the distribution of authority is consistent with the goals and objectives of the organization and that resources are used economically. A sense of justice and equity in the distribution of authority is a condition of cooperation; authority and its uses will then be seen as legitimate and worthy of commitment and work.

Although rationality and justice may appear, in principle, absolute, ambiguities arise in their implementation. People will often spend hours improving the inputs upon which rational decisions are supposedly made, while ignoring the conflict inherent in converting abstract principles into concrete action. There are practical limitations to pure rationality and justice; if there were not, the decisions concerning the allocation of authority could be programmed for a computer as a simple problem: producing the greatest output from the least input of human effort.

The limitations to rationality in the establishment of an organizational structure are imposed by several factors. First, the distribution of authority is only in part a quantitative problem (that is, how much authority to allocate among the various levels in a hierarchy). The quality of authority figures also as an important part of the problem.

We can thank Max Weber for his theoretical formulations on authority and bureaucracy, which outlined the types of authority existing in organizations. He discusses three types: traditional, legal, and charismatic.[3]

Traditional authority, Weber says, is based on historical precedents that sanction certain individuals by birth and succession to the rights and responsibilities in governing. Implicit in traditional authority is the extrarational basis on which custom and prerogative depend. By contrast, legal authority formally prescribes the rights of individuals occupying positions in the structure to issue commands. The formal rights and obligations can be found in such documents as the Constitution of the United States. Other forms of legal authority exist in the charters of corporations and in their by-laws. These documents specify offices, powers, rules of tenure, methods of selection, and, perhaps most important, the means by which modifications may be made in the structure of legal authority (in the form of amendments, additions, and deletions to the by-laws).

The third type of authority in Weber's scheme is charismatic.

Some individuals have authority, that is, the ability to influence by the nature of their personality, which seems to project a kind of spiritual or inspired leadership. Great mystics, religious leaders, and political leaders exert influence by the force of their personality. For example, Rasputin had an enormous influence in the court of the last Russian tsar because of his emotional hold over the tsarina and the hope he proffered for the cure of her hemophiliac son, the tsarevich. The emotional basis of charisma is a subject to which we shall often return, especially since the interaction of charisma and legal or traditional authority is of special interest in modern organizations. For the present, we can refer to Freud's study, "Group Psychology and the Analysis of the Ego,"[4] in which he likened the charismatic effect to the primary emotional ties of the child to the parent.

Weber's work on authority and bureaucracy provided a framework for the analysis of modern organizations, which are products of such broad technological, economic, and political forces as the Industrial Revolution, the stabilization of the nation-state, and the separation of ownership and management in large-scale enterprise. As with other theories based on ideal types, Weber's analysis spawned a generation of studies that showed how far from reality were the ideal types of bureaucracy. In Weber's ideal bureaucracy, legitimacy and acceptance of authority rested on the clear relationship of organizational resources to explicit objectives (rationality), and on the enforcement of rules designed to overcome the tyranny of men's passions and ambitions. Rationality and justice are, indeed, ideals; but, as a generation of researchers showed, the real world falls short of the ideal. The best people are not necessarily selected to exercise authority, and, instead of assuring equity, rules dominate bureaucracies and weaken the capacity of men to perform.

Any discussion of the rules for the allocation and exercise of authority does not account for motivations that bind people in authority relationships. The need for dependency, a human need seldom acknowledged in employment contracts, is characteristic to some degree of men at work in all levels of the hierarchy. Dependency needs may be expressed in the desire for approval and for close relations with an authority figure, or in the wish for satisfying relations with equals.

Departures from ideal bureaucracy also result from the complexity and specialization of work roles in modern organizations, which has led to the recognition of professional authority or expertise as a basis for power and influence in organizations. Professional authority differs from hierarchical or positional authority because it is based on the applications of expert knowledge to the work of the organization. As Philip Selznick has shown in his study of the Tennessee Valley Authority,[5] those who use knowledge and skill rather than hierarchical position for influence tend to develop their own goals and to seek independence from the dominant authority structure. It is a small step from independence to competition; one can view an organization as an arena for internal competition as well as for cooperation.

The culture of professional authority favors equality over hierarchy and builds on the notion of a "flat," "organic" organization structure. The number of authority levels between the top and the bottom of the organization are fewer in flat as compared with pyramidal, "mechanistic" structures, which are built on the principle of chain of command — a rational principle derived from an optimal number of subordinates who can report to one executive. Lateral communication is emphasized, as is the use of committees and ad hoc work groups or task forces with rotating membership. The ideals of an egalitarian culture are flexible leadership and functional influence, in which the type of leadership a group needs, depending upon its task and emotional problems, comes from appropriate members, regardless of their hierarchical position and of the formal lines of authority. Indeed, leadership, especially of the type vested in position, becomes ambiguous, if not blunted, and there is a reduction of the social distance that is in pyramids, with their clearly delineated status differences from level to level in the organization.

This brings us to another motivational constraint in the operation of different systems of authority. Social distance and status differences tend to produce anxiety — the fear of isolation felt by the leader and the uncertainties of self-esteem suffered by the subordinate. The formation of informal groupings and cliques, socially contrived means for buffering the effects of anxiety, counteracts the effects of social distance. To put the problem in another way, "love flees authority"; for many individuals, it is easier to get help from an equal than from a boss. Given the potential hazards of anxiety, especially when the nature of work requires interaction, informal groups and affiliations spring up to counterbalance the effects of hierarchy and its implications of evaluation, control, and damaged self-esteem.

The discovery (and rediscovery) of informal organization highlights the weaknesses of the various rationalistic models (including ideal-type bureaucracy) of organization and authority. An unfortunate result of the new awareness of informal organizations is the sense that they arise as a nonrational, if not irrational, response to authority. Informal structures may be irrational because they often oppose in form and content the explicit goals of the organization. But they may also be adaptive, since they siphon off tensions that, if allowed to build up, would soon impair the capacity of members to cooperate even minimally. The celebrated case of the workers on the assembly line in the Vega plant in Lordstown, Ohio, is a good case in point.[6] The workers slowed down or refused to work, contrary to the agreements in the collective bargaining contract, because the social structure — evidently — had no adaptive mechanisms to bring grievances to light and to resolve them; the only means available to the workers were slowdowns and strikes. The failure suggests the limitations of formal authority and rational organizational design as the sole regulator of human relations.

What the Lordstown phenomenon further suggests, an idea that is buttressed by the exquisite analysis in Michel Crozier's study, *The Bureaucratic Phenomenon*,[7] is a broader concept of rationality in authority relations, incorporating the universal need for power and control as motives in the formation of groups in organizations. Instead of the passive compliance of individuals with an organizational structure that establishes the distribution of authority, means can be developed for the active pursuit, whether by the individual or groups, to accumulate power for security and control. Man's striving for power may be a tactic of conservation, that is, a way to preserve and protect against encroachments, or it may be a competitive one, an expedient for increasing the capacity to control and initiate. So organizations operate as political structures. Instead of authority as a means to the end of using resources for organizational purposes, authority becomes a scarce commodity that individuals seek to secure for their uses.

Jockeying for power often takes place in business firms when the decision must be made to centralize or decentralize authority. At the time an organization reaches the stage in its growth at which it comprises several independent divisions, then the problem of centralization has to be faced. In the typical multidivisional company, the problem of distributing authority begins with the split between corporate and divisional management. The corporate organization is a superstaff, with responsibility for monitoring performance at the division level (the profit centers), approving budgets (operating and capital expenditures), financial planning, and long-range planning, including new ventures and acquisitions. There is line responsibility between the division heads and the corporate chief operating officer, but the latter cannot easily acquire the knowledge and intuitions necessary to monitor division activity closely. Moreover, the requirements of planning generally lead to the formation of a corporate staff made up of functional specialists. Or, if the corporation is large enough, there will be a new hierarchical position between the chief operating officer and the divisions, filled by a group president — a group consisting of a collection of profit centers, each with an operating head.

Because of the need for communication, both formal and informal, the division heads tend to create their own staffs to gather information and to prepare positions either in response to, or in anticipation of, initiatives coming from corporate headquarters. The proliferation of staffs, each with its own authority base, tends to act on behalf of constituents within its own organization. The constituency relationship, in turn, fosters dependencies because of the sheer weight of communication that characterizes the carrying out of business in complex organizations. A structure arises, therefore, of countervailing power, which cannot be explained by conventional rationality. In fact, it may be useful to recognize the several levels where judgments about rationality may be made. First, there is rationality at the level of the total organization, where appraisals of the effective utilization of resources may be made. Second, rationality operates at the level of the group of individuals with a common responsibility or set of interests. Third, rationality exists at the level of the individual.

These three levels of rationality, often in conflict, exist simultaneously, which accounts for many serious problems in leadership. For example, in the problem of centralization and decentralization of authority, the existence of powerful corporate staffs is often a nonrational (and even irrational) response by chief executives to their anxiety, which is created by the need to control decisions at the group and even divisional level. The corporate staffs become the "training ground" for future group and divisional officers who, while responsible for profit centers, are also loyal to their benefactors in corporate management. Treading the mobility route of corporate staff from specialist to line positions may also erode the integrity of professional authority; as in Gresham's law, "Bad money tends to drive out good money." One can convert this to mean (without taking the "good" or "bad" too literally) that, in organizations, hierarchical authority tends to drive out professional authority in direct relationship to the mobility of specialists from corporate staff to line jobs. The task, in theory at least, of rational decision-making lies with the ideals of staff specialists. But as the specialists make their assessments of rationality at the group and individual level, the ideal often suffers and further obscures definitions of rationality of the total organization.

Conflicts in assessing rationality at the levels of the organization, the group, and the individual in the distribution of authority arise with seeming regularity when decisions are made about the establishment of a formal organization structure. Here, decisions concerning the centralization of functions affect the definition of initiatives and power at all levels of the organization. Besides these structural considerations, the formal organization also reflects the ideals of the chief executive and his staff. There will be new conflicts, for example, over the issues of democracy and participation on the one hand and efficiency and control on the other. But the problems are seldom clear-cut; they are not free of internal power conflicts nor are they unaffected by the anxieties of the main actors in such corporate dramas.

There is now available an impressive array of studies involving the redistribution of authority by structural and ideological decisions. All of these studies involve the shift from pyramidal to flat organization structures, which are designed to shift the levels of decision-making downward in the organization and to secure wider participation and commitment from those who have increased authority. The ends sought are greater output and the improved quality of decisions. These ends speak to rationality at the level of the total organization. In conflict with this end, however, is the underlying effect of such decisions in squeezing senior and middle management and reducing their power. Observations of such changes, both structural and ideological, call into question the motives of executives who initiate the moves. In a significant number of cases, there appears to be confusion between what is good for the organization and what is necessary for the chief executive and his staff (given the problems of developing confident relationships with people who, at the outset, are not dependent upon the chief executive exclusively for their power base and autonomy). The squeeze, although justified by bureaucratic rationalization (an intellectual defense of one's thoughts and actions), can be understood more fully through the language of rivalry, anxiety, and the other metaphors of power conflicts.

A decision to structure and distribute authority in formal organizations can be seen as an abstract event, an outcome of impersonal forces in which the logic of costs and benefits determines the outcome. Nothing can be further from reality. How to organize is seldom a one-time decision but rather a continuous evolution that reflects, besides the "macro" forces of economics, technology, and the marketplace, the "micro" forces of human personalities that filter and define realities through conscious intentions and unconscious conflict. The myth of formal organization and the distribution of authority as a rational event dies hard. One reason the myth persists is that executives in the midst of power moves seldom evince interest in what is true; instead, they are motivated to justify and persuade rather than to understand or explain. There is, in fact, less interest in the "truth" and more in rationalization than one would expect in this age of science.

People who manage organizations are less concerned with why things happen than how they are to make things happen. They tend to be concrete in their patterns of thinking, not abstract. They prefer the "here and now" to the "there and then." Consequently, they seek to justify actions that they perceive, intuitively, as means for persuading others to accept initiatives. Persuasion all too often depends on the ability of the management to obscure conflicting group and individual interests, especially when individuals cannot negotiate conflicts of interest. The reason so much time is devoted to persuasion, even though it might obscure rather than clarify issues, is the desire to avoid the direct and naked evidences of power. Power used directly is divisive, subjecting the initiator to retaliatory measures. Therefore, the tendency is to rationalize actions, to appeal to overriding common interests, particularly in those decisions that affect the distribution of authority and the balance of power in organizations.

Management Control

One of the most important developments in managerial practice, still not fully articulated, is the concept that organizational structure is only one of a number of ways to influence and control behavior. This more balanced view suggests that authority should be distributed in harmony with specific purposes, technologies, individual motivations, work climates, and leadership styles. Flexibility, along with the capacity to adapt structure to new realities, overrides notions of optimal form, often at the expense of what Herbert Simon has called the traditional "proverbs" of organization structure.[8] Instead of such relatively inflexible principles as "span of control" to guide organizational planning, notions of designing the organization to enhance the capacity for appraising performance and results have come to dominate present-day thinking.

Control systems and procedures, such as budgets and monthly profit and loss statements, would be ineffective without the structural means to pinpoint responsibility. Therefore, organizational structure is built upon performance, or "profit" and "cost" centers, each with a clearly designated head and his appropriate staff.

The idea of performance centers permits a wider choice of formal structures and, perhaps more important, greater latitude for an executive to develop a leadership style consistent with his personality rather than with external imperatives, which may constrain his behavior. For certain purposes, organizations may be "flattened," with many heads of performance centers reporting to one executive, as contrasted with pyramid structures, which create multiple status levels and increase the social distance between the planners and policy-makers and the performers.

But flat organizations imply a high degree of autonomy at the operational level that is, perhaps, more apparent than real. There may be wide latitude with respect to the day-to-day administration of the unit but very little latitude in the techniques of work, in capital expenditures, and even in methods of communicating and evaluating results. The techniques of work can be governed by staff personnel, who develop new methods and procedures and program their use in routine operations. The policy manual may indicate that the local manager has the final say on the adoption of new initiatives on the part of staff people, but it would be an especially strong (or foolhardy) manager who would defy staff directives, no matter how tactfully they may be couched as "suggestions." The reason staff directives have clout is that line managers tend to protect their flank, particularly when there are uncertainties about achieving expected performance.

The use of capital budgeting and allocation procedures also

exerts considerable control over the direction local managers take. Generally speaking, the money limit above which the local manager cannot act without top-level approval is strict. Approval of capital expenditure requests requires justification, either in budget allocations or in special appropriation requests. Whether initially or specially allocated, capital expenditures must pass certain tests, for example, return on investment, before approval is granted. Even when they meet such tests, capital requests may be deferred in order to give priority to some other groups in the corporation, especially when capital funds are short.

The process of reviewing capital budgets and requests usually falls to corporate staffs. Here again, the monitoring function is delegated to staff specialists, even though final action in the form of approvals, disapprovals, or deferrals is given by line executives and the board of directors. When competition for funds becomes intense, the displacement of aggression onto staffs and away from the line authority acts to guard the authority structure while maintaining the myth of local autonomy. If local initiatives are blocked, pleas for cooperation may be the signal to all concerned to end contentions and to accept proposed solutions, which are usually compromises among competing line groups and staff officers.

The use of formal operating budgets as a management control technique deserves careful attention. Budgets work by committing the heads of profit centers to a stated level of sales and profits. In a literal sense, then, the budget procedure brings executives to the point of decision, committing men to action throughout the organization.

Budgets also function symbolically, a perspective that merits emphasis in managerial psychology. The symbolism underlying the budgetary approach starts with conflicts between realistic thinking and sentiment. A chief executive who, for example, is intent upon rapid growth may inform all heads of performance centers that a growth rate under 15 percent per annum in sales and profits is an unacceptable projection. Because rates of growth are under the influence of general conditions in the economy and other forces outside the manager's control, the tendency to project unrealistic forecasts curries the chief executive's favor at the expense of reality. Under such circumstances, staffs usually protect the exposed manager when the chances of meeting forecasts are slim. If the manager were held strictly accountable, he would be the victim of a "doublebind"; he makes unrealistic commitments to conform to a philosophy while, at the same time, he allows himself to be vulnerable to punishments for the failure to meet projections. To protect the exposed manager, staff people encourage him to make the forecasts, and they prepare everyone for the more probable outcome. This avoids damaging the reputation or future of heads of performance centers.

Of course, if unreality persists in the preparation of operating budgets and forecasts, the bubble is bound to burst, as the fate of the so-called growth companies and conglomerates have shown. These have often based their strategy on expanded profits and rising stock prices. The high multiple stock prices have been used to acquire companies with stocks valued at a lesser multiple. But once the profit realized falls short of projections and the stock prices fall, the strategy no longer works. If the acquisitions and patterns of growth make little inherent sense, and if the management is spread over unfamiliar areas of operation, the result may be disastrous.

Budgets reduce basic decisions about corporate strategy to numbers. Accordingly, the budget only symbolizes a deeper thought process concerning goals, purposes, and instruments. The comfort in concrete numbers, with their appearance of objectivity, will be illusory if one is unaware that there may be hidden problems in commitments made and opportunities foregone in arriving at forecasts and operating plans. Some chief executives, conscious of the symbolic aspects of budgets, purposely hold planning meetings, "think tanks," and "blue sky" sessions to break out of the molds budgeting forms around thinking.

Another symbolic and often obscured issue in the uses of budgets involves cooperation and competition. In large organizations, it is not uncommon for one division or profit center to be the customer of another division; there can be contentions about the internal market and pricing structure that should be adhered to and reflected in operating budgets and profit forecasts. Because of certain internal political considerations, the "seller" may be given an advantage in the marketplace by directives that force the "buyer" to seek his supply exclusively within the corporation. Strict control through the measurement of performance demands that a manager be free concerning decisions in buying. The rule of the marketplace and competition should govern the decision to buy inside or outside. But such hard and fast rules are naive. Where, for example, the decision to buy outside could literally destroy allied performance centers, a free market has to give way to protectionist policies. Over the long run, however, the discipline of comparing transfer and market prices permits healthy competition to rule within as well as outside the corporation.

Conflicts of interest and internal competition can be put to good use, provided there is an effective information system to expose, for realistic appraisal, the bases on which forecasts are made and costs are distributed within an organization. If management information is inadequate, the internal conflicts of interest can destroy organizations by making them unable to channel aggression and competition. In the final analysis, the operating results determine how executives are rewarded. The use of money incentives is a powerful device to control actual performance. When the information system is poor, the reward structure collapses, as does the confidence necessary to maintain authority in organization.

The problem of rewards and compensation deserves a more intensive treatment than we are prepared to offer here. We raise it briefly because underlying any program of compensation is the ultimate objective of maintaining motivation and influencing executive behavior.

Executive compensation plans are not unmixed blessings. On the one hand, they are designed to provide rewards commensurate with performance by using profit-sharing and bonus plans. (Base salaries reflect the market, both internal and external, available to the corporation, and they indicate how much money it takes to get and to keep an executive *in the race* for higher rewards.) On the other hand, when executives elevate their standards of living to meet — and often exceed — their earnings, they can mortgage their egos beyond their capacity to live with the stress they themselves engender. Instead of independence, the mortgage may foster conformity, getting along, and avoiding the dangers inherent in the errors of commission. A concrete example of such mortgaging can be seen in the sad situation of executives who exercised stock options, sometimes borrowing money to buy the stock, only to discover that stock prices go down as well as up. The result is the anxiety of debt and current interest payments, not the sought-after security of assets that can be converted to cash and retained after the smaller capital gains tax. With the realization that stock options hold perils as well as potential security, and with the maximum income tax rate at 50 percent of taxable income, the virtue of money in the hand in the form of high salaries has once again become attractive. If the executive can discipline himself to a more modest standard of living and save the residue of his income above expenses and taxes, he will not get rich, but he will avoid trapping himself in a corporate structure that, while demanding autonomy on his part, is often just as glad to see him somewhat dependent and, therefore, more controllable when he makes judgments and undertakes actions.

As formal control systems become even more sophisticated and are subtly intertwined in the basic functions of strategy and decision-making, the process of using information to control behavior will deserve even more careful study. The burden of analysis, we suggest, is to look beneath the surface in order to understand the psychological forces that act on individuals in their uses of authority and power.

Executive Action

The problem of executive action is directly concerned with how individuals mobilize and use power derived from position, competence, and personality. Ideally, only the man best qualified to hold an office should achieve it, and the authority of position, therefore, assumes paramount importance. The assumed harmony between position and competence is naive because position controls the flow of reward. (Subordinates follow directives because the superior, acting from a position of authority, can reward and punish.) The effects of disharmonies between designated authority and competence, and the psychological conflicts engendered in subordinates, are tellingly portrayed in novels like *The Caine Mutiny*.

The discrepancy between what is ideal and what is real leads inevitably to revisions in theory. One such revised theory holds that "authority is another name for the willingness and capacity of individuals to submit to the necessities of cooperative systems." Accordingly, Chester Barnard distinguishes two dimensions of authority: "authority of position" and "authority of leadership."[9] The first depends on a central location in the organization's communications system; the second depends upon the superior ability of the leader. Taken together, authority of position and of leadership determine the extent to which a superior's directives will be followed.

But the problem of executive action cannot be resolved by concentrating on, eliminating, or varying any single factor, whether it be authority of position or voluntary acceptance of authority by subordinates (itself a consequence of the use of authority inherent in competence and personal attractiveness). The problem of action boils down to the problem of how and for what purpose an executive generates and mobilizes the power and authority vested in his position, his level of competence, and the personal appeal with which he may be endowed.

As has been indicated previously, the fundamental view here is that executive action *cannot* be treated as simply an attribute of structure, but must be considered as an outcome of the behavior of an individual *within* a structure. Illustrations of this view will be made, initially, by reference to the work of political analysts, whose accounts of chief executives in office provide the clearest indication of the extent to which individual predispositions and personality have shaped and reshaped an office. Political analysts point out that the positional power of the President of the United States is always present but that there are marked variations in the ways incumbents have used their powers; the differences lie not simply in the ways in which power is exercised, but also in the individual's awareness of power processes.

As a guide in their comparisons of leaders in their exercise of power, political analysts have used the concept of "style." One can define style, following the psychoanalytic concept of "character," as *the patterns of behavior with which an individual relates himself to external reality and to his own internal dispositions.* First, we shall concentrate on descriptions of Presidents in office and on the styles of leadership with which they respond to the functional demands of their positions. The discussion will then move from what actually happens in the encounter between the individual and the situation to why it appears to happen in the way that it does.

In his book *Presidential Power,* political analyst Richard Neustadt gives a clear account of the functions a President must serve, of the means available to him for the purpose, and of the leadership styles of three different Presidents as they used their power in the execution of policy.[10]

The President is, of course, acting within a structure, and Neustadt, identifying the constitutional functions that he must serve, also brings into perspective one of the crucial dilemmas of power and position.

> In form, all Presidents are leaders nowadays. In fact, this guarantees no more than that they will be clerks. Everybody now expects the man in the White House to do something about everything. Laws and customs now reflect acceptance of him as the Great Initiator, an acceptance quite as wide-spread at the Capitol as at his end of Pennsylvania Avenue. But such acceptance does not signify that all the rest of the government is at his feet. *It merely signifies that other men have found it practically impossible to do their jobs without assurance of initiatives from him.* Service for themselves, not power for the President, has brought them to accept his leadership in form.[11]

The "constituents" of the President, those who look to him for initiatives, come from six groups: executive officialdom, Congress, political partisans, citizens at large, the press, and officials in foreign countries. Representatives of each of these constituent groups seek to develop claims on the chief executive in ways that enable them to act, and the President himself seeks to establish claims on their actions.

Presidential power, or the power to initiate successfully, according to Neustadt

> is influence of an effective sort on the behavior of men actually involved in making public policy and carrying it out. Effective influence for the man in the White House stems from three related sources: first are the bargaining advantages inherent in the job with which he persuades other men that what he wants of them is what their own responsibilities require them to do. Second are the expectations of those other men regarding his ability and will to use the various advantages they think he has. Third are those men's estimates of how his public views him and of how their public may view them if they do what he wants.[12]

The use of these powers, however, depends on an individual's conception of his role. Neustadt provides a striking example of this in his discussion of the leadership styles of Roosevelt and Eisenhower.

> Eisenhower wanted to be President [although] what he wanted from it was a far cry from what F.D.R. had wanted. Roosevelt was a politician seeking personal power; Eisenhower was a hero seeking national unity . . . He genuinely thought the President was or ought to be the source of unifying, moderating, influence above the struggle.[13]

Eisenhower's presidential style was that of a leader above the struggle. He established a staff system in the White House that

> imparted more superficial symmetry and order to his flow of information than was ever done before. Therefore, he became typically the last man in his office to know tangible details and the last to come to grips with acts of choice. His one-time chief assistant in the White House, Sherman Adams, is reported to have told a close associate: "I count the day lost when I have not found some new way of lightening the President's load."[14]

Unlike Roosevelt, Eisenhower did not want the details of every factor that could affect a decision. He wanted the details already weighed and only the final alternatives presented to him. These alternatives often reflected other men's interests more closely than his own, as Neustadt's description of the circumstances surrounding Eisenhower's 1957 budget shows. The system limited Eisenhower's ability to exploit the power available to him, since he lacked information on how and where it should be applied.

In his article "The Concept of Power," Robert Dahl, another political analyst, stresses that a power base is inert or passive; it must be exploited in some way if the behavior of others is to be affected.[15] He defines the means of power as "a mediating activity by A between A's base and B's response," and he illustrates this by suggesting that

> in the case of the President, the means would include the *promise* of patronage, the *threat* of veto, the *holding* of a conference, the *threat* of appeal to the electorate, the *exercise* of charm and charisma, etc . . .[16]

The bases of power in position, competence, and charisma are apparent, but in Eisenhower's case they went largely unused. Roosevelt, on the other hand, was a man bent on taking the initiative. The Roosevelt of the nineteen thirties wanted to make new departures, and he exploited every base of power available to him to rally support for his decisions.

> The first task of an executive, as he evidently saw it, was to guarantee himself an effective flow of information and ideas . . . Roosevelt's persistent effort, therefore, was to check and balance information acquired through official channels by information acquired through a myriad of private, informal, and unorthodox channels and espionage networks. At times he seemed almost to pit his personal sources against his public sources.[17]

In doing this, however, he not only checked and balanced the flow and validity of his information, but also insured for himself a position of the utmost centrality at every stage in the decision-making process. He could assess who wanted what and why they wanted it. He could establish his priorities and make his choices, guided by clear indications as to where his power should be directed in order to secure support. At the same time, Roosevelt's style of leadership was not just that of an initiator; it involved the use of ambiguity in interpersonal relations. The use of ambiguity provided a means for maintaining a central position in the communications network and flexibility in negotiation and decision-making.

A President can also attempt to assume the initiative with an interpersonal style that is aloof and distant. In *Woodrow Wilson and Colonel House,* Alexander and Juliette George make it clear that Wilson was dramatically aware of the chief executive's function as initiator.[18] In fact, whatever leadership position he attained, whether as president of Princeton University, governor of New Jersey, or President of the United States, Wilson initiated reforms of a sweeping nature. His style of initiation, however, reflected an emotional attachment to abstract ideals, such as justice and democracy, and his expression of these ideals involved an emotional bond between himself and the public. This narcissistic transaction proceeded through the spoken word, the "giving" in verbal imagery of strong emotional currents that mobilized and sustained idealism. The "getting" in this exchange involved the adoration of the electorate, to reinforce a self-image built on the theme of the warrior overcoming malevolent forces that impede man's struggle for justice and equality. Wilson could not function freely when action depended on negotiation and persuasion in close face-to-face relationships. In the earlier stages of his presidency, he depended on Colonel House to deal with the hard realities of negotiation, and in this sense established a relationship involving complementary role performances.

In all organizations, executives face the problem of fusing a personal style with structural realities when they assert power. Executives may or may not be conscious of the functions that they are really called upon to serve. The structure does not necessarily make clear and unequivocal what are the preferred actions. Consequently, an individual may or may not be aware of the bases of power available to him, or, as in Wilson's case, he may rely on a particular base, ignoring others that are equally available and, indeed, more appropriate means of achieving objectives.

A Psychopolitical Approach to Executive Action

A psychopolitical approach to executive action is the problem of the person-position encounter. Such analyses must relate to both structural and personality variables. The structure provides the elements for a power base as well as the definition of issues for attention. Personality is synonymous with style; it helps determine how an organization gets built, the priorities attached to objective issues, and the underlying attachment to images of the organization.

There are three basic leadership strategies: homeostatic, mediative, and proactive. The homeostatic strategy addresses the need for preserving the organization — to insure its internal stability and continuity in the face of internal disruption. The mediative strategy aims at change in the organization, made under the impact of external pressures. The proactive strategy, rather than reacting to environmental pressure, induces change in the environment to use creatively the resources of the organization. Proaction is the strategy of major innovation, which tends to induce resistance, aggression, and, in some cases, outright hostility within the organization: it forces disruption of internal relations in the interests of changing the environment.

Historically, organizations move through phases emphasizing one of these three images. For example, a brief study of management succession in Sears, Roebuck by Perrin Stryker, provides an account of the correlation between management succession and changes in corporate strategy.[19]

Richard W. Sears, the chief executive from 1893 to 1908, founded the company in partnership with Roebuck, selling watches by direct mail. As the business grew, Sears introduced basic innovations in mail-order selling, not least of which was insisting that the quality of his goods met the hyperbolic advertising copy, and this at a time when, as Stryker writes, "fleecing yokels was standard business practice." Sears kept his prices low and his markup small, and depended on high-pressure advertising to increase turnover. His advertising changed tastes and formed new ones. To compete with Sears's merchandising tactics, businessmen in the cities and small towns improved their sales and service policies, often copying his techniques outright. Sears was a proactive leader who changed the environment that merchandisers until then had taken for granted.

The man who succeeded Sears, however, adopted a different strategy. Julius Rosenwald bought a half-interest in the company in 1895 and found Sears's methods increasingly disruptive of what was, in Rosenwald's view, efficient management. Sears's advertising and promotion had sparked such a mass of orders that in ten years the company's sales jumped from three-quarters of a million to nearly $40 million. The buying and shipping departments were overburdened and confused. When sales fell in the 1907 depression, Sears argued strongly for even larger expenditures on advertising, but Rosenwald prevailed over him and began a drastic cost-cutting program. After Sears resigned, Rosenwald assumed control and stressed the importance of developing internal stability, a homeostatic position. His most far-reaching innovation improved methods of quality control, but even these were later eliminated as part of an economy drive.

Rosenwald's eventual successor was Robert E. Wood, who, as vice president of Montgomery Ward, had begun to apply statistical analysis to the mail-order market and had foreseen that the declining rural population was reducing the need for mail-order services, while, at the same time, the shift in population was increasing the need for retail stores in suburban towns. Realizing that competition from chain stores was intensifying, Wood became convinced that the future of mail-order services lay in changing the emphasis to retailing; after joining Sears, Roebuck, he immediately began to move the company into the retail trade. In 1928, the number of company-owned stores rose from 27 to 192, and the chain grew to more than 630 over the next twenty years, accounting for approximately three-quarters of Sears's total sales. Wood's contribution to the company lay in implementing a mediative strategy, adapting the business to an environment that had changed substantially. He foresaw trends and moved the organization to meet them.

In 1954, Theodore Houser succeeded Wood. As chief merchandiser of Sears under Wood, Houser had devised an unusual strategy of "basic buying," which called for close cooperation with the company's suppliers in the design of products and in the costing of materials, labor, overhead, and profit. Houser aimed to develop low-cost suppliers capable of making a steady profit for themselves. These suppliers were so located that they could save distribution costs and, assisted by Sears, Roebuck's research and volume orders, reduce their operating costs. Thus, Houser viewed Sears's suppliers as part of the company's structure, with Sears assisting each to become a more efficient producer, rather than just a source of goods at the lowest possible price.

The evolution of Sears illustrates some of the differences between mediation and proaction as business strategies. A further innovation by Houser makes the distinction even clearer. Sears had long been criticized for the cash drain its mail-order sales imposed in many rural areas. Houser found, for example, that Sears was spending less than $500,000 a year in Mississippi, while selling $8 million to $9 million worth of goods there. He felt that Sears could change the situation. Instead of continuing to rely on one very large supplier, he instituted buying policies that would encourage the establishment of several small plants spread over a wide area. On this basis, Sears acquired suppliers across the country, bringing sales and purchases into a more even balance. In the southeast alone, Sears helped to establish nearly a hundred small factories, increasing its purchases to the point where they were nearly in line with the company's sales in the area.

The discussion shows that, under its founder, Sears, Roebuck changed the mail-order environment; the organizational strategy unconsciously influencing its leadership was proactive. The internal disruption that ensued led to a homeostatic counterrevolution under Rosenwald, which was followed by Wood's successful attempts to adapt the company to an environment that had changed appreciably. Houser, in turn, reverted to proaction and innovation.

If one considers that these strategies, converted into action and decision, represent organizational reality for an executive, then we need to consider the means by which they meet or avoid functional demands. The situation in which these demands appear is interpersonal, but the first stimulus is necessarily intrapersonal, arising from the images of power formed within the personality of the chief executive.

The functional demands of organizations, described in the language of economic, political, and social realities, interact with the executive's tendencies to assume certain roles. Taking a role should not be confused with play-acting on the stage. The conscious and deliberate enactment of a role as a theatrical performance is bound in time and, although it involves the individual, it is a highly limited performance. Role-taking in organizations is part and parcel of character structure, the habitual modes of responding to internal and external stimuli. Therefore, the individual's performance serves defensive as well as adaptive purposes. Unconscious motives determine the role, and they are products of developmental conflicts as well as maturation.

The process of dovetailing individual predispositions for roles within the strategies of organizations leads to three types of objects that engage the emotions and intellect: people, tactics, and ideas. The mutual compliance of men and situations (a "best fit") can be represented in a matrix like the one shown in the diagram below.[20]

Some individuals direct their emotional energy toward tasks; they invest their attention and energies in ideas, solving prob-

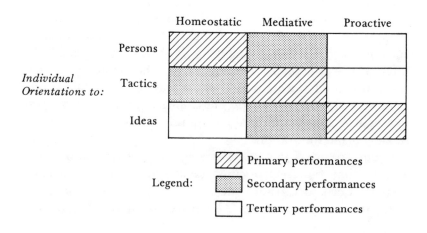

Organizational Strategies

Legend:
- Primary performances
- Secondary performances
- Tertiary performances

lems, and devising systems of doing work. They are uninterested in people and need to avoid human relationships in order to regulate their anxieties. The opposite orientation directs emotional investment toward human relationships. Tasks are unimportant to the individual's inner needs and values, and, in fact, the cognitive-technical aspects of work provoke anxiety because work seems detached from people. The third orientation is the concern for tactics, how to get things done through people. Here, the individual in his inner world weighs both persons and ideas as important to him and blends them in a concern for solving problems in a real world.[21]

The diagram suggests that orientations correspond to organizational strategies. Although individuals can shift responses to changing situations, they still select, unconsciously, a mode of acting in situations. The person-oriented individual performs most comfortably when regulating the internal relations of people to maintain a steady state. Such an individual avoids initiatives except under severe stress because he unconsciously needs to avoid aggressive behavior in his relations with others. The idea-oriented individual, on the other hand, performs most easily in initiating change, that is, in acting under circumstances in which aggression and dominance govern human relationships. Anxiety mounts when he forms attachments to people, so he avoids homeostatic functions. Organizational effectiveness would seem to require some mix in executive performance to insure that things get done and that the internal capacities of the organization are maintained.

Leadership style is the selective orientation of an individual toward a particular strategy. The means by which style becomes apparent are the ways in which the individual makes use of the bases of his power. Implicit in Neustadt's analysis of the presidency, for example, is the degree to which its effectiveness, its "success," is dependent on proactivity; the system turns on presidential initiative. But for the President to win support for his initiatives, he must be able to use the power available to him, and this, in turn, depends on his awareness of the demands placed on him and on the way in which these demands coincide with the personal predispositions that he brings to the office.

Thus, to speak of Roosevelt as "a politician seeking personal power" is to do him an injustice.[22] In Roosevelt, a predisposition for change and the functional demands of his office were effectively fused. He was psychologically free to achieve his objectives through the use of all the bases of power available to him. He could use people.

> His favorite technique was to keep grants of authority incomplete, jurisdictions uncertain, charters overlapping. The results of this competitive theory of administration were often confusion and exasperation on the operating level; but no other method could so reliably insure that in a large bureaucracy filled with ambitious men eager for power the decisions, and the power to make them, would remain with the President.[23]

In this respect, Franklin D. Roosevelt differed fundamentally from Woodrow Wilson. Wilson's emotional investment in ideas was fraught with inner conflict over the challenge to his authority that he felt in relationships with other men; in the presidency he dealt with this problem by referring it to his close associate, House, or by avoiding it entirely and relying instead on charismatic power to forge an alliance with the electorate as a means of achieving political objectives.

Neustadt's description of Eisenhower's style also suggests the contrasts with Roosevelt's:

> Eisenhower's use of men tended to smother, not enhance, the competition roused by overlapping jurisdictions. Apparently this was intention . . . Eisenhower seemingly preferred to let subordinates proceed upon the lowest common denominators of agreement than to have their quarrels — and issues and details — pushed up to him.[24]

Eisenhower evidently tried to avoid conflict and aggression, and his conscious attitude was one of altruism rather than the egoism of Franklin Roosevelt. Personal power — the means by which an idea orientation is transformed into a proactive style — held no attraction for Eisenhower. Doubting his own judgment, he relied on that of the people around him.

Another illustration of the meshing of functional demands with individual predispositions can be found in the alliances chief executives establish with their close associates. For example, in an important teaching and research hospital, three executives, all doctors who had gained recognition in their fields, were in the key positions of superintendent, clinical director, and director of research.[25] The superintendent was an active, assertive, and dominating figure, who specialized in external relations. He viewed himself very much as a builder, one who could put things together and make them run. He talked of his many activities and commitments as means to building the future of psychiatry. His memberships in professional societies, which were of immediate interest and value to him, were also part of his larger design to influence his profession.

The superintendent contributed a sense of action and movement, but more than a few of his subordinates feared him for his very qualities of assertiveness. They avoided him and weakened his lines of communication throughout the organization. To a large extent, the costs of the superintendent's style were offset in the person of the clinical director, a warm, quiet figure with close emotional ties to people in the organization and an intimate knowledge of what went on in their daily lives. The third person in this alliance, the director of research, assumed the position of a friendly uncle who gave practical advice on career while he encouraged research work.

In general, a chief executive structure usually consists of a small number of key individuals who make up an inner circle. The word "constellation," rather than "group," emphasizes the significance of the personal relations among key executives; that is, the emotional climate of the group and the psychological properties of the interactions that define the group. Constellations involve role specialization of executive members, differentiation among individual roles, and complementary roles. An executive constellation or alliance is seldom formed by individuals who are unable to define themselves in recognizable and complementary identities.

The way in which executives mobilize and redistribute power in interpersonal structures must meet the strategic problems of the organization. Taking a part in a strategy — homeostatic, mediative, or proactive — is closely related to personality structure and dynamics and, in its manifestation as a style of executive action, involves the uses of organizational power itself.

Executive constellations as structures for using power can

take a variety of forms, each with its symbolic meaning to the actors in the situation. The types of constellations include the patriarchy, built around the dominant leader as the central figure; the group, an executive system of equals; and the pair, a structure, often encountered, in which two executives relate to each other and their subordinates symbolically as parents in a family.

The acceptance of roles in constellations (this is not a reference to formalistic job descriptions, but to the functional roles that keep organizations moving) is a consequence of unconscious attachments to power. The executive acting in organizations is the center of a psychopolitical drama in which power is the focus of his attention and that of his subordinates. How he perceives power in conscious and unconscious imagery defines his mode of relating to others and his way of making decisions. The need for power does not originate in the attempts to build a career. If it did, there would be a greater degree of self-control in the executive than one usually finds. Executives appear driven in their search for power and only too painfully aware that their motives warrant some explanation beyond their reach.

CHAPTER 3

Power and Motivation

> . . . the cause of each and every crime we commit is precisely
> this excessive love of ourselves, a love which blinds us to the
> faults of the beloved and makes us bad judges of goodness and
> beauty and justice, because we believe we should honor our
> own ego rather than the truth. Anyone with aspirations to
> greatness must admire not himself and his own possessions, but
> acts of justice, not only when they are his own, but especially
> when they happen to be done by someone else. It's because of
> this same vice of selfishness that stupid people are always con-
> vinced of their own shrewdness, which is why we think we know
> everything when we are almost totally ignorant, so that thanks
> to not leaving to others what we don't know how to handle,
> we inevitably come to grief when we try to tackle it ourselves.[1]
>
> —*Plato*

FOR PLATO, "the most serious vice innate in most men's souls"[2]
is selfishness, and self-control is the essential quality that leaders
should possess to exercise power in a wise and inspiring manner.
As a moral psychologist, Plato understood that human beings
were self-centered creatures continually pursuing personal interests. Plato's conception of man may be open to question, but
it speaks to an important contemporary problem, that of achieving balance between individual assertion and collective control,
for without individual assertion, little would be accomplished
within organizations. But without collective control, man's lust
for power would unleash those destructive forces that cause human misery.

What is the nature of power and how does it motivate action?
Rollo May says that "those who turn to psychology for help
with the problem of power are bound to be disappointed. Psychologists have shared in the general avoidance of the topic
. . . that has characterized all intellectuals."[3] Poets, drama-

tists, and novelists, on the other hand, work from the conscious and unconscious conflicts surrounding images of power. The most primitive images equate power with lust. During his orgastic murder of his mistress, Camus's Caligula says:

> . . . I live, I kill, I exercise the rapturous power of a destroyer, compared with which the power of a creator is merest child's play. And this, *this* is happiness; this and nothing else — this intolerable release, devastating scorn, blood, hatred all around me; the glorious isolation of a man who all his life long nurses and gloats over the ineffable joy of the unpunished murderer; the ruthless logic that crushes out human lives . . .[4]

One reason academic psychologists and other intellectuals find power elusive is because of its relation to sexuality, the very idea that fires the imagination of artists. The one psychology that has investigated sexuality, and presumably is in a unique position to analyze the need for power, is psychoanalysis. Freud's investigations of psychological disturbances led to the formulation of the concept that sex and aggression are the two main forces underlying human development. The desire for power represents a mix of sex and aggression. Except in cases of extreme pathology, the mix is refined and attached to social realities, ideals, and human relationships.

Psychoanalysts usually avoid lists of human motives and, consequently, do not deal with a separate "power motive," but conditions of mental illness indicate that images of power appear in the ways individuals describe their symptoms, conflicts, and goals.

A young man, to take one example from clinical experience, entered psychoanalysis to help him overcome ego inhibitions. His work required ability to write, and he experienced severe anxiety whenever he had to complete a written report. He had a reputation for brilliant verbal presentations along with a puzzling incapacity to get his ideas on paper and to meet deadlines. If it had not been for his originality and intelligence, his superiors would have given up on him.

Besides his inability to write, the patient suffered from sexual impotence, which was the main reason he sought treatment. He could disguise and rationalize his work inhibitions, but the sexual impairment remained inexplicable, beyond his control, and a source of anxiety. He was driven, therefore, to find the cause and cure of his troubles.

Psychoanalysis helped the patient resolve his difficulties by bringing to consciousness the significance of his style of working and loving. The man felt torn between a conscious striving for organizational power and position and an unconscious yearning for motherly love and security in his attachment to other people. The greater his striving, the greater his underlying demand to be nurtured and loved. Verbal presentations permitted him to exhibit his assertive, independent side, without draining his limited inner resources. Writing, on the other hand, represented a permanent depletion, because the words, once they were committed to paper, took from him something permanent, and further set off his yearning to be filled, gratified, and sated. In much the same symbolic form, the sexual impotence could be equated to withholding because of his fears of depletion. To give to a woman meant relinquishing his meager supplies to someone who should have been giving to him.

Caught in the dilemma of conscious striving and unconscious longing, the patient had to deal with an inordinate amount of anger. The anger occasionally erupted in his relationships with women, but came out more frequently in his relationships to men, particularly authority figures in his organization. To his subordinates, the patient was a model of compassion, understanding, and support. To his superiors, he appeared competitive, perpetually combative. The nature of his attitudes reflected the conflict between striving for power and yearning for support. The striving appeared dominant in his behavior, and, in fact, superiors approved his assertiveness and ambition. He worked hard and frequently volunteered to take on assignments, eschewing help from others, particularly older, more senior men. He tended to dominate meetings but managed to dampen resentment by the quality of his contributions and his boyish sense of humor, which appeared whenever he seemed to offend a superior.

The language he used to describe his relationships to superiors was filled with images of combat. The world was a jungle with attackers lurking in the shadowy underside of ordinary work relationships. He had to be wary of powerful people, who could expose him as an imposter, a weakling, and without real power to present ideas and to influence. Oral presentations gave him the chance to duel, to counterattack, and rebut arguments. But the permanence of words on paper left him vulnerable to attack. There were only two positions in the power struggle, on top and in control, or on the bottom, submitting to an aggressor. Unconsciously, the bottom position meant feminine passivity, which satisfied the attacker.

The combative relationships with superiors, however, masked other, more deeply rooted ideas. To submit to men, even sexually, held out certain gratifications. The homosexual wishes underlying the conscious combative and competitive attitudes again reflected the dual conflict of striving for power and yearning for love. By submitting, one could acquire the power of the attacker and make it his own, thereby avoiding the fearful depletion of resources. Submitting could also be the route to love, because to give oneself over completely — to surrender oneself — was the ultimate in passivity, binding the weak and the strong into permanent union.

Unconscious conflict seldom appears in the stark imagery we have used to describe one individual's orientation to power. The nature of the psychoanalytic process reveals, only gradually, the intricate and the harsh demands of instinctual wishes and the modes of defense that contain these urges. More apparent, commonplace, and open to observation in ordinary human relationships are the consequences of conflict that are many layers removed from their psychological origins in time and personality structure.

For individuals to survive and to function, they must defend themselves against conflicting urges. The forms of defense reside in character traits as well as in perceptual distortions, repression, and the tendency to displace conflict from within to the outside world. Organizations assist the defensive maneuvers that arise out of anxiety over psychological conflict. The traits of assertiveness and competitiveness toward authority, alongside nurture and support of, and permissiveness toward, subordinates can effectively disguise the deeper wishes underlying the striving for power and the yearning for love. Everyday life also allows for fantasy in the rituals and games of work structures. Above all, the control of impulses depends upon compassion and awareness of the common rewards of living and working. In addition, not all individuals need to defend themselves against the erotic and aggressive fantasies of power relations. For some, the need to identify themselves with others is so strong that it overcomes rivalries and battles. Altruism and compassion originate in the conflicts of childhood, but as the tendency to submerge conflicts become self-generating, collaboration provides rewards. However, although power assumes different places in the psyches of different individuals, the origins of the need for power are the same. Differences in character structure and in personal history account for the variations in the expression and regulation of power needs. We shall try to view *power-oriented* behavior in the context of total personality development and character structure, both for so-called normal and for pathological expressions.

In formulating our position on power and motivation, we shall first turn our attention to the nature of motives and to schools of thought that include power in a long list of motives. Following a general discussion of motives, we shall review the three main theories that dominate any discussion of the psychology of power: power as a compensatory motive, power as an autonomous motive, and power as a character trait that distinguishes "political man" from other types of men.

Motives

For power to act as a motive, there must be qualities associated with it that involve mastery of nature and of other individuals. One of the chief characteristics of organization is its formal definition of power relations, which sets the stage for the expression of power needs. Power often generates conflict, arousing feelings of exploitation, manipulation, control, and dependency. Power is the potential individuals have to affect other people's behavior. It is the capacity to modify, to channel, and to persuade another person to do something he would not necessarily have done had he not been influenced to do so. The potential may be exercised through bargaining, coercion, and overt threats, but the means for exerting power are governed by the formal and informal rules and regulations of the organization and by the internalized codes of the participants.

Men differ in their desire for power. Some men appear to have little need for it. Some may use power with great confidence and conviction; other men are ambivalent in their desire for power, feel conflict about its uses, and are enraged when they discover that power and status are no guarantees of happiness and fulfillment.

Is there such a thing as a power motive? To be sure, we should be destroying our own argument to say that power as a need and the actions of men are unrelated. But here definitions become important, and not just for academic reasons. David Rapaport, the distinguished psychologist and psychoanalytic theorist, offers a valuable distinction.[5] Rapaport suggests that, as we study why men act, we should differentiate a motive from a cause of behavior. A motive is an inner tension, a need that, for its satisfaction, requires some activity, usually in the environment, and often involving other people.

Hunger and sex are examples of bodily tensions. One cannot easily conceive of a somatic tension related to tissue innervations or bodily functions. Motives have certain unique characteristics. They operate cyclically: a build-up of tension, as in sexual arousal, and release of tension, as the aim of heightened activity. Once satisfaction has been achieved with the decrease of body tensions, the motive is, for all practical purposes, nonexistent until the cycle returns to arousal. The nature of motives is such that satisfaction diminishes interest in the aims and objects associated with the release of tension. After a full meal, most people are no longer interested in food until hunger again signals the individual to act in prescribed, habitual ways. In fact, in the case of motives, there can be too much of a good thing. When hunger slackens or sexual need wanes, attention to food and love-making can be intrusive as well as irritating.

Motives are biologically derived. Although instinctual urges are subject to refinement, displacement, and elaboration, satisfaction has a primary aim that can be ignored only with difficulty, if at all, as in the case of celibacy among certain religious groups.

We referred earlier to a mix of basic energies, sex, and aggression in the orientation to power. The mix becomes evident only in the compulsive and conflicting attachments to power, as it directly involves the uses of power as expressions of unconscious wishes, to gain status and control over other people. In this sense, the desire for power causes an individual to act in definable ways, but the actions themselves cannot satisfy the need for power in the same way that energies find discharge in specific actions, such as eating and sexual intercourse. A cause of behavior results in a need-oriented activity, but it has no cyclical nature and is not extinguishable.

Another way of discussing the distinction between a motive and a cause of behavior is to differentiate primary and secondary needs. Primary needs (or motives, in Rapaport's use of the term) relate to the cyclical and repetitive tensions that generate activity and, ultimately, satisfaction and quiescence. Secondary or derived needs are more complex and elaborate aims of actions, which are only symbolically linked to bodily processes, so the study of power as a derived need brings to the fore the nature of symbolic thought processes, especially the workings of the unconscious mind.

Students of human behavior have long been tempted to differentiate motives. Lists of motives and needs, such as William MacDougall's fourteen instincts, invariably include terms that refer to power.[6] Classifications of motives stimulate research, particularly studies that use measurement and experimental techniques. Henry Murray, by classifying responses to pictorial representations into various human needs, set the stage for this type of inquiry.[7] Murray's list of human needs is long and sometimes confusing. Some researchers, however, focused their attention on a few specific needs. David McClelland studies need achievement as one of many motives, among them need affiliation and need power. Like Murray's, McClelland's methods of study consist of exposing subjects to need arousal stimuli and then asking each to tell a story about an ambiguous picture, thus projecting his inner associations.[8] A standardized scoring procedure makes it possible to score the responses with considerable reliability. Subjects can be categorized as high or low in a particular need category and then subjected to further study on the relationship of the need to performance in competitive situations or to patterns of childhood.

These studies yield many interesting findings, although studies of achievement motivation have received more emphasis than those of power motivation. Nevertheless, it is not yet evident that such studies can yield a satisfactory understanding of the psychology of power. The quantitative and experimental methods are removed from the internal experience of power and from the uses of power within organizations. These need studies, therefore, must be extrapolated from the simple experimental situation to the complex imagery of needs in the minds of people and of the expression of these needs in the structure of organizations.

Power as a Compensatory Motive

Symbolic thought processes and representations are peculiar only to man: they specifically refer to what an idea or an object means to a person. To say an individual needs power implies not one idea but an infinite number, equal to the variety of fantasies and images individuals conjure up in response to pressures to act coming from within and outside themselves. To say what something means interprets the hazy images that accompany action.

For psychoanalytic psychology, the study of meaning is the very center of technique and theory. The basic tool of psychoanalysis is to search for meaning: the most puzzling, ambiguous, and even bizarre aspects of human behavior can be deciphered or interpreted. Psychological symptoms, such as an inhibition, a phobia, an obsession, or affective reactions, such as depression and anxiety, all have meaning as compromises between instinctual urges and the forces that restrain direct action and discharge. Similarly, dreams have meaning as connections between daytime experience and the conflicts that seem to defy the separation in time of the past and the present.

In its concern for meaning and for the relationship between motives and causes of behavior, psychoanalytic theory avoids isolating for specific study secondary motives, which include power. Yet in a strange and compelling way, one of the offshoots of psychoanalysis made power central to its concern and gave to conventional wisdom the notion that the desire for power in man compensates for felt weaknesses and disabilities. The simplicity of the idea made compensatory theory extremely attractive.

Alfred Adler, the main proponent of the theory, viewed the smallness, helplessness, and dependency of the infant as the conditions that give rise to feelings of inferiority. Because any child is dependent on his environment and is therefore without the power to control, the need to compensate would seem a universal motive. But according to Adler, there is a more specific root to the inferiority complex that applies "in cases of inferior organs, in pampering and dependency, but also in neglect."[9] The negative outcome of physical impairment, excessive dependency or neglect, is a feeling of inferiority, which includes physical and psychological expressions. The mentally healthy person, according to Adler, tries to alleviate feelings of inferiority by attempting to overcome obstacles and, in general, assert himself in life. Therefore, in Adler's conceptual framework, power is man's basic motivating force organized around one overriding aim: to compensate for the injuries of early childhood.

Literature provides striking examples of how the sense of inferiority leads to the drive for power. Richard of Gloucester, the main character in Shakespeare's *Richard III,* remarks in the opening scene:

> But I, that am not shap'd for sportive tricks,
> Nor made to court an amorous looking-glass;
> I, that am rudely stamp'd, and want love's majesty

To strut before a wanton ambling nymph;
I, that am curtail'd of this fair proportion,
Cheated of feature by dissembling nature,
Deform'd, unfinished, sent before my time
Into this breathing world, scarce half made up,
And that so lamely and unfashionable
That dogs bark at me as I halt by them —
Why, I, in this weak piping time of peace,
Have no delight to pass away the time,
Unless to see my shadow in the sun
And descant on mine own deformity.
And therefore, since I cannot prove a lover
To entertain these fair well-spoken days,
I am determined to prove a villain . . .[10]

Richard attributes his villainy to one cause: his physical deformity and the consequent absence of the pleasures common to ordinary human beings. He then becomes "an exception," allowing himself aggressions denied by the common morality that governs men.

Richard's fury is compelling. It speaks to a latent identity that may, indeed, be universal; who has not suffered some real or imagined injury? In the unconscious, a grievance once felt remains as a potential claim against others and, conceivably, drives men to seek power and revenge for hurts suffered.

Alexander and Juliette George used the theory of compensatory motives in their study of Woodrow Wilson's attachment to power. The point of departure is a rather interesting fact about Wilson's experience with office. No matter what position he held, Wilson seemed to find himself in conflict-ridden relationships, usually with one individual singled out as his "enemy." When he was president of Princeton, Wilson had a deeply antagonistic relationship with the dean of his new graduate school. To others, the men seemed irrational in their behavior toward each other; they fought over the location of the graduate campus. To one unfamiliar with college politics, the fighting appeared self-defeating and even petty. Yet the antagonists, particularly Wilson, clung stubbornly to their positions and showed more than a trace of paranoia. Later, during his presidency, Wilson fought with Henry Cabot Lodge; here the issue was the confirmation of the Treaty of Versailles and the possible entry of the United States into the new League of Nations.

The compulsion to repeat a conflict is common enough. But what in Wilson's background and history drove him toward this compulsion to find an enemy? The authors write: ". . . power was for him a compensatory value, a means of restoring the self-esteem damaged in childhood."[11] To have power means to control other people. To compete and fight for power allows the person to act out a fantasy of the victor and the vanquished. The Georges explain that Wilson was driven, in his desire for power and in his need to overcome an enemy, to compensate for a personal sense (to be read as an unconscious sense) of inadequacy, which could be explained further as an outcome of Wilson's ideas of the superiority of his father. Wilson's father, a Southern minister and gifted preacher, often derided and ridiculed his son, a not uncommon form of education. This left its mark in uncertainty, and Wilson overreacted in his ambition and fear of failure.

During World War II, the U.S. Office of Strategic Services asked Dr. Walter Langer, a psychoanalyst, to reconstruct the childhood of Adolf Hitler and to explain the behavior of Der Führer.[12] The OSS also asked Langer to predict how Hitler might behave in the future, and, in fact, Langer predicted Hitler's suicide. Langer saw in Hitler's childhood a pattern of sadism connected to sexual impulses. He found many of the features that indicate motives of revenge to pay for the legacy of personal inadequacy. But Langer carefully avoided tying his interpretations to the premises of compensatory motivation.

There are many weaknesses and even distortions in Adler's theory. Its basic fault is a willingness to place overriding emphasis on one idea, the inferiority complex, and the way in which it affects character. The theory easily slides into the error of *pars pro toto,* the wrenching of one idea from a body of observation and theory and substituting the part for the whole. There are stages in human development. The experience of deprivation varies, depending on the stage of life at which it was felt. Deprivations in earliest infancy can prevent the development of psychological structure, so the individual remains dependent upon external objects, unable to rely on his own character and inner resources.

Another characteristic of development is the gradual evolution of ego functions. The means people use in dealing with reality originate in primitive splits between what is perceived as good and bad and what is experienced as inside and outside oneself. The mechanisms of defense, such as forgetting and displacing, or identifying and idealizing, come later and depend upon a substantial degree of success in the earlier critical stages of development. In any case, the person's relationship to reality and his sense of self-esteem will depend upon those aspects of development that have been mastered during the infancy years.

The theory of compensatory motivation takes a naive view of unconscious impulses and their derivatives in thought and emotion. To view the craving for power as compensation for felt deprivations overlooks the perverseness inherent in the conversion of the craving for power into action. The insatiability of power drives sharpens the observation that interests or motives can act as substitutes or derivatives of more fundamental human drives. The need for power in pathological terms can be viewed as an addiction. It is the attachment to power that is sexual, and it is the dominance over other people that provides the sexual pleasure.

One consequence of the fusion of sex with power and the wish for dominance over people is anxiety and guilt. What one wishes to do to others, one fears will be done to oneself, and this reciprocal effect of fantasy generates anxiety. A second consequence is guilt for harboring illicit wishes and failing to meet standards of conduct that the individual holds in his conscience and ideals. It is conceivable that some individuals who crave power have no conscience and a diffuse set of ideals. These people, indeed, become the criminals and the demagogues. One of the unfortunate facts of human experience is that individuals who have no internal restraints will permit themselves any conduct that will accomplish their purpose, securing power. It is, perhaps, here, as in Shakespeare's Richard, that the theory of compensatory motives works best. But in most persons there are consciences and sets of ideals to be reckoned with. The effects of guilt as a restraint on the search for power have no position in compensatory motivation. So Adler's theory remains incomplete.

The theory of power as a compensatory motive assumes that the orientation to power is uniformly pathological. There is sickness in the motive — to overcome feelings of inferiority that are angry, vengeful, and centered on the self — as opposed to altruistic ideas and social relationships. The power-hungry individual strives to overcome personal defects (felt or real) at the expense of social feelings. As a consequence, in his desires for power he disregards other people and flouts the codes of conduct that sustain a society.

Are all individuals interested in power compulsively driven to overcome feelings of inferiority? Common sense tells a different story. The expressions of interests in power, the subtlety of power relations in organizations, indicate that individuals often are capable of a great deal of self-restraint in the expression of their ambitions.

It is dangerous and misleading to equate the need for power with illness. Power can be viewed as an autonomous motive or interest that relates to an innate desire for mastery, a biological given in human beings, or to a cluster of interests that have freed themselves of infantile conflicts, such as the inferiority complex. When they are autonomous, power needs operate according to interests independent of the compulsions of neurotic disturbances.

The Autonomy of Motives

The view of power as an autonomous, innate motive existed in the days of Plato. We see, for example, how Plato divided the mind into three elements, each with its own pleasures, desires, and governing principles. He named these three elements understanding, spirit, and enterprise.[13] The element of spirit is devoted entirely to the achievement of success and reputation, a process in which honor and ambition become the governing motives. Therefore, the need for power may be equated with the fulfillment of ambitions. Plato's scheme does not presume developmental conflict, since what is innate in man — the elements of the mind — exists from the beginning, and each element follows its own course, including spirit and the desire for honor and status.

The three elements of the mind (understanding, spirit, and enterprise) follow autonomous lines of expression but have in common a positive orientation to self and society. Plato's man is highly socialized.

The English philosopher and political theorist, Hobbes, also considered the strivings for power as innate and, therefore, open to investigation as an autonomous motive. But there was nothing benign in the Hobbesian picture of man's relationships to power. Early in *Leviathan,* Hobbes discusses the nature of man as a self-centered, covetous creature — *homo homini lupus* — who possesses "a perpetual and restless desire of Power after power, that ceases only in Death."[14] Natural man is basically asocial, in continuous "pursuit of power" and engaged in a perpetual struggle for self-preservation. The capacity to control the predatory nature of man depends on the strength of a great leader, who maintains the control of both individual passion and conduct.

The basic difference between the Hobbesian view of the power-hungry man and the superficially similar view in the theory of compensatory motivation lies in the origins of the craving for power. As has been said, Hobbes believed that the desire for power is innate and independent of other motives. In compensatory theory, the desire for power grows out of a sense of inferiority, in which the relative weakness of the child, when relating to the parent, overcomes the positive self-image that grows from the mutual love and identification of child and parent.

The differences between innate characteristics and those that arise from the conflicts of development do not exhaust the possibilities for an autonomous power motive, with its selective development and expression. It is conceivable, many psychologists argue, that the autonomy of motives like power and mastery depends upon certain innate conditions of the ego and upon the capacity to remain free of conflict or to resolve conflict. Here, innate and conflicting elements are interdependent. Derived motives, therefore, become a source of pleasure and a push toward adaptive behavior. Because such derived motives are "conflict-free," they operate autonomously, and the motive seeks its own modes of expression and gratification.

The conflicts from which derived motives become liberated are both intrapsychic (within the person) and in the relation of individual and environment. To develop a conflict-free sphere of functioning, one must have had a favorable childhood environment, and one must also have developed innate ego characteristics that become activated at critical junctures in development.

The curiosity of infants, their exploratory behavior and desire for mastery, all of which could be viewed as precursors of an autonomous and highly socialized power motive, require stimulation by parents. But the stimulation alone would not provoke exploratory behavior and, ultimately, mastery, without being activated by innate perceptual, cognitive, and motor capacities.

A disquieting aspect of autonomous motives in psychological theory is the tendency to disregard analysis of the motives themselves. Autonomy of motives is a given beyond explanation. Autonomous motives are simply there, and become antecedents of behavior rather than consequences of development. Such a posture is both a challenge and a possible source of embarrassment to psychoanalytic inquiry.

Psychoanalysis depends upon a treatment situation, one that cannot readily be duplicated, for constructing its theory. The patient who comes to the psychoanalyst needs help. What motivates him to cooperate in a sometimes lengthy and expensive procedure is his determination to resolve psychological conflicts. In the course of free association and the analysis of defensive processes, developmental conflicts become exposed under the impetus of the transference to the analyst. Early emotional and stressful states, first experienced in relation to early love objects (parents, surrogates, and siblings) reappear in full intensity in attachment to the analyst. Concurrently, earlier conflicts and memories appear and can be re-evaluated under circumstances of life in which a mature ego can assert direction. Under the circumstances of psychoanalytic therapy, there is little impetus for conflict-free modes and motives to enter the treatment procedure that is the primary source of data. Changes that occur in the patient during the course of analysis reveal new motives and interests along with the appearance of the energy necessary for work and other functions. Observation of these changes does not increase one's sense of confidence in the notions of autonomous or conflict-free modes of interest and activity. Characteristics either born of conflict or free of conflict are in fluid interchange, reflecting a continuing capacity of the ego to look within the personality and to continue working through conflict between wishes, ideals, and reality.

Above all, the motive for power and its variety of expressions in organizations continually throw an individual back on himself. The fantasies of power relations, their dynamics in interpersonal relations, along with the inevitable successes and failures in reaching one's aims, impart a tension to participation in the politics of organizations and bureaucracies. Even with a secure sense of identity, leaders are often hard put to tolerate the demands of their job. It is not unusual, therefore, to find episodes of regression that reveal the conflict behind the apparently conflict-free motives or interests. If to scratch a man is to find a boy, then the reverse suggests that the ego processes associated with power maintain their solidity as an active form of psychic work rather than as a fixed structure of the mind. To dissolve all the interesting and conflicting relationships between the self and the object world by postulating power as an autonomous motive forecloses what is crucial in investigating the motivations of leaders.

Political Man: The Interpretation of Character

The orientation to power is a cause of behavior but it is neither an instinct nor an autonomous motive. Power involves all of character. The idea of character begins with the notion of the organization of personality and the self. What a person is, to himself and others, is not a random representation; nor is he simply the embodiment of the roles he is expected to play. There is both constancy and integration to character, so the person can be recognized by others while maintaining a sense of identity for himself. Interpretations of the function of the executive in politics and business often delineate the many roles he is expected to play. Roles are simply the expectations other people have of the behavior of a person who occupies some position in a recognizable structure. Individuals move from one structure to another (the family, business, community). Within any single structure, the expectations vary with the demands upon an incumbent. While it is true that roles make demands and contain variability and conflict, it is also true that personality tends toward organization, stability, and constancy. The absence of these tendencies in personality is often a symptom of emotional disturbances and psychological regression. The person under stress changes rapidly and regresses in his mental function.

One can approach character from opposite directions: from description, which consists of listing traits and distinguishing types of men according to some classification; or, alternatively, from dynamics. As we shall show, our preference is for dynamics — the play of forces in personality. Dynamics, or the interaction of forces, implies that there is both structure and function in character. The structure provides the organization and the function allows for goal-oriented behavior (either toward internal needs or external and adaptive problems). Dynamics also implies the development of structure and the elaboration of function throughout the life cycle. Because traits, on the other hand, can be used for descriptive purposes, their origins and purposes may be forgotten in the mechanics of trait analysis.

Nevertheless, the classification of character types has a long and respectable history in philosophy and psychology. Perhaps the most respected contemporary classification is in the work of Eduard Spranger, resulting in the psychological test called the Allport, Vernon, Lindzey Study of Values.[15] Spranger published a book in the nineteen twenties called *Types of Men*.[16] He describes five types: theoretic, economic, social, political, and aesthetic. As these adjectives suggest, each type represents a congruity of interests and values, the types of goals an individual pursues to satisfy perceptual habits as well as desires. Values point to what a person desires as well as what he rejects.

Theoretic man is interested in knowledge, ideas, and understanding. His heroes are the distant and great men of knowledge, and he himself appears aloof and distant in human relationships. He makes a good scientist and, perhaps, a poor lover. Economic man values things material, money for its own sake; economic man is presumably at home in business. Social man is altruistic, deeply concerned for other people, although he may feel love of mankind rather than of someone in particular. Aesthetic man values beauty and the sensory over cerebral experience. Truth may be beauty to the intellectual; it is still only an abstract idea to aesthetic man.

Finally, there is political man, who seeks power. The power he wants, while it finds expression in activity, decisions, and the sense of control over events, may require especially the dependence of other people on him. The political scientist Harold Lasswell went so far as to suggest in his book *Psychopathology and Politics*[17] that political man seeks *deference* from others. In fact, Lasswell believes that a man who is interested in power is sick, and that the interests of political man result from the displacement of his private conflicts onto public issues. In this sense, the definition of power as applied to political man is the capacity to make one's private neuroses other people's problems:

> . . . power-centered personalities are developed by individuals who come to rely upon power practices (roles) as the preferred means of maximizing their value position. This comes about in response to deprivations received from persons who are also regarded as sources of great indulgence. Strong rage and persistence responses find outlets that are successful in mitigating deprivations though not in reinstating full indulgence . . .[18]

Lasswell uses the theory of compensatory motivation to explain political man. To say what values and interests appeal to political man is to describe him. To say that he pursues these values (for example, deference from others) *because* he endured deprivations in the past and *must* mitigate rage reactions postulates a cause for an effect.

The immediate problem Lasswell presents is the equation of all interests in power with psychopathology. The notion that political man displaces his private conflicts onto public issues and then rationalizes his concern (as a means of evading the private conflict) minimizes policy issues in politics. It seems reasonable to assume that not all interest in issues is an offshoot of neurotic concerns. There are altruistic and external interests that may draw on emotional commitments but need not draw substantially on infantile reactions. There are many political men who are intent on seeing the world's work placed ahead of private interests and who, as pragmatists, try to find mutuality of interests to draw men together. These men can be distinguished by their anti-ideological positions and by their devotion to pragmatism, "the art of the possible." If any question can be raised about their psyches, it may have to do with their being too normal and well adjusted, almost to the point of denying conflict. Their credo is "getting things done through people." The less introspection, the better.

A group at the Harvard Business School undertook a study that, perhaps inadvertently, revealed the characteristics of political men who live on the surface and remain relatively detached from intrapsychic conflict and fantasy.[19] These men, whom we called "oriented managers," wrote stories about a series of ambiguous pictures (like the pictures presented in the Thematic Apperception Test developed in Henry Murray's original research on personality) .

One picture showed a man and a woman in some form of emotional distress. The oriented managers wrote clichés. Even their sexual imagery in the production of conflict themes touched on the conventional and the naive. In one of the stories, the man is agonizing over the decision to make an honest woman of his friend. He is afraid he has been exploiting her and has qualms of conscience and remorse. If he marries her, he may have to give up a chance for job advancement. He resolves the conflict by talking the problem over, man to man, with his boss, who is remarkably understanding. The boss gives him the promotion, advises him to marry the girl. He follows the advice of this wise, older man and lives happily ever after.

Anyone who sat through Saturday afternoons at the cowboy films finds the themes familiar and friendly. In fact, they reflect relatively uncomplicated minds that indeed assume responsibility for getting the world's work done. They are the minds of political men who do not have the drive for deference or compensation over felt injuries in their past.

The novelist Louis Auchincloss also takes for his hero such a political man, a rather contemporary figure attracted by the subtleties of men in organizations who try to manage human conflicts in intelligent ways despite the presence of selfish people. Auchincloss writes as a lawyer; his novels show how well adjusted political man may be.[20] In his settings, there are transgressions and violations of codes of conduct among gentlemen. But these violations are expected, and they are susceptible of reasonable solution. There are no neuroses in such characters because their roots are in an established order and they live in complete harmony with a tradition.

Although Lasswell made some generalizations about political man, he also understood the limitations of analyzing such a character type. Even at the level of description, there are many types of political man. Lasswell identified three: agitators, administrators, and theorists. Agitators were individuals who seek to disturb the existing social order; administrators keep the order going. Theorists deal with abstractions, presenting the ideologies for existing or new social systems. Presumably, each type of political man has some attachment to power. The different roles they seek and assume reflect the significance of power to them and the means by which they create harmony between their internal world and the opportunities that life presents.

There is a lot to be learned from typology; to make some order out of the chaos of extremely complex behavior is an attractive activity. But it seems that most students of political man have put the real problem on its head by starting with typology instead of analyzing the dynamic forces at play in power-oriented behavior. By looking at character, orientation to power, and self-esteem as outcomes of inner and outer processes of personality in a developmental sense, we shall facilitate explanation and avoid the limitations of typology. Only after understanding man's orientation to power in a dynamic sense can we turn the problem around and make typology more than an academic exercise.

Man's orientation to power develops gradually. Personality dynamics involves the development of a sense of self, the components of which come from two different sources — the esteem from other people and the sense of pride and achievement in mastering the environment from the individual. This developmental process also implies gradual differentiation between inner and outer sources of gratification. Through identification and differentiation, the building blocks of the ego gradually fall into place so that power can be oriented along with other interests. The same process of development, however, can go awry and result in the distortions of power. The answer to the question of why some men fall ill in the quest for power depends on an intellectual grasp of human development.

CHAPTER 4

Power and
Human Development

> People with great and splendid qualities make very little ado
> about admitting their faults and weaknesses. They regard
> them as something they have paid for or they even go so far
> as to think that, far from being shamed by such weaknesses,
> they are doing these weaknesses honour by possessing them.[1]
>
> —*Schopenhauer*

IN 1897, Sigmund Freud made an important discovery that left
him feeling like a conqueror. His new discovery overturned his
earlier conviction that neuroses in adults resulted from actual
sexual seductions that had occurred during infancy. The sexual
seductions of the child, so Freud believed, crippled sexual functioning later in life and also contributed to the formation of
other psychological symptoms. From his seduction theory,
Freud formed two ideas that were to guide his investigations of
neuroses: sexual impulses were of paramount importance in
neurotic disturbance; and development during infancy affected
psychological outcomes in the adult. Both of these ideas provoked respected medical people to attack Freud because he
questioned the conventional belief in the innocence of childhood. In the face of the criticism, Freud lamented that, at
times, he believed his lot in life was to discover what every
competent nursemaid already knew: children had sexual feelings and masturbated.

The main evidence for Freud's early theories came from
women patients who told him of sexual seductions — usually
involving adults who appeared as father figures. From such information, Freud concluded that the seductions overwhelmed
the infantile ego, and he confidently developed a formula that

related particular neuroses to types of sexual seductions (active or passive). Although he was assured by his explanation, Freud continued to listen to his patients. But, in due course, he became suspicious of what he was hearing and, eventually, of his own theories. It did not seem possible for these seductions actually to have taken place, especially the repeated implications of father figures in what appeared to be remarkably similar circumstances. The doubts gained support from the results of his self-analysis. Freud began to realize that patients were reporting sexual *fantasies,* not real events, and that they were presenting him with wishes and fears rather than describing experiences.

At first glance, it would appear that Freud had been defeated in his attempt to find the cause of neurosis. Freud's original conception of neurosis did not grant to fantasy the power to cause illness. The idea of trauma involved a real event of a damaging and overwhelming nature. How else could sexual impairment be explained, and how else could infantile sexual development carry forward into adult disturbance? But Freud's mood suggested he had come upon a more important explanation; he seemed more the victor than the vanquished. In a letter to his friend and confidant, Wilhelm Fliess, Freud said:

> It is curious that I feel not in the least disgraced, though the occasion might seem to require it. Certainly I shall not tell it in Gath, or publish it in the streets of Askalon, in the land of the Philistines — but between ourselves I have a feeling more of triumph than of defeat . . .[2]

The sense of triumph came from discovering the importance of unconscious fantasies and wishes and in turning psychoanalysis into the study of what goes on within the mind. Because the content and function of the unconscious, except in the cases of severe psychoses, were obscure (they usually contained unacceptable ideas and feelings), methods had to be provided for the study of unconscious thought. The royal road of the dream, and the psychoanalytic method of free association, became the window on the world of unconscious mental life and the development of the psyche.

The Discovery of the Oedipus Complex

More intriguing than the path Freud followed in his investigations were his discoveries about the evolution of unconscious mental activity. Perhaps the most monumental theme in the discovery of the unconscious was the Oedipus complex. Freud postulated, through an intricate reconstruction of infancy, that all children experience an intense triangular love affair, from about the third through the sixth year of life, modeled on the myth of Oedipus.

According to Greek legend, retold in Sophocles' *Oedipus Rex*, the oracles told King Laius that his son would kill him and succeed him on the throne of Thebes. To ward off the disaster, the king had his newborn son left in the wilderness, exposed, with a nail through his feet, to die. Instead, a shepherd took pity on the infant and delivered him to royalty, who raised him as a son. Oedipus had no knowledge of his real parents. On a journey to Thebes, Oedipus met a chariot on a narrow road. The passenger, King Laius, ordered the driver to force Oedipus off the road. In the altercation, Oedipus killed the passenger, unaware that he had murdered his father. Oedipus continued his journey to Thebes and, before entering the city, solved the riddle of the Sphinx. For this accomplishment, he was named king, and married Queen Jocasta, his mother. Oedipus, unknowingly, committed incest, and the gods took revenge by visiting plagues on Thebes. Because he was the king, Oedipus had to learn the cause of the gods' displeasure. He discovered his own sin. To expiate his guilt and sin, Oedipus plucked out his eyes and wandered the earth, homeless and bereft of the love and support of his fellowmen. He eventually died, hounded by the Furies.

The tragedy of Oedipus provided the metaphor for conclusions Freud reached through his self-analysis. Writing to his friend Fliess on October 15, 1897, Freud said of his self-analysis:

> It is no easy matter. Being entirely honest with oneself is a good exercise. Only one idea of general value has occurred to me. I have found love of the mother and jealousy of the father in my

own case too, and now believe it to be a general phenomenon of early childhood, even if it does not always occur so early as in children who have been made hysterics . . . If that is the case, the gripping power of Oedipus Rex, in spite of all the rational objections to the inexorable fate that the story presupposes, becomes intelligible . . . the Greek myth seizes on a compulsion which everyone recognizes because he has felt traces of it in himself. Every member of the audience was once a budding Oedipus in fantasy, and this dream-fulfillment played out in reality caused everyone to recoil in horror, with the full measure of repression which separates his infantile from his present state.[3]

The pull of the Oedipus tragedy comes from self-recognition. What was repressed reappears, momentarily renewing familiarity with childhood.

A young man entered psychoanalytic treatment because he had repeated difficulties in working with superiors. He felt anxious and uncertain about his career. He was a gifted economist who had achieved considerable recognition for his doctoral studies and showed promise for a successful university career. Because he had such a strong antipathy toward his superiors, he tended to avoid them. As a consequence, the communications between superior and subordinate were very poor, a cause of considerable tension for him and his seniors. In addition to his difficulties with authority, this young man also suffered from depressive reactions, though he scarcely recognized them for what they were. He would experience an emotional vacuum, a void, an emptiness, and he would complain of not feeling anything, of being bored and fatigued. His marriage was not successful, but it offered him the only hope that he would be able to enjoy deep emotional closeness to another person. He hoped to improve his marriage, raise a family, and be a strong and good father to his children.

The course of his psychoanalytic treatment revealed a history of a very close, prolonged attachment to his mother. Like many young men of his generation, his father had left home to serve in the military during World War II. At the war's conclusion, his father returned home, but was a stranger to his son. The father resumed normal activity in his work and family, but the young man resented his father's presence. He saw his father as a powerful interloper who had taken his mother away from him. Even more significantly, the young boy experienced a shock when his baby sister was born. He now realized he had been displaced from the number one position in his mother's affection.

The patient's psychological difficulties arose because he had repressed his anger and rage and, consequently, was afraid of the effects of his hostile impulses toward his father as his competitor. He felt his mother had misled him; in his eyes, she was a deceitful woman, and he turned cold toward her. The defense against his own anger was a form of psychological overkill. He would not permit himself to experience his rage and anger, and, in a self-punitive manner, he also would not allow himself to feel anything. He was afraid that if his anger came to the surface he would become a killer, and he would then be cast out, rejected from the family, much as Oedipus had been, left to wander from place to place without a home and people to love him.

In another case, this one of a young woman, the appearance of the Oedipus complex brought up conflicts of unfulfilled wishes in her early erotic attachments. Academically gifted and very ambitious, the young woman felt that she wanted to forge a career for herself and, unlike her mother who was very much oriented to the family, to gain recognition and esteem in the academic community. She undertook advanced studies in her field, but in the course of these studies she found herself in deep conflict with authority figures and also in hostile and emotionally destructive relationships with men. She had had no satisfactory love affair with a man, one that combined sexual feelings, tenderness, and respect over a sustained period of time. Any man for whom she felt sexual attraction was younger than she, because with a younger man she felt confident, in control, and powerful. Yet she idealized older men, particularly men who had achieved outstanding success in their careers. She easily identified herself with the type of young woman who lives in an asexual relationship with an older man. For such a relationship to work, the man had to be a genius — an Einstein, a Frost, or a Picasso.

Her history indicated angry reactions toward her parents at the birth of her younger siblings. She sometimes acted in a seductive manner toward her father, but at other times she made fun of him or appeared cold and uninterested in him. In her fantasies, she had taken over the position of the mother, but, simultaneously, she experienced deep anxiety and had to run away from these fantasies. By rejecting her parents, she idealized distant geniuses in her field, which, paradoxically, helped her academic career but left her anxious, unhappy, and depressed. She got little (and gave little) in real relationships.

The most convincing evidence of the dynamics of the Oedipus complex comes not in the recounting of personal history, but in the patient's attachments and emotional reactions to the psychoanalyst. These reactions occur in a transference to the analyst of attitudes, unconscious wishes, and inhibitions felt toward parents early in life. Under the influence of the transference, the patient gradually remembers more about his past, seeing the distorted consequences of the infantile past in the present. The convictions of the transference neurosis are far different from conventional intellectualizations and ruminations about one's past as they bring together memories of emotions as well as of events and ideas.

Other evidence of the existence and effects of the Oedipus complex come from the psychoanalytic treatment of children and from the observation of children in normal development. The significance of childhood is available to parents who can observe their own children. It is not uncommon, for example, for parents to hear their child say that he wants his father to leave the house so that he can take over and marry his mother. But the main impact of the Oedipus complex is often lost on parents because it is contained in fantasies the child may express in play but will seldom put in words. It is also inaccessible because the repressions of infantile experience by parents leads them to overlook or to deny what occurs in their children.

Freud reported a very vivid example of the Oedipus drama in childhood. A father of a five-year-old boy came to Freud because he was concerned about his child's phobic reactions. The description of the now celebrated psychoanalytic case, "Little Hans," is the earliest recorded material on psychoanalytic observation of childhood, and, probably, on the psychoanalytic treatment of a disturbed child.[4]

Little Hans's father became worried because his son would go out of doors only reluctantly and only when accompanied by his mother. He had a fear of animals. These fears could be attributed to his having observed an accident involving a horse and carriage when the horse fell. But the real events took on significance beyond the disturbances that occur when one observes a frightening scene. In the course of reporting the child's associations, Freud was able to point out to the father that Hans was very deeply attached to his mother and that the symptom enabled him to cling to her and remain with her. The fear of animals and his preoccupation with horses were displacements of his fear of his father. Hans's fears, of course, were unrealistic, since in no sense did the father hold malevolent intentions toward the boy. Rather, the child read his own unconscious hostility toward his father, and, following the law of the talon ("an eye for an eye, a tooth for a tooth"), he was afraid that his father would do to him what he, the boy, wished to do to his father out of rage, jealousy, and disappointment in his deep love affair with his mother. As is common in so many cases, little Hans was jealous of a younger sister whose birth gave him overwhelming evidence of a special relationship between the mother and father and also evidence that in his mother's life there was room for others besides himself.

The resolution of the Oedipus complex in normal childhood begins when the child willingly relinquishes his wishes to displace his father and possess his mother for his own. The pressure of reality helps children give up their infantile wishes. But reality alone does not account for the child's readiness to give up oedipal wishes. It is here that one encounters the hazards of development in childhood. If the child remains fixed in the oedipal triangle, his capacity to grow, to attend school, to learn, and to broaden his experience are seriously impaired. What helps move the child from the triangle, besides reality, is the recognition that the father is, indeed, larger and more powerful than he. The anxiety the child experiences in his fears of the father leads him to make an identification with this powerful figure and to adopt the formula: "If I cannot take his place I will wait, grow up, and be like him."

There is, of course, considerable controversy about children fearing their father, and, if they do, whether the fear is a good thing. The evidence suggests that fear of the father and castration anxiety serve as impetus to give up infantile longing and striving. But if the child's relationship with his father is based only on fear, the child will remain crippled in his capacity to have positive relationships with authority figures and to function as a man. Pervasive fear of the father leads to identification with the aggressor. The individual lives his life subordinated to people more powerful than he, while he is a tyrant in his relations with those who are weaker and are dependent upon him. Such individuals are "authoritarian personalities," acting in limited and restricted ways.[5] It is possible, in instances in which fathers and sons relate harshly in culturally prescribed ways, for a national character that fosters authoritarianism and dependency to emerge. In such cultures, the end result of the Oedipus complex follows the prescribed path of identification with the aggressor.

A more positive and healthy resolution of the Oedipus complex is the converting of fear of the father into respect. Children learn from their fathers, deriving pleasure from a close relationship (one that is not seductive yet that has significant substance). The child begins to sense the possibilities of mastery through the example his father establishes and through learning ideals, skills, and attitudes from his father.

The Orientation to Power and the Oedipus Complex

The passing of the Oedipus complex affects the structure of personality and the development of character. The identification with the father allows the child to absorb moral codes and beliefs that ultimately belong to him and help him govern his conduct. Moral precepts and the knowledge of right and wrong become part of the internal structure of the individual, affecting his behavior. The internal structure takes the form of restrictive conscience (possibly with a mild punitive quality). The conscience, however primitive, enforces a code of conduct that relies on fantasy and anxiety to prevent impulsive action. The individual feels the pangs of conscience and avoids acting against his standards.

In addition to restrictive codes (the rules of "thou shalt not"), the child also adopts ideals that direct him toward activity and accomplishment. Some success in meeeting the ego ideal produces a sense of security and of self-love that helps sustain the self in the face of the real adversities of life. A conscience may be overly harsh and restrictive, producing a sense of guilt; ideals may be overly lofty and unattainable, producing a sense of shame. A sense of failure produces hopelessness and depression, as though one were missing a love relationship.

The unhappiness people experience in life often comes less from their inability to develop satisfying love relationships with others than from their failure to develop a loving, gentle attitude toward themselves. The qualities of gentleness and love for oneself reflect the gratifying sense of internalized love from one-time authority figures. These images of parents can also cast foreboding shadows, which darken the self and generate self-loathing. Internalized images sometimes do not portray accurately how parents actually behaved during the formative years. The images of parents take shape and color, in part, from the emotions of the child and from the tendency to take the worst from a projection of one's own unacceptable impulses.

The orientation to power is a particular way of organizing the legacies of human development that pervade an individual's feelings about himself (whether he is self-loving or self-punitive), his attachments to other people (whether they are realistically based or highly charged with unrealistic and ambivalent reactions), and his attitudes toward work and career. Individuals, for example, often leave the oedipal stage with many developmental problems unresolved. They find themselves in continuous struggle with authority, unable to use power because of guilt and anxiety. Such individuals may seek to estrange themselves from others, to approach decisions with a feeling of remoteness and isolation. There are many rationalizations (the myth of the loneliness of command, for example) that people use to justify themselves in the lonely uses of power. Rationalization allies itself with the defenses that help the individual to cope with the deeper conflicts he feels about himself, about the source of his power, and about its legitimacy in the eyes of others. A more satisfactory resolution of the Oedipus complex leads the individual to accept his own authority and power and to give recognition to the authority and power of other people. He invests in abstract ideals; justice, equity, and reason mean something in his dealings with other people. They balance the effects of pragmatism, expediency, and compromise.

A corporate chairman engaged a consultant because he felt misgivings about changes he had made in his organization's structure. The chairman of this privately held business took over as chief executive when his father died unexpectedly. After he became head of the company, he managed to buy his brother's stock interests, so he and his mother owned the business outright. His arrangement with his brother made certain that all stock ownership would pass to him upon his mother's death. The estate arrangements insured his control of the business.

The chairman felt that he needed to strengthen his organization so that he could be free from operating responsibilities. He elevated himself to the position of chairman of the board and appointed one of his vice presidents to the job of president and chief operating officer of the company. He expected to devote most of his time as chairman of the board to the exploration of new business ventures, because he wanted the company to grow through acquisitions. Eventually, he wanted to sell stock to the public. He had outlined for himself an ambitious, but apparently not unrealistic, program. The man he appointed to the presidency of the firm was considerably older and more experienced in many aspects of the business than he was. The new president had a good reputation in the industry and appeared to meet the qualifications for the job.

The chairman of the board moved his offices from the operating center of the business to symbolize the change. The new president took over the chairman's old office with assurances that he had the authority and responsibility for the operation of the business.

Not long after the changes were made, the chairman had doubts about his decisions. He felt isolated from the business; he had more time to himself than he needed. He wondered if he had appointed the right man to the presidency. To find out, he intruded into operating affairs. He would attend meetings but say that he was only observing and no one was to pay attention to him. When the new president went on a short vacation, the chairman of the board took over. He decided (all in the space of a week) to let key executives go. He threatened others with dismissal. He shut down a plant and ordered the sales program revamped. The chairman also encouraged the vice presidents, who were supposed to report to the new president, to come to him, and they entered into collusive relationships. Men talked against each other, and all were encouraged to criticize the new operating head.

One of the unstated reasons why the chairman sought outside consulting help was to get support to dismiss the new president. There were, in fact, no grounds for taking such action. The consultant tried to show the chairman that he had some responsibility for the unfolding events and his own dissatisfactions. The consultant tried to show the chairman how he had set up another individual to become a victim of his own angry impulses and personal insecurities.

When conflicts are unconscious, even if they erupt into action, the individual will hear only what the current state of his anxiety and the solidity of his defenses will permit. It is as though a psychological economy creates a balance between instinctual wishes on the one hand, and a punitive conscience on the other when there is an attack on one's self-esteem. The medium of exchange in this economy is the defenses, a repertoire of unconscious techniques for dealing with disruptive ideas and anxieties.

The orientation to power is a link between the state of the self and reality. People with active oedipal conflicts see events and situations in competitive terms, a view that has some basis in the real world. But those with oedipal anxieties have a particular sensitivity to competition, qualitatively different from those who have long since resolved the battle to displace their father.

The damaging aspects of the Oedipus complex are its active demands on the psyche long after the stage in development (ages three to six) when it first takes hold. The experience with the triangle and the intense emotions aroused in the relations with parents paves the way for constructive activity in vertical relationships of authority.

Organizations and positions of leadership draw people into a hierarchy. What makes it possible for people to accept and implement roles while according recognition to the actions of others? Surely self-interest is important in motivating people to behave in prescribed ways and to meet the obligations of organization. But beyond self-interest stand other, perhaps more abstract, principles, which take hold once the Oedipus complex is resolved. A sense of justice, equity, and fairness, without which hierarchical relationships would become totally irrational, flowers when the individual can escape from what is purely personal in the immediate pressures to act. The difference between an active oedipal conflict and the resolution of competing attachments to authority figures turns on new perceptions of old struggles. Authority figures are not simply there to be loved or hated, to gratify or deprive. They occupy positions only temporarily. They are therefore obliged to meet commonly held goals, to find out and give expression to what people value. These same authority figures are as trapped in obligations as the less powerful, and are subject to evaluation; authority figures, too, can be judged, but according to accomplishment over time and not in the minutiae of immediate expectations. If one submits to authority figures (and submission hardly characterizes the give and take possible in hierarchical relationships), the forms of acquiescence express the fact that there are many ways to live with authority. To acquiesce is only one act in a relationship over time. One remains assured that other occasions and events may elicit different responses and even may result in a new perception of alternatives and, therefore, new ways of acting.

The shadow of the Oedipus complex provides a sense of drama in organizations. It sharpens acuity for what is out of the ordinary and often leads to planning ahead, thus allowing one to avoid the pressures that come with making decisions and acting on them. It is, finally, a healthy antidote to depersonalization in hierarchies, since, without the need to repress what one feels, the capacity for communication makes human what all too often appears machine-like.

In short, the orientation to power becomes a collective phenomenon (not simply one man's struggle for power) linked to survival, to the perpetuation of structures, to change in the social order, and to enjoyment of the temporary quality of authority that organizations confer on their leaders.

Otto Friedrich chronicled the decline and fall of the *Saturday Evening Post*. He stood the death watch of the *Post* and later wrote a book about it.[6] The *Saturday Evening Post* grew out of, and gave voice to, middle America of the late nineteenth century. Its founding genius, Cyrus Curtis, understood a rural America that believed in an order where each man could work his way up the ladder, enjoy the fruits of his labors, and live and let live. Families grew up on the stories in the *Post* and took heart in the optimism captured in the Norman Rockwell covers. The delivery of the *Post* marked the end of a week's good labor, joining families in the reaffirmation that all was right in America and would eventually be right in the world once this nation's mission took hold. The boys who delivered the *Post* were part of the optimism. They could see themselves on the lower rungs of the ladder on the move up.

The *Post*'s management, after Curtis passed from the scene, perpetuated his vision. Their belief in the magazine led them to keep the publication going, not as an idea, but as an institution that controlled the forests that made its paper and the printing plant that stamped it out week after week and year after year. The signs of change — the growth of labor unions, the wars in Europe, the devastating unemployment of the Great Depression, and the rise of pictorial journalism in Luce's *Life* and later television — made little impact on the thinking of the

Post's executive group. Their belief in the legacy of Cyrus Curtis seemed as fixed as a tribe's worship of its totem. When the changes took hold, it was past the time for the leadership to undo the effects of the rigid hold on their idol.

The actions the *Post* executives finally took — bringing in a succession of supersalesmen and financial wizards — only added up to the substitution of one form of magic for another. As the crisis deepened, infighting and intrigue overwhelmed the community of interest that had been held together by the optimism of its founding father.

The story of the *Saturday Evening Post* suggests a conflict higher than the suppression of the Oedipus complex. This higher conflict, which Freud referred to as the demands of the reality principle, simply indicates that survival in a hierarchical order falls to the impersonal effects of change. Those who seek stability ignore reality at their peril. It is here that different orientations to power take over and result in a defiance of hierarchical stability.

Pre-Oedipal Development

The orientation to power represents a partial compromise between internal demands and external reality. The notion of compromise immediately suggests conflicting forces within the person and in his relations with other people. The compromises lead to the formation of defenses by which the structural devices of organizations are used as auxiliaries. We mentioned, for example, the depersonalization of authority, in which one escapes conflict by paying deference to institutions rather than to men.

Before a defensive apparatus and a psychological structure are firmly established, the individual moves through three stages of development. The Oedipus complex is the third stage in the series, after the oral and anal phases. The pre-oedipal stages of development establish a basis for the ego functions of cognition, memory, perception, and reasoning, as well as a sense of self-esteem.

There is no psychological structure at birth, only innate

equipment and potential. Behavior during the earliest infancy period is largely determined by primary motives. Only gradually does the psychological apparatus begin to grow in complexity, progressively adding new functions and capacities to the innate psychological potential.

The pre-oedipal stages of development, from birth until about the third year of life, are closely tied to the ebb and flow of instinctual excitation. The symbolic representations that accompany oral and anal tensions are primitive, not yet susceptible to ego control. The pre-oedipal mental life, therefore, requires artful interpretation and a considerable ease with the language of unconscious expression. In human beings, the knowledge of this early period comes from the study of severely disturbed individuals (those suffering from psychotic, borderline, and narcissistic disturbances) and a still tenuous interpretation of what the behavior of infants means. After all, infancy is preverbal, and one can draw ambiguous conclusions, at best, from the observation of an infant's actions.

Yet it would be a mistake to relegate pre-oedipal mental life to psychosis. It enters into normal psychology because of its legacies in the field of creativity and in the formation of character, and because it forms the pathway of regression to which individuals retreat when they undergo stress.

A man in his mid-forties had a dream in which a small child was going out on a Sunday morning to get the comics. The boy approached the newsstand and asked the man behind the counter for a paper. The boy worried about having the money to pay for the paper. The man behind the counter offered him the comics from somebody else's newspaper and the dreamer became upset because someone might be cheated. The newsdealer insisted the boy take the comics, offering them to him with a wink.

The fact that the man dreamed he was a child indicated that regression, the return to earlier modes of thinking and feeling, was well underway. The causes of the regression were many, including intense dissatisfaction with life and a feeling of disillusionment with his career and marriage. His wife behaved toward him in an inconsistent manner. At times, she would cradle him and stroke his neck and head, like a mother with a small child; at other times, she would be cold and withholding, particularly in their sexual life. His relationship to his wife repeated his early life experience with his mother, who also appeared inconsistent. Unable to absorb his own rage and tolerate his anger, he gradually became passive; he developed a sense of powerlessness and demanded that others take care of him.

The anxiety in the dream reflected his underlying fear of men. He interpreted the offer of the comics and the wink as seductive actions. Manifestly, he was being given something free, but beneath the surface was the conviction that he would have to pay by sexual submission to the man. The level of his sexual function in real life was simulated. His wishes tended to be perverse, but he did not act on these wishes and so could not feel gratified in genital sexual activity. Basically, he felt pulled to suck, to cuddle, and the objects of his needs were men. He despised women as he had rejected his mother. In his work, he persuaded others to take care of him, thus satisfying his need to be dependent. His behavior patterns and character structure were dominated by pre-oedipal wishes. The nature of these wishes, their appearance in the developmental series, and their effects on the orientations to power take us back to earliest infancy, before words and symbols command thinking and communication.

For the newborn baby, the mouth is the most important zone of activity. In the oral period, which usually lasts about one and a half years, closeness to the mother is all that matters. Although little that is definite can be said about this very early stage in life, we can argue that, initially, the baby does not cry for the mother; the process of crying is caused by bodily discomfort, which can be eased only through maternal activity. The early relationship of mother and child is symbiotic; there is no separation between the self and non-self, the infant and mother, the subject and object. Only gradually is the mother perceived as a separate entity. The capacity to delay while developing anticipatory fantasies directs the mother-infant relationship from symbiosis to one of mutuality and individuality. At this stage in the life cycle, the infant turns to the mother, who seems omnipotent, as the sole source of gratification and, at the same time, the focus of reactions to frustration. A sense of boundaries between the self and objects is vague and undefined. Body tension is the predominant force, reflecting needs that demand instant gratification. The correlate of the body tensions is the "oceanic" experience of unity with the mother and, on the other side, a terror of being overpowered by impulses.

The oral stage of development provides the bedrock experience of unity with the omnipotent mother, or, conversely, rage and helplessness in face of a threatening environment. The child internalizes both the omnipotent and the threatening object; these internal objects are the source of later ambivalent reactions to the self and to the object world.

Experiences at the oral stage account for later egocentric behavior, the dual emotions of mania and depression, elation and despair, the experience of oral gratification and deprivation. The representation of power at this early phase of development is the oceanic feeling, the infant's perception of boundlessness and unity, along with the ill-defined sense of the self.

Gradually, the psychological apparatus becomes more sophisticated — the child learns how to differentiate and anticipate from the trustworthy and repetitive experiences of tension followed by pleasure. The infant accepts the possibility of restraint and delay in the modification of his demands. The separation from mother usually is accelerated by the growth of the teeth, the capacity to bite and hurt. This initiates control over the impulse to bite, which again leads to an experience of frustration. The urge to bite, possibly to devour and incorporate the good mother, is a way of making permanent what seems to be changing — the stage of oral sadism. This later development of orality leads more fully into a period of sadistic fantasy, when the infant and mother are engaged in the tasks of control.

Depending on the reliability and care of mothering during the oral stage, the child forms the rudiments of a world view, sometimes in optimistic, trusting images of warmth, friendliness, and security. Or where there is continuous frustration, the world view is in dark and foreboding images of possessiveness, dependency, greediness, suspicion and lack of trust. Either world view is carried over into the adult's orientation to power.

The second psychosexual stage of development begins with a sadistic component, proceeding in the images of dominance and submission, of controlling and being controlled. The anal zone is sensitized, and awareness of eliminating functions, of retaining and releasing, is pleasurable. The mother toilet trains and, depending on what came before and on the degree of rigidity in the training, the child learns something about friendly compromise, or about manipulation, exploitation, and conflict of wills.

During the anal stage of development, the infant becomes aware of power relations, his own will and his mother's will, which reflect the norms of society. The rudiments of bargaining between mother and child cover sadistic impulses in a relationship where the need for love and security still exists. The child realizes that he can give and withhold, capitulate to the demands of society or rebel. He learns that powerlessness can mean power, and, consequently, that powerful adults can be manipulated. It is a period in which stubbornness may prevail, testing a person's limits of power. But if the limits are narrowly defined, if, in the bargaining process between parents and child, excessive control is used, forcing the child to capitulate, a behavior pattern of superficial compliance and obedience may cover an enraged and injured self-esteem.

Franz Kafka describes the effects of conflict of wills between parent and child in a very touching way when he recalls an incident from his childhood in a letter to his father (which he never delivered) :

> . . . There is only one episode in the early years of which I have a direct memory. You may remember it, too. One night I kept on whimpering for water, not, I am certain, because I was thirsty, but probably partly to be annoying, partly to amuse myself. After several vigorous threats had failed to have any effect, you took me out of bed, carried me out to the *pavlatche,* and left me there alone for a while in my nightshirt, outside the shut door. I am not going to say that this was wrong — perhaps there was really no other way of getting peace and quiet that night — but I mention it as typical of your methods of bringing up a child and their effect on me. I dare say I was quite obedient afterwards at that

point, but it did me inner harm. What was for me a matter of course, that senseless asking for water, and the extraordinary terror of being carried outside were two things that I, my nature being what it was, could never properly connect with each other. Even years afterwards I suffered from the tormenting fancy that the huge man, my father, the ultimate authority, could come almost for no reason at all and take me out of bed in the night and carry me out onto the *pavlatche,* and that meant I was a mere nothing to him.

That was only a small beginning, but this sense of nothingness that often dominated me (a feeling that is in another respect, admittedly, also a noble and fruitful one) comes largely from your influence. What I would have needed was a little encouragement, a little friendliness, a little keeping open of my road, instead of which you blocked it from me, though of course with the good intention of making me go another road . . .[7]

Obedience remained an area of conflict for Kakfa all his life. Furthermore, this episode left him puzzled about the possible connection between acts and their consequences, a theme that dominates much of his work. Kafka may have been unique in the way he transformed his broodings about causality, morality, and authority into artistic achievement; ordinary children learn in interpersonal terms the idea that submission often insures affection, and that dominance falls to those in power and control. This sadistic orientation to power covers over the strivings for attachment and security.

Oceanic Power

The primary effects of the oral stage of development on the orientation to power lie in the experiences of omnipotence and the oceanic feeling of unity, the inseparability of the self and the object. Here, power is total; it exists within the unformed self. There are no limitations to the fantasy of oceanic power until one experiences deprivations from the loss of the mother. At first she seems omnipotent; later, the feeling about her is re-experienced in the urge to possess what is lifegiving.

Oceanic power is madness; indeed, if it is untransformed it

leads to an autistic, psychotic existence. Equally strange, however, is the relationship between oceanic power and creativity. There is increasing understanding, certainly in the realm of artistic creativity, that in the search for unity with an omnipotent object the individual turns inward, investing in his ideas, feelings, and fantasies. A gifted individual achieves a kind of omnipotence when the turning inward results in some special work, like a poem, a book, or a painting. The performance, however, depends not simply on the investment in oneself (the turning inward), but also on the nature of discipline and craftsmanship, subjects about which we know too little. But without the capacity to invest inwardly, there is little raw material for the application of discipline and craftsmanship. In creativity, there is also the problem of letting go, of relinquishing the product of one's imagination and effort. It is not uncommon to find that the gifted individual, in the grip of oceanic power and of the search for union, is unable to relinquish what he has produced. The act of separating means to endure again the trauma of loss and separation from the giving object. Even if the artist can let go of his work, he may experience a depressive reaction, as though to mourn a deep loss or even destruction of the self. It is no wonder, therefore, in the case of gifted people, to find repeated instances of severe depression and suicide.

Our interest here is the relationship between oceanic power as a developmental phenomenon and political behavior. Oceanic power and political behavior take us into the realm of charismatic leadership and of emotional ties between leader and the led. We shall discuss charismatic leadership in Chapter 11. Here, one illustration should give a good indication of the ties between earliest infancy and charisma.

Erik Erikson published a provocative study of Mahatma Gandhi, in which the theory of maternal union and the oceanic experience play a significant part in explaining the development of a charismatic leader. The focal point of Erikson's study is how Gandhi initiated passive resistance (Satyagraha) as a new form of social aggression in a national power struggle. The struggle assumed spiritual dimensions, and Gandhi's leadership became a religious movement. In Erikson's words:

> . . . I can only view with awe a man who (making himself more transparent than any of the saviors and saints of mythological past) improvised every item in the inventory of saintliness — nakedness, poverty, silence, chastity, and charity — without being baptized or ordained in any traditional investiture; and who attempted to apply the power of that position in every waking minute to the Here and Now as lived by the masses of men . . .[8]

Self-rule for India became Gandhi's ultimate goal in the political sphere. To reach it, he assumed prophetic heights in dealing with his audience. Fasting, an old ritual act, became the bond between him and his audience and, simultaneously, a provocation to his opponents. For example, his opposition to the "Black Act," the Indian government's antisedition law, resulted in major disturbances and, eventually, in his arrest. But Gandhi's involuntary passivity and physical isolation while he was imprisoned paradoxically reinforced the union between himself and the masses.

> . . . I am perhaps the happiest man on earth today. I have during these two months experienced boundless love. And now I find myself arrested, although I bear no ill will to anybody and although I am the one man who can today preserve the peace in India as no other man can. My imprisonment, therefore, will show the wrongdoer his nakedness. And he can do me no harm, for my spirit remains calm and unruffled . . .[9]

The isolation of prison buttressed the union within the self. Instead of despair, he felt elation, boundless power, and the omnipotence of one who needs no one person for gratification or support. He could renounce his wife (sexually), and he could force his followers to renounce appetites in order to strengthen the union of leader and led through abstinence and heightened awareness.

Oceanic power transcends institutions and rules. But it would be a mistake to interpret historical change on the basis of the mystical unity of leader and led, itself predicated on the archetypal experience of maternal union. A catalyst for change, oceanic power can prevail over institutions and custom only when there is a special readiness. Devotion to a maternal leader is a study in manipulation. If people are faced with hardship, deprivation and suffering, which accompany the inequalities of power in rigid organizations and societies, then they can be manipulated. A history of real deprivation together with rising aspirations creates readiness for the maternal leader. Oceanic power, therefore, is a study of the fusion of primitive symbols with current realities, and in the gradual transformation of elementary human needs into sophisticated institutional forms.

Sadistic Power

Sadistic power aims to dominate other people and to secure their deference. The forms of sadistic power range from sexual dominance, with the aim of inflicting physical pain, to regulating in detail what people do. In the case of sexual perversions, there is little transformation from the primitive instinct to the overt activity. The control of behavior through regulation and prescription represents a highly modified use of aggressive and sexual urges. But in both primitive and transformed sadism, the defense against internal conflict on the part of the aggressor connects the behavior of the adult with the developmental experiences of the child, particularly during the anal-sadistic stage of development.

Historically, one can attempt to trace the changes in industrial organization — from a highly controlling and punitive form of work to efforts at democratization — as movements in the transformation of sadism. Organizations would hardly have fostered sadistic control were it not for the capacity of individual leaders to draw from within their psyches capacities for inflicting punishment on others. It is true that in the early days of industrialization, through slavery and the rise of the labor movement, the notion of human dignity was carefully limited and was rationalized in favor of a minority. Sometimes the minority was defined as property, predestined to be so; this made legitimate the right of some to dominate and punish others. The need to control has a psychological as well as cultural basis.

William Manchester's striking study of the Krupp family

documented the interlocking of individual, family, and nation in patterns of cruelty.[10] The value of Manchester's book lies in its disclosure of the sexual perversions of the various Krupp leaders and of their compulsion to dominate the lives of their workers and even to rationalize slave labor in the name of the Nazi cause. Sadism was the predominant feature of the *Familien Geist,* the family spirit, which was handed down from one generation to the next. It is not pure coincidence that sadistic power in the hands of the Krupp family was directed toward the production of weapons. The inventiveness of the family produced larger and larger cannons; these symbols of death and destruction related to a paranoid fear that dangers lurked without, requiring extreme vigilance to maintain control of the empire. Alfred Krupp warned about the necessity for total control by:

> . . . a constant quiet observation of the spirit of our workers, so that we cannot miss the beginning of any ferment anywhere; and I must demand that if the cleverest and best workman or foreman ever looks as though he wants to raise objections, or belong to one of those unions, he shall be discharged as quickly as practicable without consideration of whether he can be spared . . .[11]

> . . . The full force of authority must be used to repress disloyalty and conspiracy. Those who commit unworthy acts must never be permitted to feel safe, must never escape public disgrace. Good, like wickedness, should be examined through a microscope, for there truth is to be found. Even as a seed bears fruit in direct ratio to the nourishment or portion it is given, so is it from the spirit that an art, benign or evil, arises . . .[12]

In 1944, the Krupp empire was supported by approximately 280,000 Kruppianer. In addition, 100,000 persons worked as slaves for Krupp in Germany, the occupied territories, and concentration camps.[13] The Krupp leaders were cruel, but they also practiced paternalistic control toward the Kruppianer, the working force. However, the façade of paternalism disappeared in Krupp's dealings with foreign civilian workmen, prisoners of war, and concentration-camp prisoners. As Manchester comments:

No one knows who coined the ingenious phrase "extermination through work," but . . . Krupp put it to the Führer. Ignoring the language rules, he said that every party member favored liquidation (*Beseitigung*) of "Jews, foreign saboteurs, anti-Nazi Germans, gypsies, criminals, and antisocial elements" (*Verbrecher und Asoziale*), but that he could see no reason why they shouldn't contribute something to the Fatherland before they went. Properly driven, each could contribute a lifetime of work in the months before he was dispatched . . .[14]

Brutality and complete disregard for human lives became common practice under the last ruler of the Krupp empire. His slave-labor force worked twelve hours a day, seven days a week, without respite. These workers had no names, only numbers, and they were without sufficient shelter, clothing, and food.

Gustav Krupp von Bohlen und Hallbach, perhaps making up for the fact that he was not a Krupp by blood (he married the heiress, Bertha Krupp), embraced the *Generalregulativ*. His obsession for order and punctuality was renowned. The fact that he read railroad timetables for pleasure typifies his obsession with regulation and control. His personality and the Krupp family spirit were well matched.

Alfred Krupp, the last and most powerful ruler of the Krupp empire, grew up under the continuous surveillance of his father, Gustav, who received daily reports on his activities.

Not only did Alfred look like his great-grandfather, but it was his great-grandfather's rule that was continuously set up as an example of the behavior necessary for continuing the Krupp company in the *Familien Geist*. The orientation to sadistic power turned, for the rulers of the house of Krupp, into a legacy, an inheritance to pass from generation to generation.

The transactions in organizations, from the dominance of men to the rule of law and to the application of principles of justice and equity, reflect basic shifts in the orientation to power. The shifts are made from cruelty and the desire for dominance to compassion and the need for abstract principles that merit universal application. From the rule of men to the rule of law, some parallel shift occurs in the psychological development of leaders and in the integration of their personalities. The development of a sense of self, an identity that includes benevolent caretakers, makes possible the evolution from primitive passions to abstract principles governing the exercise of power. How the self becomes cohesive and, conversely, how fragmentation of the self inflicts risks on leadership are aspects of the constructive and destructive attachments to power.

CHAPTER 5

Power and
the Fragmented Self

Do you not know that there comes a midnight hour when everyone has to throw off his mask? Do you believe that life will always let itself be mocked? Do you think you can slip away a little before midnight to avoid this? Or are you not terrified by it? I have seen men in real life who so long deceived others that at last their true nature could not reveal itself; I have seen men who played hide and seek so long that at last in madness they disgustingly obtruded upon others their secret thoughts which hitherto they had proudly concealed.[1]

—Kierkegaard

THE GREEK MYTH tells of Narcissus who, on seeing his image reflected in a pool of water, fell in love with himself. The love of the self detaches the individual from his need of others. Leaders who are narcissistic experience a freedom of action not usually available to other human beings. Such leaders also have no sense of conscience or guilt and, above all, lack empathy to human needs.[2]

The narcissist, despite his seeming independence, often has an uncertain sense of identity and serious disturbances in self-esteem.[3] The disturbances arise from an inner fragmentation of self-images, some conscious and others, more damaging, unconscious.[4] What are the conditions that prevent the cohesion of the self? How does the fragmentation of the self affect the search for power and its uses in positions of leadership? What are the consequences of a search for power as a means to achieve unity of the self or as a means to prevent the further fragmentation of an already shattered self? Does a fragmented self always result in the pathological attachment to power, or, in an effort to bring together what is partially split, can certain positive outcomes develop that appear as constructive uses of power?

As these questions suggest, the relationship of power to narcissism, self-hatred, and esteem for oneself moves even further from a strictly motivational view of power toward a developmental perspective, in which problems of adult function and maturation assume major importance in the orientation to power.

Omnipotence and Helplessness

On May 21, 1949, James Forrestal killed himself. A successful investment banker and government official (the first secretary of defense), he had, by all accounts, realized great achievements; yet he became depressed, despairing, and paranoid to the point where he could no longer tolerate himself. Arnold Rogow, who wrote *James Forrestal: A Study of Personality, Politics and Policy,* traced Forrestal's last moments. Rogow records that, just before he threw himself from a window at the Bethesda Naval Hospital, Forrestal sat at a table writing feverishly. He was copying passages recited by the chorus in Sophocles' *Ajax:*

> Fair Salamis, the billows' roar
> Wanders around thee yet,
> And sailors gaze upon thy shore
> Firm in the Ocean set.
>
> Thy son is in a foreign clime
> Where Ida feeds her countless flocks,
> Far from thy dear, remembered rocks,
> Worn by the waste of time —
> Comfortless, nameless, hopeless save
> In the dark prospect of the yawning grave . . .
>
> Woe to the mother in her close of day,
> Woe to her desolate heart and temples gray,
> When she shall hear
> Her loved one's story whispered in her ear!
> "Woe, woe!" will be the cry —
> No quiet murmur like the tremulous wail
> Of the lone bird, the querulous nightingale.[5]

The sense of hopelessness and despair in the passage, and the raging fury it conveys, spring from separation and detachment. The lamentation for the son in a foreign land, a child detached from his mother, projects a condition of hopelessness. No one can comfort, so hope and interest in life disappear. But the sense of loneliness does not come simply from the absence of objects. The deficit resides in the self, in its lack of cohesion and in the fragments that epitomize the conflicts of love and hate. If it is "Woe to the mother in her close of day/Woe to her desolate heart and temples gray," her woe is the result of revenge against her representation in the self. This mother is uncaring, cold, and hated. The suicide will destroy her and, in doing so, excise the hated aspects of the self and, possibly, permit the remnants of a loved self to survive and grow.[6]

At crucial stages in individual development, the objects of life (mainly the parents) become an internal part of the personality through a process of introjection (which literally means "taking in") and also through identification (the desire to be like the object). The incorporation of objects is a universal phenomenon that generally assists development. It is also dangerous, since what is incorporated can include representations of what one comes to hate and fear in the objects.

The tragedy of life is that one can never get enough of what is good. No matter how good and giving the parents (especially the mother during the child's earlier years), they must sooner or later deprive in order to foster growth and development of the young. The image of the depriving parent will, even in the most beneficial relationships, potentially be a source of self-hatred and devaluations. (After all, if one were perfect there would be no cause for deprivation by, or of loss of, the one who gives.) Perfection, an idealized condition of union with a fulfilling object, becomes an unconscious goal toward which the individual must strive. The striving for perfection involves an unconscious self-humiliation, an excision both of the fragments of the self that appear contrary to the idealized self and of the internalized figures who were once loved and then hated before they were incorporated.

In part, the orientation to power is a consequence of the aims of drawing together the self. We should distinguish two primary modes through which the moves toward cohesion take place. The first mode can be described as excision and exclusion; it involves defensive maneuvers to eliminate the hated and unacceptable fragments of the self. If one can destroy what one hates within, the potentially positive fragments can come together and thrive, as removing weeds from a garden permits room and nutriment for the desirable plants. Suicide is the most violent act of excision. Acts of excision short of suicide, such as depressive withdrawal and inhibition of activity, are also destructive, because the individual is forced to relinquish real gratification to close off undesirable self-images.

A second primary mode for achieving cohesion of the self is through healing the splits in the ego and reconstituting the fragments of the self to which aggression is attached. Healing comes about in normal development when there has been a "good enough" maternal relationship so that a sense of basic trust and benevolence within the self has been established. In the absence of adequate mothering, the capacity to test reality is impaired, leaving the ego vulnerable to the effects of malevolent internal figures incorporated in reaction to the loss of love.

Healing also occurs in special therapeutic relationships (psychoanalysis being the most intensive), in which the patient reactivates incorporated fragments of lost objects. Following this reactivation, which in psychoanalysis takes place in the transference, the splits in the self heal. Primitive fears originating in instinctual demands become conscious and, simultaneously, new understanding of one's parents (even compassion) takes the place of an unforgiving hatred. Distortions and exaggerations that have become dominant characteristics of the fragmented self are corrected by remembering other aspects and qualities of past relationships. This can lead to a reconciliation with the past.

Between normal development, in which healing is effected by experience built upon a sense of basic trust, and the special healing that occurs in psychoanalysis, quasi-therapeutic relationships sometimes spring from individuals who have empathy and who spontaneously reach people in special need.

Erik Erikson refers to one such quasi-therapeutic relationship in his description of Martin Luther's identity crisis. Luther's ambivalence toward authority in general led him into all sorts of difficulties with real authority figures, often to the point where the overscrupulous young man could only irritate those around him. There was, however, one exception, a superior named Dr. Staupitz. Luther, in a procession behind a figure of Christ, had an anxiety attack. (He was prone to anxiety attacks when faced with events that aroused anger and other repressed impulses.) Erikson describes the therapeutic event as follows:

> It seems that [Luther] always remembered most vividly those states in which he struggled through to an insight, but not those in which he was knocked out. Thus, in his old age, he remembers well having been seized at the age of thirty-five by terror, sweat, and the fear of fainting when he marched in the Corpus Christi procession behind his superior, Dr. Staupitz, who carried the holy of holies. (This Dr. Staupitz . . . was the best father figure Luther ever encountered and acknowledged; he was a man who recognized a true *homo religiosus* in his subaltern and treated him with therapeutic wisdom.) But Staupitz did not let Luther get away with his assertion that it was Christ who had frightened him. He said, *"Non est Christus, quia Christus non terret, sed consolatur."* (It couldn't have been Christ who terrified you, for Christ consoles.) This was a therapeutic as well as a theological revelation to Luther and he remembered it.[7]

The healing of splits in the ego can even take place in the most impersonal superior-subordinate relationships. Dwight David Eisenhower described (although not in the terms of psychological healing) a turning point in his career.[8] Shortly after World War I, Eisenhower, then a young officer somewhat pessimistic about his career chances, asked for a transfer to Panama to work under General Fox Connor, a senior officer whom Eisenhower admired. The army turned down Eisenhower's request. This setback was very much on Eisenhower's mind when he was hit by the tragic death of Ikey, his first-born son. The infant succumbed to the influenza epidemic, and the young parents were grief-stricken. By some sense of responsibility for their own, the army came through with orders transferring

Eisenhower to Panama, and he took up his duties under General Connor with the shadow of his lost son very much upon him.

Eisenhower reverted to being the son he lost in a relation to the kind of father he would have wanted to be; in this highly charged situation, Eisenhower began to learn from his mentor. General Connor offered, and Eisenhower gladly took, a magnificent tutorial on the military. The effects of this relationship on Eisenhower cannot be measured quantitatively, but, in Eisenhower's own reflections and the unfolding of his career, one cannot overestimate its significance in the reintegration of a person shattered by grief.

One characteristic of grief and mourning is the working through of conflicting emotions centered upon the lost object. One is at once angry with the dead person (a seemingly primitive reaction, yet one that recurs frequently during mourning), guilty at having failed him, helpless because of events beyond one's control, and bereft of the love given and received in a human relationship. The work of mourning entails incorporation of the lost object — he is taken into the self, and all the conflicting emotions now rage within the self. The individual is very vulnerable in the face of the psychological regression that takes place during incorporation, but he is also susceptible to influence. This explanation accounts, in part, for the effect General Fox Connor had on his junior, Dwight Eisenhower.

People who are not fortunate enough to find or use therapeutic relationships often engage in the excision of unacceptable fragments by themselves, rather than seeking modes of healing through the help of others. Suicide, the extreme example of excision, enables one to understand other futile and destructive attempts to rid the self of what is experienced as bad, dangerous, and ungiving. In other forms of excision, the psyche may temporarily obtain relief from oppression from within but at the expense of reality-testing and genuine personal relationships.

Sigmund Freud wrote a remarkable study of a psychotic man who, in reaction to the dangers of helplessness and, ultimately, of self-destruction, unconsciously modified his internal world so that he became grandiose and megalomaniacal.[9] For this man, Paul Schreber, power was incorporated inside himself; there was no limit to his grandiosity. Schreber was an influential German jurist who became depressed upon receiving a promotion. Following a long and recurring psychosis, he began to write his memoirs as a natural history of a mental illness. He believed, in his grandiosity (and, paradoxically, with merit), that his experience would prove to be a revelation to the world. Freud interpreted the autobiography to show scientifically how the ego defends itself even at the cost of reality. Schreber held to a system of delusional ideas. He believed that he had a special relationship to God in which God sought to penetrate him with rays. Schreber adopted a feminine attitude toward God, and in this sense he became androgynous: he could conceive and give birth to a perfected self, so that he would need no one, and would be free of dependency and the sense of indebtedness.

This last grasp for power is evidence of sickness; indeed, the delusional ideas become the reality. However, given the fragmented self, the delusional system, with all its grandiosity, is a form of excision, a way to rid oneself of bad objects that have become tormentors of the psyche. Freud mentioned in this context that "the delusional formation, which we take to be the pathological product, is in reality an attempt at recovery, a process of reconstruction."[10] This basic defense against assaults from within, when it remains delusional, affects only the individual, not the outer world.

Self and Objects

One of the fascinating dramas in the history of industrial management is the life of Henry Ford and his development of the Model T and the assembly line.[11] Ford was determined to gain complete control of all aspects of the manufacture and sale of his car. That he nearly succeeded testifies to his genius. That he also failed indicates the limits of his capacity to translate fantasy into reality. There was a rather strange quality to

Ford's human relationships. Compare, for example, his attachment to Harry Bennett with his relationship to his own son,
Edsel. Harry Bennett came from a shady background in De-
troit; he had associated with gangsters and thugs. By contrast,
Edsel was a sensitive, well-educated man who was averse to
using aggressive tactics in his dealings with other people. Bennett took the lead in Ford's strike-breaking activities, encouraging sabotage and spying on employees even remotely suspected
of disloyalty to Ford. Ford developed a very close relationship
with Bennett, but he rejected and humiliated his son. When
the Ford Motor Company found itself in trouble because of its
antiquated organization and product line, Edsel attempted to
remedy the situation by making proposals for new methods of
organizing the company and for the development of new product lines. Ford cruelly rejected his son's help and seemed to
draw ever closer to Bennett, whose advice and suggestions only
fed Ford's paranoid and distrustful thoughts.

Common-sense observation of Ford's relationship to subordinates fails to explain his perverse attachment to an aggressive
and devious man and his simultaneous rejection of his constructive and well-meaning son. But this bizarre and self-defeating
attachment is part of a compulsion to defend oneself against
unconscious objects that are represented in the self.

Individuals attach themselves to real objects who meet the
requirements of fantasy. The fantasies include opposing images
of what is good and bad in relationships of power, love, and
dependency. Ford could not resolve his attachment to his parents; he carried a legacy of anger toward them. He split his
perceptions of parents, just as he created split images in his
relationship to subordinates. At a conscious level, he idealized
his mother and hated his father. His father, in effect, became
the carrier for the negative reactions of a dependent child to a
powerful parent; his mother reflected what he idealized but
probably never realized. The split images of loving and hating
parents and of good and bad sons were the precursors of his
reactions to Harry Bennett and Edsel Ford. By projecting these
split images on to them, he was able to create a drama in the
real world by unfolding images of his past. In this way, Ford

attempted to excise the hostile images that he was unable to put away or to heal. His acceptance and overvaluation of Harry Bennett as the angry, aggressive, harsh side of himself enabled Ford to regulate his anxiety over being rejected and cast out. Bennett also acted out for Ford the side of himself that wanted revenge on siblings and on others who came between himself and his parents. Edsel Ford, who represented the image of the good, loving son, had to be rejected and dealt with harshly, because this tender and loving self reflected Ford's own wishes for a close relationship to his father, which he also unconsciously feared. Closeness to his father was a source of anxiety because it involved unconscious homosexual impulses. Unable to tolerate these impulses, he had to reject and cast aside his son. Ford prevented himself from accepting and using the help offered to him.

The projection of internal split images on to people in the real world is one way of using power relations to regulate personal anxiety. The capacity to establish relationships with others based on objective assessments of self and object is a psychological achievement of major proportions. Yet this achievement frequently occurs at the expense of deep feelings and emotions in human relationships. Often, the individuals who value objectivity in dealing with others are people who avoid deep emotional attachments and relationships. They avoid attachment to others in order to repress memories of infantile relationships and the painful experience of dependency.

There is no logic to love. Emotion follows its own path in making human attachment, and the path inevitably leads back to the past. The influence of the past is not necessarily pathological. The sense of continuity in life arises in the reflection of oneself in another without the distortions that arise when people seek to merge their identities. But the difference between identification with empathy and the defensive projection of intolerable self-images on to others determine whether power relationships serve human purposes or individual narcissism. As people learn to trust their capacity for closeness and love for other people (when they no longer must destroy what they need), it gradually becomes possible to be both objective and tender with others. This dilemma between objectivity and emotionality is caused by the difficulty of binding together a fragmented self.

The development of human relationships progresses from a stage of total narcissism, or love of the self, to object love, which involves the relationship of two separate individuals. Pure narcissism exists during those early stages of development when the individual is incapable of acknowledging, or being aware of, a separation between the self and the object world. Separation and individuation occur gradually under the beneficial effects of good care, on the one hand, and, on the other, the gradual development of perceptual capacities for distinguishing the self from the outer world. Secure separateness leads also to the capacity to form an objective valuation of objects and to adjust responses to the needs of others as well as to one's own. This awareness is often referred to as mutuality — the capacity for give and take — which, as we indicated in the previous chapter, is also the basis for relationships of order and hierarchy in organizations.

Studies in the development of children and the disturbances of narcissism indicate that establishing a self-object relation based upon separateness is a hazardous procedure.[12] The hazards are controlled by an intermediate stage in object relations, in which the individual creates ties through the fantasy that his love-objects are part of his self-image. In this intermediate stage, the person incorporates these objects into his self-image while he attaches himself to them. As we have indicated, however, it is not only the benevolent sides of objects that are incorporated and infused with love and attachment. The individual also incorporates the hostile, negative images, and these unacceptable fragments of the self become available for projection on to others. Through projection, individuals create a drama in the real world in which they fuse the past and the present through the images of the self that they invested in other people.

Objects become a mirror of the self, aiding in the transition from absolute narcissism and complete object love. The evidence for the intermediate stage can be seen by observing children. It is not uncommon, for example, to find that a young child struggling with the need to separate from his mother will find an inanimate object to which he becomes closely attached.[18] The object may be a soft blanket or a cuddly toy, which the child refuses to relinquish. He must maintain possession of the object and use it to control his anxieties over loss and separation from his mother. The toy becomes a transitional object between the stages of total self-absorption and complete object love. The use of transitional objects to regulate anxiety serves a purpose in development, but it is only a temporary solution to the problem of separation.

We can summarize these three stages of the self and its relation to objects in the following diagrams.

Self and Objects

A *Self*	B *Self*	C *Self*
Self Absorption	*Reflected Object*	*Object*
The condition of narcissism where the self is taken as the object.	The transitional phase where the self image contains the representations of the object.	The reciprocal relation of self and object where two separate people can give and take.

Diagram A shows the self taken by the individual as an object of his own attachment, a stage of narcissism that exists in everyone during the early years. This is not necessarily experienced only once. Under stress or traumatic loss, individuals revert to this narcissistic stage and, when the condition is most extreme, show a total psychotic withdrawal from reality.

The study of psychotic individuals, however, warns us that we should not assume that the individual has given up completely his relation to reality. The fantasies of even the most severely disturbed people, those with shattered self-images, show that the inner world still contains the images of objects that were once real, but that now exist in fantasy only.

The second stage in the relation of self to objects, Diagram B, is attachment to the transitional object, in which the world of people reflects the images of the self, much as the little child invests his favorite blanket or toy with significance. In the example of Henry Ford's relations with Harry Bennett and Edsel Ford, the elder Ford was functioning at this intermediate stage of object relations. Edsel became invested with images of an unacceptable self, of a son homosexually attached to a father; Harry Bennett became invested with the angry, hostile self-image, which had to be protected to preserve the self. In other words, the transitional or intermediate stage in object relations regulates the anxiety the individual experiences from unresolved attachments of the past. The individual infuses his current reality with shadows of past objects. It is in this intermediate stage that the individual's orientation to power becomes most problematic; he is attempting to solve an unconscious conflict by using power in the real world.

The third stage, shown in Diagram C, involves a reciprocity between two separate individuals. The self and the object are differentiated. Qualitatively, the relationship may range from an objective contractual bond to a deeply emotional tie, in which the individual has a capacity to endow people with selective self-images without losing his objectivity.

We can look once again to Henry Ford to understand more fully how reality enters into the play of individual attachment to fantasy. One of the legends about Henry Ford, backed by significant fact, is that he remained completely attached to the Model T, for him the instrument of perfection. When subordinates attempted to show him that new market conditions made the Model T less than the ideal car, Ford resisted their suggestions. On one occasion, when Ford returned from a trip abroad, subordinates brought him into a room to see a mock-up of a new car that could replace the Model T. Ford walked around the car, inspecting it, and then tore it apart with his hands. He refused to entertain any possibilities that the perfect product of his imagination was no longer acceptable in the real world. Ford carried his attachment to the Model T to such an extent that competitors, like General Motors, gained positions in the market that threatened the very existence of the Ford

Motor Company. How can one explain this irrational attachment to an inanimate object? The explanation lies in the investment of inanimate objects (as a substitute for people) with meaning from self-images. The car carried symbolic content for Henry Ford. It signified a particular attachment to him, a method of reconstituting his relationship to his father. In this sense, the car became a transitional object, defending him against the loss of his father. Ford built the car for the farmer. It was to be simple in design. Above all, it had to be designed so that the farmer could maintain the car independently (and so that it was serviceable over the rough roads that the farmer generally had to travel). Ford's father was a farmer (an occupation that Ford consciously rejected). The car became the link to his father and the past. Ford paid a price for this link; he lost objectivity about the car's purpose and mutability, and diminished his capacity to be a father to his son.

Anxiety and the Problem of Mastery

The fear of destruction of the self and the anxiety over loss of identity are primarily internal conflicts. There is no single internal conflict that accounts for the pervasive anxieties for the survival of the self. Instead, each developmental stage contains specific conflicts that require mastery. These developmental conflicts begin with the demands of instinctual drives and their derivatives in fantasy.

The stimulation of the infant occurs when there is actual dependency for control of instinctual forces. When the infant experiences hunger and other bodily discomforts, the primitive fear of being overwhelmed by these experiences is mitigated by the repetitive presence and activity of a caring mother. The cyclical experience of feeling arousal, having a mother attend to needs, and then slipping pleasurably into the security and comfort of quiescence constitute the underlying basis for a sense of trust and for the capacity to experience greater delays between the arousal of impulses and their gratification. The anxiety connected with instinctual arousal typifies the fear of being rendered helpless in the face of forces that are completely beyond control. If the mother fails, in some way, in her caretaking responsibilities, then an underlying problem of mastery remains; the individual will constantly be struggling to control his impulses. In the extreme case of psychosis, for example, the withdrawal from reality and the resultant total self-absorption is a basic, though faulty, effort at mastery through the denial of the real world and its threats. Or, when individuals become addicted to drugs or alcohol, the aim is mastery and control of primitive rage and anger at ungiving objects that appear to destroy the self and at the image of the uncaring mother that is lodged within the psyche. Addictive behavior results from the craving for a sensation to overwhelm rage and to ward off depression that occurs when anger and debasement are turned inward.[14]

Primitive anxiety connected with the fear of loss of the self also causes sexual perversions. Like addictions, the motivation is defensive: to master anxiety, rage, and helplessness by flooding inner reactions with sexual fantasies and putting these fantasies into action that has some relationship to the mirror images of the self. Perverse sexuality and the preservation of the self is at the heart of Philip Roth's novel *Portnoy's Complaint*. As long as Portnoy floods his consciousness with erotic feelings both in masturbatory fantasy and in heterosexual activity, he controls rage directed toward his parents and their representations in the self. Although the theme of power indirectly expresses Portnoy's grandiosity, it is implicit in the aim of sexuality: to feel control over other people by picking them up, using women and caricaturing their manners, discarding them to suit the needs of the moment. The craving for power is an addiction. The erotic sensations that power-hungry people experience during moments when they feel dominant becomes a compulsion. They need the elation of power; if they do not achieve it, they suffer anger, depression, and the humiliations of dependency.

In each of these three examples (psychosis, addiction, and sexual perversions), the primitive anxiety centers on the problem of mastering inner impulses that, if uncontrolled, can lead to further fragmentation of the self and its destruction. The individual is in a life-death struggle. The annihilation may appear metaphorical, but, nevertheless, has a primitive force for the person. In the defensive struggle, the ego resorts to drastic measures and pays dearly for survival.

Individuals acquire certain characteristic modes of relating to reality through which, by getting power and securing control, they attempt to resolve the conflicts of helplessness, dependency, and the fear of being overwhelmed by the forces within the personality. But not all kinds of power wishes involve the problem of mastery at this primitive level of survival. Assuming a condition of "good enough" maternal care, the individual may not be faced with the fears of being overwhelmed by his own impulses. But there are other conditions of anxiety and parallel problems of mastery that trigger defensive reactions involving activity in the real world.

One such condition of anxiety is the wish to control the movements and activities of objects. Sigmund Freud described such anxieties and attempts at mastery in his observations of an infant at play.[15] The child takes a toy to which a long piece of string is attached, throws the toy away, and slowly draws it back toward him with obvious satisfaction. Or a child plays a game of throwing a favorite toy that an adult retrieves. The familiar childhood game of peekaboo represents another variant of loss and retrieval. The child covers his eyes with his hands and the object disappears; when the child removes his hands, the object reappears. This play produces feelings of great power and control over important people; objects appear and disappear at the whim and wish of an otherwise weak individual.

These games involve complicated mental work that includes the use of magic to secure a sense of omnipotence. During the course of the child's development, these transitory phases of magical thinking and omnipotence help to regulate anxiety. He can continue developing so that reality-testing gradually assumes an importance greater than magical thought and action. If, however, the problem of mastering anxiety leads the individual to fix on magical ideas and to equate power with magic, there is little chance for effective activity in solving problems.

In an earlier chapter, we referred to the history of the *Satur-*

day Evening Post, which illustrated how, under crisis conditions, the regression to magical thinking was a defensive reaction to restore confidence in the future of an enterprise about to go under. The original idealization of the *Saturday Evening Post* and the legacy of Cyrus Curtis represented a form of magical belief in the omnipotence of an idea (the *Saturday Evening Post* as a fixed reflection of permanence in the American society). The directors and executives of the *Post,* without being conscious of their dependency, were so reliant on magical formulas that, in a crisis, they merely substituted one form of magic for another in a futile attempt to solve the corporation's problems.

The problems of mastery arise also in the dilemmas of moral sanction and control. Individuals normally develop a sense of conscience in the form of internal standards. When their behavior fails to measure up to the standards of their conscience, they feel anxious, remorseful, and guilty. The effect of moral anxiety on behavior inheres in the Protestant ethic; when an individual does not work and meet set standards, he tends to feel anxious and guilty, and he will take steps to alter his behavior toward the desired standards.

A group of workers in a factory dominated by an urban, Catholic population had minority members who had been raised under the influence of the Protestant ethic.[16] These individuals were isolated from the group whose cultural beliefs supported hostile attitudes toward authority. The isolates came from rural backgrounds, mainly Protestant, and felt that authority was to be respected; they believed in meeting the standards and requirements of employment. During interviews, the minority members of the group would speak of the importance of a fair day's work for a fair day's pay, and of conforming to the directives of management. They criticized the dominant group for failing to meet expected standards of conduct. The records of daily production showed that the worker oriented to the Protestant ethic turned out considerably more than the average amount of work.

When individuals are susceptible to moral anxiety, they can fall under the influence of leaders and group cultures, even to the extent of violating commonly held precepts. If the individuals turn over moral control to others, the effect of individual conscience is weakened. An exchange of this sort must have occurred in the Nixon administration, and it led to the crimes of Watergate and other violations of moral standards. The tape transcripts show clearly that the President and the members of his inner group gave priority to narrow and immediate political interests, especially those concerned with winning and surviving. Watergate raises questions about whether the individuals concerned simply had no well-developed standards against which to judge behavior, or whether, under the sway of the presidential mystique, they relinquished their "ethical compass." Undoubtedly, the explanation for the behavior of one individual in the group will not be the same as that for the behavior of the others. In some, ethical failures were probably the result of defective consciences. In others, consciences weakened by awe of the President permitted participation in illegal acts that he sanctioned. In either case, when an individual has no conscience or when he turns over the regulation of his behavior to authority, he is free of anxiety and develops, if only vicariously, a sense of mastery and control.

The intriguing case of Jimmy Hoffa, the former president of the International Brotherhood of Teamsters, raises important questions about the uses of power in mastering conflict and regulating anxiety.[17] Hoffa resolved as an adolescent never to allow himself to fall under the control of another individual. His course was to gain power and to use it to control the actions of others. His standards of behavior were influenced by the paramount purpose of his life: to achieve dominance. Hoffa used his drive for control in very shrewd ways. He learned how to cause divisiveness among truck owners and isolate them into relatively weak bargaining units, while he organized the Teamsters to assert central direction of the union. He developed a bargaining tactic of divide and conquer. Instead of negotiating an industry-wide contract, he would go after a region. The strike weapon could effectively stop over-the-road traffic in one region; for all practical purposes, this had the same effect as a nationwide shutdown without incurring for the Teamsters the

costs of a massive strike. The settlement in one region established the pattern for the entire industry.

Hoffa's standards of behavior — justified by higher wages and
better working conditions for his teamsters — flowed from an
overriding need to master his environment and to control the
actions of other people. He resisted using structural devices to
create objective relationships (in managing the pension fund,
for example). Instead of seeing legitimate constraint, he saw
antagonists, people who were battling to seize his power. In the
end, James Hoffa went to jail. For someone who abhorred having others dominate him, submitting to the stringent regulations and restrictions of prison must have been a horrifying
experience. In addition, he lost his power and position in the
Teamster's union, even though he battled to retrieve what he
had lost.

Two biographies of James Hoffa indicate why power became
his personal instrument for mastery and control. He lost his
father at a relatively early age. His mother was a hardworking
woman, who raised her children strictly and perhaps even
harshly. For Jimmy, the world appeared to be hard and ungiving. In his early years at work, he was under the authority of
autocratic, tyrannical bosses, men who appeared arbitrary in
their actions. But in the course of this work experience, Hoffa
discovered that countervailing power could be obtained by
leading and organizing workers. He found a few older men
who served as his mentors, but he concentrated primarily on the
techniques of gaining and holding power. He had difficulty,
however, in understanding the initiatives and constraints of
independent groups. Without a realistic grasp of the limits of
power, Hoffa lacked self-control, and this lack proved to be his
Waterloo.

The Grandiose Self

There is a high risk in striving for power when a grandiose
self-image splits apart from other internal images during the
defensive struggle with and against objects that are partly real
and partly fragments within the psyche. The grandiose self re-

sults from "concentrating perfection and power upon the self [while] turning away disdainfully from an outside world to which all imperfections have been assigned."[18]

Why the need for perfection and why the concentration of power in the self at the expense of other people and reality? On a cultural level, perfection and grandiosity can be attributed to the innate helplessness of the human being. (He is born totally dependent and is destined to die.) But such cultural attributions say both too much and too little. How does grandiosity work in and for the individual?

A young man who refused to accept limits developed a defense against anxiety and depression that consisted of a fury of activity. He was a hard worker but also a believer in his future omnipotence. The problem, simply put, was how to realize the omnipotence and grandiosity in which he believed. One way was to find someone who seemed to be perfect and powerful and to get from him the key, the magic substance, the source of perfection. His beliefs in omnipotence, the conviction that one could really fulfill the image of the grandiose self, affected his life and work, since he did not dare confront his beliefs by real performance, whether in writing, sex, or other human relationships. The problem was how to avoid this confrontation.

There are a number of ways to avoid the truth, especially to by-pass the inevitable depressive feeling that sets in when one recognizes limits. One avenue of avoidance is to become passive and to find people who like to be exploited. When one plays the game of taking from others, he feels no need to decide, commit, or think about someone else.

Exploitation is most evident in the unhappy love affairs experienced by many young women. Their attraction to passive men is like that of the moth to the flame. The unconscious motive behind this attraction is to *feel* powerful, controlling conditions of intense emotional reactions. But the guilt caused by these wishes and the pull of masochism guarantee that, instead of dominating, the women submit. They then become substitute mothers who must take care of a dependent child and submit to his aggression, which is born of his hatred toward the mother who has failed to give enough.

It is not uncommon to find women at the height of their

exploitation in an affair experiencing and expressing serious discontent with the limitations of their jobs and the restraints of competitive relationships with men. They are, indeed, capable of abstract arguments about the limitations of freedom in corporate relationships but are, at the same time, blind to their willingness to give up all freedom in the service of a neurotic attachment.

Another line of defense exists in pre-emptive action: to escape the danger of being suddenly overwhelmed by anxiety, a person initiates moves toward the dangerous situation. One cannot then be rendered helpless and passive as though caught by surprise in some ridiculous and shameful position.

During World War II, Drew Pearson, the originator of the newspaper column, "The Washington Merry-Go-Round," broke a story about General George S. Patton, Jr.[19] Patton was a military hero of the old mold and very different from his boss, General Eisenhower. Patton was an expert horseman, a military dude in his choice of uniforms. He carried two pearl-handled revolvers on his hips and in other ways portrayed a figure afraid of nothing. He hated the restraints placed on him during the war by agreements among Allied officers. His idea of combat was to attack, to keep moving, and to disregard coordination and grand strategies. During the campaign in Sicily, he raced to get to Messina ahead of General Montgomery, commander of the British forces. Patton was under a great deal of pressure, because of heavy casualties, battle weariness, and the urgency he felt to beat Montgomery to Messina.

Patton took to visiting wounded soldiers in evacuation hospitals. On two separate occasions, he saw a man who was not obviously wounded, and approached the soldier to find out what was wrong. The soldier in each case appeared anxious; one said, "I guess I can't take it." Patton became enraged, slapping the soldier and swearing at him.

The general's loss of control came about for many reasons, including worry, fatigue, and concern about the morale and battle capacity of his troops. In addition to the objective difficulties of the campaign and his sense of urgency, Patton had to cope with a grandiose self. This grandiose self felt compatible with Patton's bravery but not with his fears of cowardice. In hitting the soldier, Patton lashed out at his unconscious fears, which contradicted the grandiose self portrayed in his outward appearance and manner. The side of himself that he feared contained images of his father, who had disrupted the family tradition of the military and become an intellectual as well as a gentleman. The pattern of intense activity, which sometimes was expressed in compulsive work or bravado, led inevitably to his anxiety.

What makes men anxious, at odds with themselves, and so trigger-like in their reactions to real as well as psychic danger? In popular terms, the danger exists in the expectation that one will be exposed as an inadequate male. Barbara Tuchman elevated the conflicts of masculinity to a hypothesis about leadership in a speech to the American Foreign Service Association. She said that one of the psychological problems affecting a leader's ability to deal with unpleasant truths is his "fear of not appearing masterful, or a ruler's sense that his manhood is at stake." Continuing, Tuchman said:

> Proving his manhood was I imagine, a factor pushing President Nasser of Egypt into provoking war with Israel in 1967 so that he could not be accused of weakness or appear less militant than the Syrians. One senses it was a factor in the personalities of Johnson and Nixon in regard to withdrawing from Vietnam; there was that horrible doubt, "Shall I look soft?" It was clearly present in Kennedy too; on the other hand it does not seem to have bothered Eisenhower, Truman, or F.D.R. . . .[20]

Masculinity and potency are by-products of the demands of a grandiose self. Richard Nixon needed to feel he was masterful, in control, able to deal manfully with crises, rather than submissive, weak, and, by implication, castrated. He therefore accepted American withdrawal from Vietnam, but only after he ordered savage bombing and thereby asserted our awesome military power.

The notion of secrets figures in psychoanalysis, the art and science of delving behind the veneer of character and manners. Patients can often be anxious about revealing secrets. Secrets pertain to the body: they are attached to images of sexuality and to associations of cleanliness and filth, purity and debasement. Secrets go beyond the body, too. Sometimes the need to hide fortifies resistances to the recalling of events from the past; sometimes secrets appear in the confessions of minor sexual perversions or of perverted ideas. Sometimes the images take on an intense quality, in which the patient expresses driving needs for the key that will unlock secrets. Here, he begins to come closer to the truth. He may reveal his sense of sexual inadequacy, fears that he is homosexual, and that analysis will establish this as the truth about himself to which he will have to conform. This idea is only a short step away from another truth — that perhaps there has been, in his longings to love and be loved, an underlying wish to be a woman. But the notion that a man may wish to be a woman, or even hate a woman because of envy, can be misunderstood if one neglects the narcissistic component of the idea. This idea is not a homosexual wish to be a woman with a man; it is, instead, a wish to become reunited with a lost mother and, in the process, to recover the lost part of the self that is at the base of one's grandiosity. This reunification of the self then gives a greater capacity for action — it is the stuff of which heroes are made, though they can be tragic when reality overtakes fantasy. The tragic heroes of political leadership fail to reckon with the destructive potential of grandiosity and the divided self.

There are two distinct types of career in politics. The first is characterized by the achieving and securing of power; the second, by the use of power. In the first kind, the laws of success involve the psychology of deference. One cannot be too humble, too serving, too responsive to the wishes of others. Ask me to appear at a testimonial dinner, and I shall be there. Present me with the complaints of my constituents, and I am alert and sympathetic. Face me with a mirror of myself, and I shall be sincere and compliant.

The rule of ascendancy in bureaucratic politics is deference. The psychic assets one uses are selflessness and masochism, the capacity to suffer and, above all, to survive. There is no place for the grandiose self; the person remains divided, in a state of repressed longing.

A political man on the make avoids becoming depressed by activity. The activity of political and organizational life presents numerous auxiliary defenses against the frank appearance of the grandiose self and against the depressive reaction that occurs when the comparison is made between one's real and one's ideal self. In activity, exhibitionistic needs find satisfaction in the stagecraft of career. Latent wishes for omnipotence find expression in situations that demand reciprocal activity: if one does for others, they enter his debt and are on call for payment as time and circumstances may demand. Corporate man seeks deference from others, and he knows that, in the climb to the peak of power, he must show deference. According to the laws of reciprocity in human affairs, it is better to give, at least at first, if one wants, eventually, to receive. Like Uriah Heep in Dickens' *David Copperfield,* "your 'umble servant" ingratiates himself while climbing, but once he has reached the top of the ladder, he can shift from deferring to demanding deference.

Holding the peak of power may mean becoming the object of deference where defenses against grandiosity are tested. There have been safeguards against grandiosity in the history of American politics. An established elite, an aristocracy like the one that produced a Franklin Roosevelt, in which the sense of noblesse oblige prevented the flourishing of a detached and grandiose self, is an example of these safeguards. In the times of machine politics, the kind of politics that nurtured Harry Truman, similar protections existed in the code of loyalty one lived by during one's rise to power. A third kind of protective shield exists in the codes and commitments that characterize large organizations like the military. This was President Eisenhower's source of nurture and perhaps accounts for the way he avoided grandiosity by subordinating himself to a code and community.

Leadership in the nineteen sixties and nineteen seventies has fallen to self-made individuals who avowed no allegiances to codes and communities and whose Achilles' heel was a secret and grandiose self. In the rise to power, deference politics fosters ambitions and suppresses grandiosity. But once the prize has been obtained, controls give way and hubris takes over. If one of the important tasks of leadership is to establish communication with people, grandiosity will always get in the way. Under these circumstances, both leader and led alike become isolated, detached, and victimized by the elation and despair that accompany the victories and defeats of short-range decisions and policies.

The self-made man has long been an ideal in American leadership, probably reflecting our origins in overturning established authority and moving toward an open society. Recent history warrants a closer examination of what being self-made entails. It is not simply ambition and the climb from humble origins to lofty position. Maintaining inner cohesion while moving away from early attachments, integrating past and present identities, acknowledging grandiose images while valuing reality — these become the psychological tasks of the self-made man in his role as leader. The tasks are especially difficult because the leader who becomes too self-aware, that is, painfully absorbed in his inner psyche, feels incapacitated for action. Leadership exists in the real world just as power can be used to solve real problems. In the background stands the image of self that sustains or threatens a leader's grasp of power and the politics of organizations.

CHAPTER 6

Power and Politics in Organizations

It would be equally unreasonable to imagine that men at first threw themselves into the arms of an absolute master, without any conditions or consideration on his side; and that the first means contrived by jealous and unconquered men for their common safety was to run headlong into slavery. In fact, why did they give themselves superiors, if it was not to be defended by them against oppression, and protected in their lives, liberties, and properties, which are in a manner the elements of their being? Now in the relations between man and man, the worst that can happen to one man being to see himself at the mercy of another, would it not have been contrary to the dictates of good sense to begin by making over to a chief the only things they needed his assistance to preserve? What equivalent could he have offered them for so great a right? And had he presumed to exact it on pretense of defending them, would he not have immediately received the answer in the fable: What worse will an enemy do to us?[1]

—Rousseau

EXECUTIVE CAREERS depend upon securing power. Power transforms individual interests into coordinated activities that accomplish valuable ends. The executive incorporates power into his self-image, but the base of his power is in political structures. Organizations are political structures because people compete for power in an economy of scarcity. Power cannot be had for the asking; it must be distributed according to rules and codes that establish the legitimacy of authority in a hierarchy. Power is scarce because it is usually measured by comparing individual against individual and group against group. Comparisons are made when individuals gain power, usually at someone else's expense, or when a shift results in a relative change in the allocation of authority even if no one loses in a literal sense. The ratio of power held changes, so that people feel their value is either enhanced or depreciated in the power structure.

Paradoxically, although individuals use comparisons to assess their self-worth, the assessment, once made, feeds back on self-esteem. A man may compare himself with others and decide that his absolute or relative loss of authority forecasts more attrition in his power base. He may also compare his position relative to others against a personal standard and *feel* a sense of loss as a result. This tendency to compare is deeply ingrained and takes hold in the family, where early life experience shows that time and attention (if not love and affection) go to the most dependent member.

Corporate acquisitions illustrate the effects of comparisons. In one case, the president of the acquired corporation resigned because he could not accept the relative displacement in rank that was a consequence of his no longer being chief executive officer. Two vice presidents vied for the position of executive vice president. The expedient of making them equals drove their competition underground, but not for long. The vice president with the weaker power base soon resigned because he could not formulate a workable definition of his responsibilities. His departure resulted in increased power for the remaining vice president and the gradual elimination of "camps," which had been covertly identified with the main contenders for power.

The pyramidal structure of organizations produces a scarcity of positions as one moves higher up in the hierarchy. This scarcity, coupled with inequalities, needs to be recognized. It may be humane and socially desirable to say that people are different instead of unequal in their potential; executive talent, nevertheless, is in short supply. The end result of organizational planning should be to move the abler people into the top positions and to accord them the pay, responsibility, and authority to match their potential. On the other hand, the strong desires of equally able people for the few top positions available means that someone will have to confront unfulfilled ambition or shift his interest to another organization.[2]

Power Relations in Organizations

Organizations must deal not only with scarcity and competition, but with the politics that will always exist where there are constituencies. A superior may content himself with shifts in the allocation of resources, but he represents subordinates who, for their own reasons, may be unhappy with the changes. These subordinates affirm and support their boss. They can also withdraw affirmation and support, isolating the superior, with all the painful consequences isolation entails. As a result, subordinates are also constituents who, as in party politics, may ask the boss, "What have you done for me lately?" when he tries to defend his acceptance of current organizational changes on the basis of past performance. Appointments to positions come from above; affirmation of position comes from below. The only difference between party and organizational politics lies in the subtlety of the voting procedure.

In a large consumer products corporation, one division received almost no capital funds for expansion, but another, which had developed a new marketing approach for products common to both, expanded dramatically. The head of the static division found his power position diminished considerably; this was reflected in the degree of seriousness with which his subordinates accepted his efforts to influence activity (for example, programs to increase the profits from existing volume). He initiated one program after another, with little support from subordinates because he could not make a claim for capital funds. The flow of capital funds in this corporation provided a measure of power gains and losses both absolutely and relatively.

Still another factor heightening the competition for power that is characteristic of all political structures is the incessant need to use whatever power one has in a job. Corporations have an implicit banking system in power transactions. The initial "capitalization" that makes up an individual's power base consists of three elements: the quantity of formal authority vested in his position relative to other positions; the authority vested in his professional abilities and reputation for competence (a factor weighted by the importance of the expertise for future growth) ; the attractiveness of his personality (which is a combination of respect as well as affection, although these two sources of attraction are often in conflict) . This capitalization of power reflects the total esteem with which others regard the individual. The individual *knows* he has power, assesses it realistically, and is then willing to risk his personal esteem to influence others. But there are dangers. The individual must perform *and* obtain results. If he fails to do either, there will be an attrition in his power base directly proportional to the doubts other people entertained in their earlier appraisals of him. An erosion of esteem occurs; it will lead to self-doubt and will undermine the psychological work that produced the self-confidence preceding action.

A psychopolitical analysis of organizational planning is rather like a performance of a play. Each actor's job has been conditioned by a story — a plot and script — which is the invention of the playwright. The play is the acting out of the playwright's invention. The actors interpret, but they do so within the limits of the writer's imaginative construction. Similarly, organizational planning is the dramatization of someone's ideas, usually the ideas of the "power figure" or chief executive. But these ideas, which may be called rationalizations, are derived from the chief executive's fantasies; or we may prefer to say that the rationalizations of organizational planning begin in some imagined ideal state, a preferred order of highly charged emotional relationships in the mind of the central figure in the dramatization. This analogy does not suggest that the "play" is unreal or irrational. Whatever the fantasies behind an organization's structure, their effects are all too apparent to individuals who make major commitments to their job.

What distinguishes organizational planning involving alterations in the authority structure from other types of organizational change is a direct confrontation with the political character of corporate life. Such confrontations are real manipulations of power, not the indirect approaches that deal with ideologies and attitudes. In the first case, the potency and reality of shifts in authority have an instantaneous effect on people's actions and interactions and upon their self-images. In the second case, the shifts in attitude are often based on the willingness of people to respond according to the desires of authority figures, but usually these shifts are temporary expressions of compliance.

One of the most common errors executives make in organizational planning is to confuse compliance with commitment. Compliance is an attitude of acceptance to the request of an authority figure for change in an individual's position, activities, or ideas. The individual complies or "goes along," often because he is indifferent to the scope of the directive and to the changes it proposes. If he complies from indifference, the authority figure will have little difficulty implementing the directive.

Commitment, on the other hand, represents a strong motivation on the part of an individual to adopt or resist the intent of a directive. If the individual commits himself to a change, then he will use his ingenuity to interpret and implement the change in a way that insures its success. If he decides to fight or block the change, the individual may act as if he complies, but reserves other times and places to negate the effects of directives.

In a large company, the top management met regularly to discuss organizational planning. The executives responsible for implementing planning decisions could usually be counted on to carry out intentions when they had fought hard and openly in the course of reaching decisions. When they seemed to accept a decision, giving all signs of compliance, the decision usually ended up as a notation in the minutes. Surface compliance occurred most frequently when problems involved loyalties to subordinates. In one case, a divisional head agreed to accept a highly regarded executive from another division to meet serious manpower shortages in his organization. When the time came to effect the transfer, this divisional general manager refused, with some justification, to allow the executive to join his division, on the grounds that bringing someone in from outside would demoralize his staff. He had used compliance initially to respond to the problem of "family" loyalties, to which he felt committed. The existence of these loyalties was the major problem to be faced in carrying out organizational planning.

Compliance as a tactic to avoid changes, and commitment as

an expression of strong motivation in dealing with organizational problems are, in turn, related to the definition of individual interests. In the power relations among executives, the so-called areas of common interest are usually reserved for the banalities of human relationships. The more significant areas of attention usually force to the surface conflicts of interest, including, especially, competition for positions of power.

Organizations demand cooperative endeavor and commitment to common purposes. The realities of experience in organizations, on the other hand, show that conflicts of interest exist among people who share a common fate and who are supposed to work together. The overriding importance of conflicts of interest renders business more political than ideological.

If an individual (or group) is told that his job scope is reduced in either absolute or relative terms for *the good of the corporation,* he faces a conflict. Should he acquiesce for the common good, or fight for his self-interest? Any rational man will fight. (How constructively he fights depends on the absence of neurotic conflicts, and on ego strength.) His willingness to fight increases as he comes to realize the intangible nature of people's definitions of what is good for the organization. And, in fact, his willingness to fight may serve the interests of corporate purpose by highlighting issues and by stimulating careful thinking before final decisions are made.

Fortune magazine, in an article on IBM's decision to concentrate on a new computer line, described the consequences of the move for power relationships.[3] Individuals in charge of various divisions seemed quite capable of assessing the effects of the proposal on their authority and influence, and they tried aggressively to preserve their positions. The article suggested the difficulty in drawing a line between the desire to preserve an acquired position of power and the merits of the proposal for a new product line. One fallout of the decision was the shift of key people to positions of greater or lesser authority, depending on their stance for or against the proposal. What was unambiguous, to say the least, was the intensity of involvement for all concerned in working through the related problems of personal power and corporate decisions in product development.

Conflicts of interest in the competition for resources are easily recognized — in capital budgeting, for example, or in the allocation of money for research and development. But these conflicts can be subjected to bargaining procedures that all parties to the competition validate by their participation. The secondary effects of bargaining do involve organizational and power issues. The fact that these power issues relate to debate on economic problems minimizes distortions that are brought about when individual self-esteem is more directly at issue, when, for example, changes are about to occur in the authority structure. When organizations plan new formal structures, management succession, promotions, corporate mergers, and entry of new executives, the conflicts of interest are severe and direct because there are no objective measures of "right" or "wrong" courses of action.

There is a sizeable literature on organizational behavior dealing with the design of formal structures. This literature states that organization structures should be fitted to certain environmental-task conditions, suggesting that "tight and hierarchical" structures work best with programmed and competitive activity and that "loose and egalitarian" organizations work best in problem-solving and innovative activity. These suggestions have a certain superficial validity, but they avoid the main political problem of organizational planning. The critical question to be answered in a specific action is a "micro" event: who will be placed in a position of power? This involves particular people with strengths and weaknesses and a specific historical context in which actions are understood in symbolic as well as rational terms.

The literature on organizational planning, on the other hand, deals with structure as a "macro" event. The aggregate of decisions based upon criteria of tasks, environments, and the interplay of "systems" ignores people and the meanings they attach to events. All too often, the language of "macro" events serves the purpose (intentionally or not) of divorcing the decision-maker from reality, rather than bringing him closer to it, in order to help him escape the painful emotions that arise when he deals with conflicts of interest.

A new president of a large corporation wanted to appoint an executive vice president. The candidate he had in mind was one of six vice presidents equal in authority. To elevate one person from a group of peers (in effect, to name a second in command), would alter the formal authority structure. It also, as later events showed, stirred up feelings of deep anger, envy, and disappointment, as the change affected individual evaluations of the self and others in the currency of power and self-esteem.

The board of directors of a large corporation received a letter from the president saying that he intended to retire. The members of the board knew very well that the president had wanted to retire for some time. The reason he had stayed on was simply that naming his successor would mean making the painful decision of by-passing a man who wanted the job but who, because of age and a troublesome personality, seemed unsuited to the position. The problem the board faced was not that of reaching a correct decision. Indeed, there were actually several valid alternatives. The more serious question was how to meet and deal with the reactions of people who, as is true of most human beings, are busy deciding where they stand in their careers.

A family business, run very successfully if it were judged by sales and profits, had drifted into a committee system for formulating policy and making critical operating decisions. Every individual who was a part of the committee complained about the cumbersome, time-consuming, and inefficient decision apparatus. Yet they were helpless to remedy a self-made problem. To do so would have meant a shift to executive leadership and the delegation of authority to one of their number. Such a shift was not possible because of mistrust, envy, and the fear of domination, submission, and control in the executive power structure.

General Motors inadvertently confirmed what every seasoned executive knows: that coalitions of power to overcome feelings of rivalry and the play of personal ambitions are fragile solutions. The appointment of Cole to the presidency of General Motors followed by Semon Knudsen's resignation shattered the illusion that the rational processes in business are separate from human emotions and the ties that bind men to one another. General Motors prides itself on rationality.[4] To allow the public to infer that major corporate life, particularly at the executive levels, is not so rational after all can be damaging to the sense of security people get from belief in an idea as it is embodied in a corporate image. The fact that Knudsen was subsequently discharged from the presidency of Ford, an event that will be discussed later in this chapter, suggested that personalities and the politics of corporations are common conditions of life in large organizations.

But just as General Motors wants to maintain an image, many executives, as well as students of organizational theory, prefer to ignore what these illustrations suggest: that organizational planning is a *political event* that triggers and then feeds on the psychology of comparison. To analyze political events means to think about power relations in symbolic and subjective terms. The psychology of comparison involves the theory of self-esteem, both in its conscious manifestations and in its unconscious origins. There are practical benefits and general enlightenment to be gained from such analyses. The practical benefits include increased freedom to act more directly — instead of trying to "get around" a problem, one can meet it; greater objectivity about people's strengths and limitations, and, therefore, the ability to use them more honestly and effectively; more effective planning in organizational design and in distribution of authority — instead of searching for the "one best solution" in organization structure, one accepts a range of alternatives and then gives priority to the personal or emotional concerns inhibiting action.

Symbolic Meaning of Coalitions and Collusions

As a political event, organizational planning is a series of contradictions. It is an exercise in rationality, but its energy comes from ideas in the minds of power figures, the content and origins of which are only dimly perceived. It deals with sources of authority and its distribution, yet it depends in the first place on the existence of a balance of power in the hands of an individual who initiates and moves organizational planning through its various stages. The formal organization structure, usually the main outcome of planning, implements a coalition among key executives; the emotional basis of this coalition is a precondition for the acceptance of the formal structure. Finally, there are many rituals associated with organizational planning (such as participation, democratization, the sharing of power). Yet the real outcome is the consolidation of power around a central figure to whom other individuals form emotional attachments.

To take one case, the newly appointed director of a research and development center started organizational planning. The purpose was to establish a structure that would encourage innovation, participation, and responsibility for decisions at levels in the organization closest to the actual performance of technical work. The main idea behind the projected organizational changes was to eliminate the third level of authority and shift the power base of the second (the level just below the director) from direct to indirect influence. The net effect would be to "flatten" the organization structure, reducing the vertical distance between the top and bottom levels.

The redistribution of authority in this example of organizational planning used a latent coalition between the new director and the group leaders (fourth level of authority). The strength of this coalition depended upon the power of the director (derived from corporate headquarters, which made and supported his appointment) and the individual desires of group leaders for more authority. It depended also on the willingness of the director and the group leader to sever their ties with the second-level people. The net effect was a transfer of authority from these intermediate levels. The group leaders benefited from this shift, and the director's power base increased considerably; more people were directly dependent upon his evaluations and upon his control of information, activities, and budgets.[5]

In the discussions of organizational change in this case, the words "coalition," "balance of power," "gains and losses" never appeared. Yet these words are closer to the realities of the change, its causes and the reasons for its success, than the statements of objectives and the emphasis on improved technical performance. The statements of objectives and other rationalizations were attempts to make credible and legitimate changes that had deeper significance to all the individuals involved.

A coalition is successful when the interests of its participants are served. In this case, the value of additional power offset the disturbed relationships or losses endured by the managers excluded from the coalition. But this "trade-off" is a subjective evaluation. It would be years before one could determine whether the benefits of a flattened organization would be realized in motivation and performance. If performance depended on the technical competence already existing, then it is conceivable that the new arrangements would have little long-range effect. But here again, one is weighing intangibles against the reality of a coalition favored by an individual in the primary position of power to build and sustain it.

A coalition of some sort exists in all formal organizations. The forms and the psychological significance of the various sorts of coalitions differ. But no organization can function without a consolidation of power relationships between a central figure and his select group. As the previous illustration shows, the coalition need not exist between the chief executive and his immediate subordinates or staff. It may, indeed, by-pass the second level, as in the case of Presidents of the United States who do not build confident relationships within the cabinet but, instead, rely on members of the executive staff or on selected individuals outside the formal apparatus.

The failure to establish a coalition within the executive structure of an organization can produce such problems as the inability to make decisions and to evaluate performance, and infighting and overt rivalry within the executive group.

The president of a medium-sized corporation found himself besieged with requests to make decisions but hamstrung by the unwillingness of subordinates to make recommendations. Analysis of the organizational structure showed that no coalition existed in the form of close working ties between the president and key subordinates. The closest ties he had managed to establish were with individuals in relatively peripheral areas of the business. The consultant, whom the president asked for advice, deliberately shifted the president's attention to the key positions and helped him allocate authority necessary for a coalition of the president and three vice presidents, each of whom was given a major area of responsibility. The new allocation of authority was the easy part of the job; the more difficult part was convincing the president to make the mutual ties necessary for the coalition actually to take effect.

When a chief executive finds it difficult to create confident relationships, an effective coalition cannot be formed. The causes for this failure are many and complex; they usually involve the nature of the chief executive's defenses and his means of alleviating stress.

"The palace revolt," in the words of the *Wall Street Journal*,[6] that led to Semon Knudsen's departure from Ford Motor Company illustrates a failure in the formation of coalition. It is true that Henry Ford named Knudsen president of the company, but his actual position of power as a newcomer to an established power structure depended on the formation of an alliance. The individual with whom an alliance seemed crucial was Lee Iacocca. For some reason, Knudsen and Iacocca became competitors instead of using cooperatively a power base to which both contributed (as is done in most workable coalitions). In the absence of a coalition, the opposing postures of rivalry were assumed and the battle for control was waged. Ford ultimately responded by weighing his power with one side over the other, thus determining the outcome.

It is not at all clear why the coalition failed to develop. The personalities of the main actors and the nature of their defenses, which made certain coalitions improbable (no matter how strongly other realities indicate their necessity), may give a clue.

Defensiveness on the part of a chief executive can preclude the building of a realistic and workable coalition, so that he suffers self-enforced isolation.

The president of another medium-sized corporation established a coalition or working alliance with two of his vice presidents. He had, without conscious intent, excluded a very competent vice president who was in charge of a key functional area in the business. This vice president also happened to be a major stockholder. Dissipation of authority resulted because formal power derived from stock ownership and competence lay outside the main orbit of the president. The situation caused confusion on the part of subordinates and created suspicion and rivalry among the vice presidents. Again, this president sought a consultant, who recommended dissolving the existing coalition and reconstructing it around the two major stockholders: the president and the vice president. It was fortunate for this company that the stockholder–vice president was a competent person. In some cases, when coalitions based on the power of ownership do not coincide with competence, the results are unfortunate.

One of the most frequently encountered defensive maneuvers leading to the formation of unrealistic coalitions, and to the isolation of the chief executive, is the fear of rivalry. A realistic coalition matches formal authority and competence with the emotional commitments necessary to establish and maintain the coalition. The chief executive's fear of rivals, and the subordinates' jealousy of the chief executive's power, can result in paranoid distortions. People become suspicious of one another, and, through selective perceptions and projections of their own fantasies, create a world of plots and counterplots.

In a large advertising agency, a very gifted account executive, who was unsure of his real abilities, competed fiercely with other account executives and with the chief account officer who was his immediate boss. During account group meetings, this executive would become quarrelsome and aggressive. If marketing programs for his accounts were under discussion, he would dominate the meetings and fight any criticism of the plans. The problem appeared especially severe when the meetings included the heads of the creative departments, such as copywriting and art. The account executive ran into difficulty when, at his insistence, the creative departments developed an advertising campaign for a children's product that featured guns and other symbols of destruction. The chief account officer and other managers felt that parents would be offended by such an advertising campaign.

In decision-making, the displacement of personal concerns onto the substantive material is potentially the most dangerous form of defensiveness. The need for defense arises because people become anxious about significance of evaluations within existing power coalitions, and because all coalitions are susceptible to fear and rivalry, given the nature of the investments people make in power relations. Although it is easy to dismiss such reactions as neurotic distortions, their prevalence and impact deserve careful attention in all phases of organizational planning.

All individuals, and, consequently, groups, experience areas of stress that cause them to mobilize their defenses. Coalitions employ defensive maneuvers on those occasions where stress goes beyond the usual level of tolerance. A more serious problem occurs when the main force that binds men in a structure is the need to defend against, or to act out, the conflicts that individuals cannot tolerate alone. Where coalitions represent the aggregation of power with the conscious intention of using the abilities of members for constructive purposes, collusions represent predominance of unconscious conflict and defensive behavior. Before changes can be implemented, one must explore the causes of these collusions.

A young executive took over the presidency of a business in which his father had invested, gradually assuming control. The young man brought with him to his new job two friends with whom he had worked in another company. He appointed them vice presidents and assigned to them the functional areas of manufacturing and sales. The president had managed to inform his friends that he was unsure of himself, that he doubted whether he deserved to be president of the company and whether he was as good a man as his father. In effect, the president had communicated a basic motive for his attachment to his two friends: they were to provide the reassurance that he deserved to be president and that he was, if anything, more competent than his father. The three executives set out to prove the point by proposing ventures in new products and markets that would give the company a "new look." They also criticized the lack of management sophistication, particularly in the older executives, who had been with the company for some time. In at least one case, the group impulsively bought a company with a product line of dubious value. They also alienated an older executive, whose technical ability could not be matched within the company.

The collusion of latent interests among executives can become the central theme and sustaining force of an organizational structure of top management. For a collusion to take hold, the conflicts of the "power figure" have to be communicated and sensed by others as an overriding need that seeks active expression. Needs vary just as the structures that constitute collusions vary. For example, there is the need to take control; there is the need to be admired and idealized; and there is the need to find a scapegoat.

One can find parallels between the collusions in work situations and those in marriage and family. Very frequently, the strongest bond in a marriage is the expression of the unconscious and often unacceptable needs of one or both partners. A man who is very inhibited in his character and rigid in his self-control marries a woman who is just the opposite. He experiences through her behavior how he himself would like to be. The marriage may work until the point where the man's guilty conscience takes over and he has to punish his wife, as he himself would be punished if he were to act as he implicitly had encouraged her to behave.

If people could hold on to and keep within themselves areas of personal conflict, there would be far fewer collusions at work or in the family. But part of the human condition is that conflicts and needs take over life situations. As a result, one finds numerous instances of collusions' controlling the behavior of executives.

A multidivisional corporation found itself with a revolution on its hands. The president was very sensitive to the opinions of a few outside board members who represented important stockholder interests, and he was so afraid of being criticized by these board members that he demanded from vice presidents full information on their activities and complete loyalty to him. Over a period of years, he moved divisional chief executives to corporate headquarters so that he could assure himself of their loyalty. Other executives joined in to gratify the president's need for control and loyalty. The result of this collusion, however, was to create a schism between headquarters and field operations, and some of the staff members in the field managed to inform the board members of headquarters' lack of attention to, and understanding of, field problems. Discontent grew to such an extent that the board placed the president on early retirement. The new president, with the support of the board, decentralized authority, appointing new division heads who were to make their offices in divisional headquarters with full authority to manage their respective organizations. The new president faced the problem of the dissolution of the collusion at headquarters without the wholesale firing of vice presidents.

Just as the distribution of power is central to the tasks of organizational planning, the conservation of power is often the underlying function of collusions.

A manufacturing vice president of a medium-sized company witnessed over a period of fifteen years a procession of changes in top management and ownership. He had managed to retain his job because he had made himself indispensable in running the factory. To each new owner he stressed the importance of "home rule" in insuring loyalty and performance in the plant. He also tacitly encouraged each supervisor to go along with whatever cliques happened to form and to dominate the shop floor. A gradual loss of the company's competitive position, together with open conflict among cliques in the form of union disputes, led to the dismissal of the vice president. None of his successors could reassert control over the shop, and the company eventually moved or liquidated the operations in the plant.

Critical Episodes in Organizational Politics

Faulty coalitions and unconscious collusions, as we have illustrated, can result from the defensive needs of a chief executive. These needs, which often appear as a demand upon others to bolster the self-esteem of the chief executive, are tolerated to a remarkable degree. Often they persist for a long time before harmful effects become apparent to outside stockholders, bankers, or boards of directors, who exercise the final control over the distribution of power and authority in organizations. Occasionally, corporations undergo critical episodes in organizational politics that cannot be ignored in the conscious deliberations affecting how power is distributed and used. One such critical episode is outright revolt, as in the case presented earlier of the field managers who took their complaints against a chief executive to outside directors. This "revolution" resulted in the dismissal of the chief executive and, subsequently, in a counterphase of organizational planning aimed at decentralizing authority and restoring the coherence of power relations within the various divisional units.

Intertwined with the various expressions of power conflicts in organizations are three underlying "life dramas" that deserve careful attention. The first can be called "parricide"; it dramatizes the theme of stripping the powers of a "parental figure"; the second leads to the predominance of "paranoid thinking," by which distortions of reality result from the surfacing of conflicts that formerly had been contained in collusions; and the third is "ritualism," in which real power issues are submerged or isolated in compulsive behavior at the cost of real problem-solving and work.

PARRICIDE

The chief executive in a business, along with the heads of states, religious bodies, and social movements, becomes an object for other people. (The term "object" should be understood in its psychological sense: a person who is the recipient of strong emotional attachments from others.) It is patent that chief executives are objects because they control so many of the levers that direct the flow of rewards and punishments. But there is something to say beyond this obvious calculation of rewards and punishments that forms the basis for the emotional attachments between leader and led as object and subject.

Where a leader displays unusual attributes in his intuitive

gifts, cultivated abilities, or deeper personal qualities, his fate as object is governed by powerful emotions. We have used the word "charismatic" to describe such a leader. The word refers to a mystique, but also to the "great" man as charismatic leader; it expands to superhuman proportions what really belongs to the psychology of everyday life.

What makes for strong emotional attachments exists as much in the need of the "subject" as in the qualities of the "object." In other words, the personalities of leaders take on proportions that meet what subordinates need and even demand. If leaders, in fact, respond with the special charisma that is often invested in them at the outset, then they are parties to a self-fulfilling prophecy. Of course, the qualities demanded have to be present in some nascent form, ready to emerge as soon as the emotional currents become real in authority relationships.

The emotional attachments referred to usually contain mixtures of positive and negative feelings. If the current were only of one kind, either admiration or hostility, for example, authority relationships would be simple to describe and to manage. The blend of positive and negative feelings sets off secondary currents of emotion that intensify the relationships.

Norman Podhoretz in *Making It* provides a beautiful insight into the subtleties of emotional currents that charge the dependencies of those who need power upon those who have it. In his case, the example comes from the literary world and the reactions of his friends to his success as an undergraduate at Columbia. It applies equally to the power structures of business organizations, where the admiration of authority figures becomes infused with hostility. Podhoretz, recognizing the nature of ambivalent feelings, draws a distinction between jealousy and envy:

> Children are jealous creatures but not envious ones, the difference between the two passions lying in this: that jealousy says, "I wish I were as good a pitcher as you," whereas envy says, "You're not really a good pitcher even though you've fooled everyone into thinking so; if they weren't all so dumb, and if I felt like it, I could show them what pitching is." Where a precise ranking of best and second-best is not significantly relevant — in, for instance,

the area of money — jealousy would say, "I wish I had as much money as you, but I don't mind if you have it too," whereas envy would say, "I wish I were as rich as you and you were as poor as I." Jealousy is thus the covetous emotion appropriate to a situation of abundance and envy the covetous emotion appropriate to a situation of scarcity . . .

[Envy] is an imperialistic passion with an inherent tendency towards expansion into territories of the spirit that do not belong within its natural sphere of influence. And it is, in addition, an ultimately cannibalistic passion: it aims at the expropriation of the enemy's power and can conceive of no other way to get it than to destroy and then gobble him up . . .

In any event, while I myself from a very early age knew everything there was to know about jealousy, and from both sides of the fence, I knew almost nothing about envy, having experienced so little of it either as subject or object. Not only did I not recognize it when I saw it, I was scarcely aware that such a thing existed; and this remarkable obtuseness was of course compounded by my adored-child illusion that the world around me would declare a holiday whenever I won a prize. Hence my incredible stupidity in failing to anticipate that my friends at Columbia would be envious when, after absorbing the blow of the Kellett, they would also have to endure seeing me win the only Fulbright any of us was to get. Hence too my incredible insensitivity in expecting them to be happy for me and my amazement when I realized they were not. And hence, finally, my inability to understand the intention behind their effort to persuade me that glibness and an adaptability bespeaking flabbiness of soul, rather than any virtue of mind or character, accounted for my success. Not perceiving the envy in this assault — taking it, indeed, just as my friends themselves did, for the honesty of a courageous love (we were great believers in telling one another the "truth") — I was altogether helpless before it and before the guilt and self-doubt it aroused.

It was the first time I had ever experienced the poisoning of success by envy. Because it was the envy not of enemies but of friends, and because it came at me not naked and undisguised but posing as love and masked in ideologically plausible rationalizations, it was hard to identify as envy — and harder still because in my instinctive terror of becoming the object of this expropriating and cannibalistic passion, I was unwilling to admit to myself that it was in fact being directed against me. And no doubt in my terror of it, I was also trying to ward the envy off by allowing my friends to make me so miserable that they would finally have nothing to envy me for. Theirs the virtue of failure, mine the corruption of success: who then was the enviable one?[7]

Podhoretz may show a certain naiveté when he says that envy has no place in the psychology of childhood. There is much evidence for the case that envy in Podhoretz' usage indeed begins in childhood as an aspect of the sense of helplessness that besets the young in their fantasies about powerful adults. But putting aside questions about its origins, one can see that envy affects the quality of authority relationships, particularly because it is intertwined not only with jealousy (in the positive sense that Podhoretz uses the word), but also with simpler emotions of admiration, affection, and even love.

On the one side, subordinates cannot help having fantasies about what they would do if they held the number one position. Such fantasies, besides providing fleeting pleasures and helping one to regulate one's ambitions, also provide channels for imaginative and constructive approaches to solving problems. It is only a short step from imagining what one would do as chief executive to explaining to the real chief executive the ideas that have been distilled from this flight into fantasy. If the chief executive senses envy, he may become frightened, rejecting ideas that might be used quite constructively.

But imagine a situation where not one, but several subordinates enjoy the same fantasy of being number one. Imagine, also, subordinates who feel deprived in their relationship with the chief executive. Imagine, finally, that an organization is faced with substantive problems that are more or less out of control. The stage is now set for a collusion which, when acted out, becomes a critical episode of "parricide," or displacement of the parental figure.

In November 1967, the directors of the Interpublic Group, a $700 million complex in advertising and public relations, moved for the resignation of the leader and chief executive officer, Marion Harper, Jr. Harper had managed, over a period of eighteen years, to build the world's largest conglomerate in market services, advertising, and information on the base of a personally successful career in the McCann-Erickson agency. In expanding from this base, Harper made acquisitions, started new companies, and widened his orbit to include international branches and companies. As often happens, the innovator and creative person is careless about controlling what he has built, so financial problems become evident. In Harper's case, he appeared either unwilling or unable to recognize the seriousness of his financial problems, and, in particular, the significance of allowing cash balances to go below the minimum required in agreements with lending institutions.

Harper seemed careless in another, more telling, way. Instead of developing a strong coalition among his executive group, he relied on individual ties, in which he clearly dominated the relationship. If any of the executives "crossed" him, Harper would exile the offender to one of the "remote" branches or place him on partial retirement. When the financial problems became critical, the aggrieved executives, who had once been dependent upon Harper, then cast out, formed their own coalition, and managed to gather the votes necessary to fire the head man. Although little information is available on the aftermath of this "palace revolution," the new coalition had its own problems, which one would reasonably assume included contentions for power.[8]

A cynic viewing this illustration of the demise of a parental figure could conclude that if one seeks to maintain power by dominance then one should go all the way. This means that to take some, but not all, of the power away from rebellious sons sets the stage for a cabal among the deprived. Because they have a score to settle, they await only the right circumstances to move in and depose the aggressor.

This cynical view has its appeal, but it ignores the deeper issues of why otherwise brilliant men fail to recognize the realistic need for a coalition in the relationship of superior and subordinates. To answer the questions, we need to understand how powerful people operate with massive blind spots that limit their vision and their ability to maneuver in the face of realistic problems. The purpose that coalitions serve is one of guarding against the effects of blind spots; two people seldom have identical limitations in vision and ability to respond. The need to control and dominate personally is perhaps the most serious of all such limitations that can affect a chief executive; he makes it difficult for people to help him at the same time that he creates grievances that sooner or later lead to attacks upon him.

The unseating of a chief executive by a coalition of subordinates seldom reduces the emotional charge built up in the uncertain attachments to the ousted leader. A new head man has to emerge and establish a confident coalition. Until the contentions for positions of power subside and the guilt reactions attached to deposing the leader dissolve, individuals remain hampered by their own blind spots and their unconscious conflicts over power.

The references to "parental figure" may appear to exaggerate the meaning of power conflicts. In whatever ways it exaggerates, it also condenses a variety of truths about coalitions among executives. The chief executive is the central object in a coalition because he occupies a position analogous to that of parents in the family. He is at the nucleus of a political structure, whose prototype is the family, in which jealousy, envy, love, and hate find original impetus and expression, as in the relationship of child to parents.

It would be a gross error to assume that, in making an analogy between the family and formal organizations, the parental role is strictly paternal. There are also characteristics of the mother figure in certain types of chief executives and in combinations of mother-father in the formation of executive coalitions. A chief executive can also suffer from depersonalization in his role, and can, as a result, become emotionally cold and detached. The causes of depersonalization are complex, but they can be connected to those narrow definitions of rationality that exclude the importance of emotions in guiding communication as well as thought. There is some truth to the suggestion that the neutrality and lack of warmth characteristic of some leaders results from the fear that they will become objects for other people. To become an object may arouse fears that subordinates will become envious and compete for power.

PARANOID THINKING

Paranoid thinking is the distortion of thought and perception to which all human beings are susceptible from time to time. For those concerned in their work with the consolidation and uses of power, suspicion, the attribution of bad motives to others, jealousy, and anxiety (characteristics of paranoid thinking), may be more than a passing state of mind. In fact, such ideas and fantasies may be communicated to others; they may be the main force that binds men into collusions. Organizational planning is particularly vulnerable to the effects of paranoid thinking, since such planning stimulates comparisons while evoking anticipations of added power or fears of diminished power. Even without the stress of formal organizational planning, the fears and attributions of paranoid thinking can enter into communications. The mere passage of time and the weighing of realizations against the expectations of power and influence often aggravate tendencies to blame dissatisfactions on malevolent forces and individuals beyond immediate control.

Behind the suspicions and jealousies inflaming thought often lie kernels of truth. These complicate decisions and issues, often turning them into ambiguous combinations of truth and fantasy. Personality conflicts do affect decisions to allocate authority and responsibility. An individual may not be distorting if he senses through undercurrents in his relationships with others that he had been excluded or denied an ambition. To call these sensitivities "paranoid thinking" may be a gross misconstruction. But in spite of actual events, the potential for paranoia as a fallout from organizational planning and action is high.

Paranoid thinking goes beyond suspicion and distrust. It may take the form of grandiose ideas, the overestimation of one's position and control. This form of distortion leads to swings in mood from elation to despair, from a sense of omnipotence to one of helplessness. Again, when acted out, the search for complete control produces the tragedies that the initial distortions attempt to overcome.

Occasionally, we encounter a serious form of paranoid thinking, short of outright psychosis, which combines suspiciousness, personal omnipotence, and the obsessive attachment to an idea. This combination seemed to characterize the late Sewell Avery.

Avery had a truly remarkable career as a chief executive. After successfully managing the U.S. Gypsum Company, he took on the job of turning Montgomery Ward from a loser during the early Depression years into a profitable business. Avery was so successful that he must have had good reasons to believe, with reinforcement from grateful stockholders, that his business acumen and ability to foresee the future could not be questioned. The end result of these beliefs was the firing of more than forty vice presidents and four presidents between 1939 and 1955, the inability to arrange for management succession, and a weak business strategy for the postwar years. Avery held the conviction from 1941 until 1955 that the country would fall into major economic depression. He kept Ward liquid at the expense of store expansion, sales, and profits. Sears adopted just the opposite policy, with good results. In 1955, Sewell Avery resigned as chairman and chief executive officer. Then eighty-one years old, Avery finally responded to moves of dissenting stockholders and board members, as well as to pleas from family and close friends. But his resignation followed a personal humiliation in his confused final appearance before a stockholders' meeting.[9]

An executive can be just as much a victim of his successes as of his failures. If past successes lead to the false sense of omnipotence that goes unchecked in, for example, the executive's control of the board of directors, he and his organization become the victims of changing times and of competitive pressures, and may suffer, too, the weakened perception and less acute reasoning that often accompany aging. We could speculate that paranoid distortions are the direct result of senility and of the inability to accept the fact of death. Sewell Avery expressed his struggle with this grim fact when he said: "It grinds my insides to think of leaving this organization in hands that were incompetent, or in a condition in which it could not carry on successfully after the inevitable overtakes me." Although he was intellectually aware of the inevitability of death, Avery, like other men, could not accept emotionally the most ineluctable limitation of power. The disintegration of personality in the conflict between the head and the heart is what we come to recognize as the paranoid potential in all forms of collective relations.

RITUALISM

Any collective experience, such as organizational planning, with its capacity for changing the atmosphere and the imagery of power conflicts, can fall victim to rigidities. The rigidities consist mainly of the formation and elaboration of structures, procedures, and other ceremonials that create the illusion of solving problems but, in reality, only provide a basis for the discharge of valuable energies. The best example of a ritualistic approach to real problems is the ever-ready procedure of bringing people together in a committee in the naive belief that the exchange of ideas is *bound* to produce a solution. There are even fads and fashions to ritualism, such as the sudden appearance of overused words like "brain-storming" and "synergism." It is not that bringing people together to discuss problems is bad; it is that the faith that is invested in such proposals deflects attention from where it properly belongs.

In one research organization, professionals faced severe problems arising from personal jealousies as well as from differences of opinion about the appropriate goals and content for the research program. Someone would periodically suggest that the problems could not be solved unless people came together, preferably for a weekend away from the job, to share ideas and *really* work on the "nitty gritty" of the problem. (It is interesting to note that no one ever defines the nitty gritty.) The group would, indeed, follow such suggestions, usually ending the weekend with a feeling of euphoria induced by considerable drinking and a sumptuous meal. The most concrete idea to emerge from the weekend's discussion was that the basic problem stemmed from the organization's increased size, so that people no longer knew one another and each other's work. The solution that appeared, only to disappear shortly afterward, was the publication of a laboratory newsletter that would keep people abreast of their colleagues' newest ideas.

In another company, where major conflicts between line and staff people provided a constant source of tension, the meetings of both groups could not begin until the members carried through a ritual of fining people who arrived late. The least powerful "punished" the most powerful by imposing the fines. The fining proceeded with much joviality and talk about how the fund would allow the group to enjoy a weekend of spring skiing. There undoubtedly was some reduction of tension because of this ritual, but there were few substantive changes in the real power conflicts. The fact that the head of this organization was eager to participate in the ritual signaled to all concerned that he had neither method nor solution for dealing with the problems.

Ritualism can be readily seen in the behavior of factory work groups.[10] In one example, the workers, typically, had very little real influence on the making of decisions, and their position of power derived from union membership, which pitted one institution (management) against another (the union) in negotiating collective agreements. There were few uses of power available to the workers, so their behavior was turned inward to solve the problems of interpersonal relations of mixed ethnic groupings, the sexes, and the generations. The presence of these conflicts and the larger issues of authority and dependency compelled the group to establish rituals for the channeling of aggression.

One cannot assume that ritualism is an exclusive feature of work groups in factories. It is true that the absence of power, along with the limitations of sublimation characteristic of members of lower socioeconomic strata, sets the stage for the peculiar rigidities found in factories. But ritualism seems to exist universally, quite apart from differences in social class and occupational status.

The function of group rituals has its origins in individual psychology. There is a kind of mental conflict that individuals commonly experience while growing up and that, in its more pathological forms, finds expression in the complex of symptoms known as the obsessional-compulsive neuroses. Here, the individual is beset with alien thoughts over which he has little control. For example, a conscientious, hard-working executive driving along a highway suddenly panics at the idea that he had struck and left for dead a pedestrian several miles back on the road. He may realize that the idea has no basis in reality, but he cannot control his anxiety without turning back and retracing his journey in some ritualistic way, such as stopping at every second gasoline station to ask if there has been a report of an accident. Few individuals will fail to recognize this conflict in the benign practices of childhood, where the child, walking along the street, feels compelled to hit every tree he passes on the left-hand side with a stick, or to avoid stepping on cracks in the pavement because, "step on a crack, break your mother's back."

The rituals are magical formulae that regulate anxiety in their assurance that the strict performance of the acts in the ritual will ward off some danger. The danger connected with ideas that, for example, one has struck down a pedestrian or that mother will be hurt comes from one's own hostile-aggressive wishes. The function of the rituals is to control one's actions, to limit or restrict thought and action that could get out of control and result (at least in one's fears) in the dreaded wish. More generally, ritualism can be invoked to deal with any real or fancied danger, with uncertainty, ambivalent attitudes, a sense of personal helplessness. Rituals are used even in the attempt to manipulate people. Power relations in organizations is a fertile field for ritualism.

As had been indicated before, the problems of organizational planning involve the dangers associated with loss of power; uncertainties are legion, especially when one recognizes that, though there is no best way to organize and distribute power, individuals must make a commitment to some form of organization. Ambivalent attitudes, the simultaneous experience of love and hate, are also associated with authority relationships, particularly when dependency reactions appear in the superior-subordinate relationship. In addition, a person may feel helpless when confronted with events that could result in loss of status and influence. Finally, superior and subordinate are constantly tempted to manipulate each other as a way of gaining control over environment, a temptation that becomes stronger when there is a lack of confidence and credibility in the organization's efforts to solve problems in realistic ways.

There are negative effects to ritualism. A great deal of energy is expended in following the rituals and too much hope is invested in the magical formulae at the expense of accurate diagnoses and effective solutions to the problems of organizational life. When the heads of organizations, unsure of the bases for the exercise of power, become defensive, the easy solution is to play for time by invoking rituals that may temporarily relieve anxiety. Similarly, when executives fail to understand the structure and potential of the power coalitions they establish (either consciously or unconsciously), they rely more and more on rituals to deflect attention from their responsibilities. And when leaders are timid men, incapable of initiating or responding, their spontaneous reaction is to use people to act out rituals. Usually, the content and symbolism in the rituals provide important clues about the underlying defensiveness of the executive.

In one company, a vice president struggled with a sense of inadequacy that began in his family relations and found conscious expression in a highly ambivalent reaction to a very successful older brother. This executive constantly tried to prove himself by creating the image of "professionalism." He was the first to attend management seminars, to introduce new control methods, and to practice the latest techniques of managing. His subordinates would react with consternation when, for example, he adopted delegation as a technique. The subordinates would ask to review important problems, only to hear him say that they should work them out because he had complete confidence in them. He reached the height of absurdity when he introduced a pension plan and held a luncheon to honor the first employee to retire under the plan. This employee and his wife, both elderly, sat through a long afternoon of laudatory speeches, much to everyone's embarrassment, since the couple could barely understand English. The executive's downfall was precipitated by his adoption of a new technical method in manufacturing, which proved an utter failure and almost bank-rupted the company.

Obsessional rituals in organizations appeal to obsessional leaders; the gravitational pull to ceremonials and magic is irre-sistible because, in positions of power, these men use for public performances the mechanisms of defense originating in their private conflicts. These defenses include hyperrationality, the isolation of thought and feelings, reactive behavior in turning anger into moral righteousness, and passive control of other people, as well as of their own thought processes.

Very frequently, particularly in this age of psychologizing conflict, obsessive leaders try to convert others to some new religion. The use of sensitivity training, with its attachment to "openness" and "leveling," seems to be the current favorite. What these leaders, and the consultants with whom they form an alliance, do not understand is the fallacy of imposing a total solution for the problem of power relations where reality dic-tates, at best, the possibility of only partial and transient solu-tions. To force openness through the use of group pressure in T-groups, and to expect to sustain this pressure in everyday life, is to be supremely ritualistic. People intelligently resist saying everything they think to other people because they recognize that such a course leads to emotional overextension and, per-haps, to sadistic relationships. The choice, fortunately, is not between ritualistic civility and naive openness in human rela-tionships, particularly where power is concerned. In between lies the choice of defining those problems that admit of solu-tions, through which bright people can learn something about the intelligent uses of power.

In a large corporation, the newly appointed president pan-icked at the magnitude of the task of shifting from a relatively stagnant and traditional marketing approach to one of long-needed innovations. The introduction of changes brought him into conflict with vice presidents who had formidable and well-entrenched constituencies. Instead of selecting one area for change in a long-range plan, the president chose the route of conversion. He instituted, with the aid of university consult-ants, group approaches along the lines of sensitivity training.

On one occasion, to stress the importance of listening as well as to control his own anger, he placed adhesive tape across his mouth so that it would be impossible for him to speak. The vice presidents viewed this behavior with contempt, and thus the president destroyed whatever hope he had had for establishing confident and credible authority relations.

This example could be dismissed as an extreme instance of compulsion, but it contains a basic lesson: people in positions of power differ from ordinary human beings mainly in their capacity to impose their personal defenses on to corporate life. They can force others to act out, through collective rituals, the personal enigmas of behavior in relationships dependent on power. Fortunately, the relationships are susceptible to intelligent management.

A Search for Substance

The main job of organizational planning, whether it concerns developing a new organization structure, making new appointments to executive positions, or undergoing management succession at top levels, is to bring talented individuals to top positions, where they can exercise power. In the previous discussion, we indicated that organizational planning is bound to be a highly charged event because of the real changes in the distribution of power and because of the emotional reactions people experience when they gain or lose power.

The demand of organizational planning is for objectivity in assessing people and needs (as opposed to pseudorationality and rationalizing). But this objectivity has to be salvaged from the impact of psychological stresses that impel people to act out fantasies associated with power conflicts. The stresses of change in power relations increase defensiveness, to which counterreactions of rationalizing and myth-making contribute little, except, perhaps, to drive underground the concerns that make people react defensively in the first place.

Thought and action in the politics of organizational planning are subject to the two kinds of errors commonly found in practical life: those of omission and of commission. What people do and what they do not do both result in the outweighing of positive by negative effects. But besides the specific errors of omission and commission (the tactical aspects of action), there are the strategic aspects of action, which have to be evaluated in considering organizational planning. The strategic aspects deal with the aims and objectives of planning as well as with the style of the leaders who initiate change.

In general, leaders approach change with certain stylistic biases over which they may not have too much control. There is a preferred approach to power problems that stems from the personality of the leader and his defenses as well as from realities of the situation. Of particular importance as stylistic biases are the preferences for *partial* as contrasted with *total* approaches, and the preferences for *substance* over *form*.

The partial approaches attempt to define and to segregate problems that are amenable to solution by directive, negotiation, consensus, and compromise. The total approaches usually magnify the issues in power relations so that people act as though it were necessary for them to undergo major conversions. The conversions can be directed toward personality structure, toward ideals and beliefs, or toward values that are themselves connected to important aspects of personal experience. When conversions become the end products of change, we usually find anxieties about who dominates and who submits; who controls and who is being controlled; who is accepted and who is rejected. The aftermath of these concerns is the heightening of fantasy and defense at the expense of reality.

It may come as something of a disappointment to realize that, although organizations have an impact on the attitudes of their constituent members, they cannot change personality structure or carry out therapeutic procedures. People may become more effective while working in certain kinds of organizations, but only when effectiveness is not dependent on the solution of neurotic conflict. The advocates of total approaches seem to miss this point in their eagerness to convert people and organizations from one set of ideals to another. A person, therefore, would be a good deal wiser, if these propositions are true, to scale down and make concrete the objectives he seeks to achieve through organizational planning.

Leaders can also present a stylistic bias in their preference for substance and form. Substance, in the language of organizations, is the detail of goals and performance — *who* has to do *what* with *whom* to meet specific objectives. Form directs attention to the relationship of "who to whom" and attempts to achieve goals by specifying how the people should act in relation to each other. There is no way in which matters of form can be divorced from substance. But students of organizations should, at least, understand that attention to form *ahead of* substance threatens people's sense of what is reasonable in action. Attention to form may also present an implicit attack on people's conceptions of their independence and freedom from constraint.

Making form secondary to substance has another virtue: it can secure agreement on priorities without predetermining those who will have to give way in the final give-and-take of the negotiations that must precede decisions on organization structure.

The two dimensions of bias appear in the following matrix. Each of the four cells describes a different executive approach to power.

Cognitive Management Styles in Organizational Life

Selection of Goals

Partial

	Bureaucratic		Problem Solving	
Orientation to Action	Form			Substance
	Conversion		Compliance	

Total

Two dimensions define the executive's cognitive biases in selection of goals (partial versus total), and in orientation toward action (form versus substance). In the *bureaucratic* approach (partial goals and attachment to form as a mode of acting), the emphasis is on procedure and the establishment of precedent and rule to control the uses of power. The appeal of this approach lies in its promise of certainty in corporate relationships and in the depersonalization of power. A man does not *act* but, instead, *invokes* a procedure or rule that has the confidence of the organization based on the acceptance of traditions. Personality conflicts and contentions for power are subordinated and suppressed in the attachment to the past. The weaknesses of the bureaucratic approach are too familiar to need further description. Its major defect, however, is its inability to separate the vital from the trivial. It more easily commands energy over irrelevant issues because of its tendency to by-pass conflict, to adhere to the notion that few important problems can be attended to without conflict of ideas and interests. Eventually, organizations become stagnant because bureaucratic approaches seldom bring together power and the vital issues that make organizations dynamic.

The *conversion* approach (total form) can be found in religious and national movements. It has a special appeal to the suffering and the deprived; it depends on a coalition of a dramatic leader and the masses, often founded on love and acceptance. Its presence in business is evident through the human relations and sensitivity-training movements, as well as in ideological programs, such as the Scanlon Plan and other forms of participative management. The popularity of "management by objective" bears some scrutiny as a conversion movement directed toward power figures.

The second total approach, which differs from conversion in its emphasis on substance, is *compliance* with the directives of the powerful leader, the authoritarian personality whose personal power is expressed in some higher ideal that makes it possible for him to justify means by ends. The ideal may be race, used by Adolf Hitler, welfare, manipulated by Huey Long,[11] or religion, employed by Gerald L. K. Smith and

Father Coughlin in the Depression and early war years. In business, the illustrations are of a technological variety, as in Frederick Winslow Taylor's "Scientific Management"[12] and the elder Henry Ford's automobile and assembly line.[13]

Almost any technology can assume the proportions of the total approach if it is advanced by a charismatic leader and has deep emotional appeal. For example, "management information systems," "value analysis," and "program planning and budgeting" can provide a belief system based on order, rationality, and action, to counteract the fears of chaos and loss of control. The effects of these fears on the arrangement of power relations in business, government, and the community cannot be overestimated.

It is precisely such realistic action that is referred to as problem-solving. From observation of highly competent executives, one can assume that their effectiveness derives from their ability to define problems worthy of thought and action and from their skill in utilizing the organization to evolve solutions that characterize their style. The contrary notion — that executives are primarily caretakers, mediators, and seekers of consensus — does not accurately portray how the competent ones attain positions of power. To have power without directing it to some substantive end that can be achieved in the real world is to waste energy. To solve problems is to risk power in fostering a substantive solution. There are no absolutely right answers in solving problems, but there are ways of evaluating the correctness of a program and plan. With a little luck and more correct than incorrect decisions, the executive finds his power base enlarged and his ability to take risks increased.

The problem-solving approach to organization structure operates according to certain premises:

1. That the organization structure is an instrument rather than an end. This means that a structure should be established or modified quickly; the process of making changes should not be prolonged as if it were a search for a "best and single" solution for the problem of allocating power.

2. That organization structures can be changed but should not be "tinkered with." This means that members of an execu-

tive organization can rely on a structure and can work with it without the uncertainty that comes from the constant modification of the organization chart.

3. That organization structures express the working coalition attached to the chief executive. In other words, the coalition has to be established de facto for the structure to mean anything. If the structure is out of line with the de facto coalition, there will be an erosion of power and, consequently, of effectiveness. If no coalition exists in the minds of its participants, putting it on paper in the form of an organization chart is nothing more than a confusing academic exercise.

4. That organization structures represent a blend of people and of job definitions, with the structure designed to accommodate competent people. The reason for developing a structure to suit key people is that competent executives are hard to find. Therefore, in principle, one should insure the effective uses of the scarcest resources rather than conform to some ideal version of power relations.

5. That the organization structure is a product of negotiation and compromise among executives who hold semiautonomous power bases. The more the power of an executive is based on his demonstrated competence, the greater his autonomy of power and, therefore, his capacity to determine the outcome in the allocation of power.

The basic criticism of the problem-solving approach is that narrow definitions of issues may undermine the moral-ethical basis of leadership. This criticism, as with so many problems in practical affairs, can be overcome only by leaders who are able to see beyond the limits of immediate contingencies and whose thinking is free of the disabilities of emotional conflict. For it is the limitations of leaders, their way of handling superior-subordinate relationships, both in their cognitive and emotional capacities, that cause power problems.

CHAPTER 7

Subordinacy

Man is the only creature who refuses to be what he is. The problem is to know whether this refusal can only lead to the destruction of himself and of others, whether all rebellion must end in the justification of universal murder, or whether, on the contrary, without laying claim to an innocence that is impossible, it can discover the principle of reasonable culpability.[1]

—Camus

"WITH DEEP REGRET, I have concluded that General of the Army Douglas MacArthur is unable to give his wholehearted support to the policies of the United States Government and of the United Nations in matters pertaining to his official duties. In view of the specific responsibilities imposed upon me by the Constitution of the United States and the added responsibility which has been entrusted to me by the United Nations, I have decided that I must make a change of command in the Far East. I have, therefore, relieved General MacArthur of his commands and have designated Lieutenant General Matthew B. Ridgeway as his successor."[2]

With this terse statement to the press, President Harry S. Truman asserted his authority and fired General MacArthur. This bold action was, however, more cautious than it appeared; Truman had already extended himself in every way possible, short of surrendering presidential power to MacArthur. The final action was precipitated by a series of behind-the-scenes comments from MacArthur to the press and to Congressman Joseph Martin about the general's opposition to the government's policy of containing the Korean War and working out a negotiated settlement. MacArthur, badly burned after his defeat at the Yalu River, wanted to go after the Chinese. His views might have triggered another world war. MacArthur's aggressiveness appealed to the right wing of the Republican party and the China Lobby; President Truman consistently advocated the more cautious path of stopping North Korea's aggression and settling the war through negotiation.[3]

General MacArthur's insubordination, which included, besides the countermanding of directives, extremely rude behavior toward his commander in chief, raised the sensitive problem of subordinacy: how to be loyal yet independent, how to be a team player and remain an individual. If General MacArthur could not agree with the decisions of his superior, it was incumbent upon him to resign once he made known his own views. But he neither resigned nor accepted the policy about which he was fully informed. Instead, it seemed clear that General MacArthur's hubris warped his judgment, leading him to overestimate his power and to underestimate his responsibility.

Insubordination is only one side of the manifest difficulties encountered when one works under another in a chain of command. Another way for subordinates to fail is by an excess of loyalty and acquiescence — even to the point where the subordinate permits his boss to get into trouble. This type of acquiescence occurred during the cover-up of Watergate. It appears that all of Nixon's subordinates shared his fear that a disclosure of the events and decisions leading to the break-in would threaten Nixon's election campaign. The commitment to law (if, indeed, such a commitment had been felt) succumbed to the desire to preserve the chief's power at all costs. What fortified the misjudgments and immoral behavior of both the President and his subordinates was a psychological collusion fed by ambition and the desire to maintain supremacy against real and imagined rivals.[4] In this sense, the fallacy of extreme loyalty and the offense of insubordination have a common genesis in a kind of egoistic sense of power. Either one feels superior to one's boss, or a group in power feels itself special and beyond the accepted codes of conduct. In each case, there is contempt for accountability and worship of power.

With so much attention given to leadership and its aura of mystery, observers often forget that the path to leadership is successful subordinacy. People who advance in large bureaucracies generally understand this principle; it is even possible that the subordinate's role comes to be valued more than the chief's because of its usefulness and its capacity to fulfill a career. In the extreme, subordinacy may become more than a career; it may turn into a challenge to, and a caricature of, society.

"Humbly report sir, I'm an official idiot," is one of the recurring but surprisingly cheerful remarks by the hero-subordinate of Jaroslav Hašek's novel *The Good Soldier Švejk*.[5] Hašek has an uncanny talent for describing the dilemmas of subordinacy in bureaucratic situations.

Although Švejk may appear a simpleton, a former peddler of dogs with forced pedigrees who turned soldier, he ingeniously changes every apparent defeat at the hands of authority into a personal victory. Humor and shrewdness accompany modesty and innocence, making Švejk an enigma to his superiors. He is a master of evasion, adaptability, and often unwarranted initiative. Švejk turns into a modern hero who, confronted with impossible odds, always emerges successful in the end. His professed patriotism and monarchism, his apparent respect for authority, lead to a succession of disasters, but Švejk manages to keep his wits and to survive.

Subordinacy often provokes emotional conflicts of dependency, control, and aggression. Unifying these conflicts, which are usually unconscious, are the search for a parent and the wish for attachment. Discontents with the subordinate role make it difficult to carry out an effective work relationship and soon reveal themselves in behavior. The surface conflict may take the form of outright rebellion, as in MacArthur's defiance of Truman. There is a relation between manifest behavior toward authority and unconscious conflicts of attachment to a parent.

The chief scientist of a biomedical laboratory engaged in the clinical testing of new pharmaceuticals became severely depressed and entered a psychiatric hospital for treatment. The onset of the depression came after the chief scientist had, almost singlehandedly, saved the laboratory from a disaster over some strange and contradictory results in an important clinical testing program. The symptoms of the depression consisted of withdrawal (he would sit behind his desk for hours, hardly acknowledging the presence of other people), loss of weight, insomnia, and, eventually, delusional ideas. The symptoms suggested a psychotic breakdown, which led to hospitalization. After a time, the man made a good recovery.

Once the events leading up to the illness and the dynamics of his personality were reconstructed, it became very evident that there were no indications of depression during the stressful work period. The president of the laboratory, a highly respected scientist, reported that he had never found his chief scientist as effective or as much in control of his thoughts and actions as during the recent crisis. The president doubted that the laboratory could have survived without the chief scientist's abilities and diligence. One is reminded of the instances in which soldiers who hold up extremely well in battle become anxious and depressed after they leave the military and return to civilian life, far from the dangers of warfare.

There were two important features of the crisis period that changed as soon as the problems had been solved. First, the chief scientist had worked very closely with the president of the laboratory; they were in constant communication, spent nights at the laboratory, took their hurried meals together, and, in all respects, devoted themselves to the clinical testing problems. Second, the nature of the problem made it natural for the president and others to look to the chief scientist for leadership and guidance. The president and the laboratory were dependent on him. He became the object of the needs of other people, including the president, who, as indicated, was a gifted and highly respected person.

When the crisis had been averted and life in the laboratory returned to normal, the chief scientist saw the president only periodically, and he was no longer the person on whom the president relied to the exclusion of other professionals and executives.

Perhaps the most significant clue in an explanation of the psychosis was the content of one of the chief scientist's delusional ideas. He thought that he was in love with the president's daughter and that the president would object to their marriage. He hardly knew the girl. She was considerably younger than he, and she had never expressed any interest in him. As far as one could tell, the chief scientist's thoughts about this young woman appeared in conjunction with his depression. His interest in the president's daughter resembled the plot of some novels about military bases: the young lieutenant falls in love with the colonel's lady.

The chief scientist's problem was how to manage strong dependency feelings toward the president of the laboratory. Like many talented people, the chief scientist transferred his search for a strong and good parent to his superior in the laboratory. The dependent longings became highly erotic because of the close working relationship with the president during the crisis. He could tolerate and defend himself against these sexual feelings toward a man because the work structure actually reversed the dependency trend. Instead of his needing the president, the president needed him. In addition, the intense activity and the pressing demands to solve problems involving detailed experiments and the review of masses of quantitative information helped to contain the fantasies of a close attachment and to suppress homosexual longings.

When the work pattern returned to normal, the chief scientist missed the contact with the president. He also missed being the center of attention, the hero of the moment, which had added immeasurably to his self-esteem. The delusional idea of wanting to marry the president's daughter substituted for the wish to be close to his boss, disguising the homosexual feelings that came to the surface following the disruption of an intense but satisfying work period.

The psychology of subordinacy is the capacity to work closely with an authority figure and to involve oneself with work without the intrusions of infantile dependencies. The failures in subordinacy that frequently occur in business, government, and universities usually wreck the careers of otherwise gifted people. For example, the behavior of "drifters" can be interpreted as one manifestation of the problems of subordinacy. These people seem unable to hold a job; they continually get into trouble with their superiors, and they have an uncanny knack for putting themselves into impossible situations, antagonizing others and eventually provoking dismissal or avoiding the inevitable only by resigning. In a strange, compelling way, the need for punishment and a sense of rebelliousness coincide, with disastrous results for the individual in whom these feelings exist.

An advertising executive seemed genuinely surprised by his apparent inability to hold a job longer than a year. If questioned, he always blamed his superiors for their stupidity, jealousy, vindictiveness, or generally negative work attitude. On his entry into a new organization, he showed great promise, but his achievements never lived up to the initial impression. He managed over and over again to irritate his superiors by forgetting appointments, making poor presentations to customers, and sometimes executing advertising campaigns badly. And when his superiors criticized him, he usually took an aggressive, uncompromising stand, which eventually caused his departure. After working for a number of different agencies, he found it increasingly difficult to acquire new jobs. Word of mouth about his work traveled fast. At last, unwilling to face the depreciation of his sense of self-esteem, which the acceptance of a lesser job implied, he decided to go back to the university and start on a new career.

One explanation for his provocative behavior, which resulted in defective work performance and job-hopping, might be found in the persistence of a fantasy of rejection, a personal myth, recognized at a conscious level, that he was unworthy of acceptance. To prevent further damage to his already deficient self-esteem, he exaggerated his importance and appeared angry and irritable without cause. He engaged in provocative behavior, which converted what he feared in fantasy into a reality.

The instances of sudden attitude reversals are equally instructive in understanding subordinacy problems. Some people begin a relationship with an authority figure by overidealizing their boss, overestimating his strengths and capabilities. To these persons, idealization of a superior enhances their self-esteem. But the reality of everyday interaction makes it impossible to sustain the fantasy. There soon follows the opposite extreme of depreciation and underestimation. These individuals seem to be in pursuit of a goal that cannot be attained and suffer the inevitable disappointment. The disappointment resembles early frustrations and humiliations from childhood, a time when intense reactions of rage and anger follow injuries to self-esteem. Depreciation of others expresses the rage while it shifts attention away from one's own sense of depletion. For these individuals, parental or authority figures are viewed as "good" or "bad." They seem never to have acquired the ability to integrate these split images. Persons who polarize their feelings toward authority are compelled, in their evaluations of authority, to create and then destroy unrealistic images of other people. The persistence of fantasy and the unwillingness of these individuals to relinquish those images for reality illustrates the complexity of the emotional conflicts surrounding subordinacy.

The behavior of individuals in large bureaucratic organizations is a symptom of other conflicts pertaining to subordinacy. In these organizations, we often encounter those who accept projects initiated by others but who are very reluctant or unable to take any initiative themselves. We are reminded of the Japanese film *Ikiru* by the film-maker Kurosawa. Fascinated by the darker side of bureaucracy, the director presents a caricature of bureaucracy, showing the apparent unwillingness or inability of any city official to take initiative. In the first scene of the film, a group of women petitioners goes from department to department in a vain attempt to obtain city hall's cooperation in turning a swampy piece of land into something more usable. Dejected, the petitioners eventually end up where they started. The shock that one of the bureaucrats experiences after a physician tells him he has cancer and only a limited amount of time to live makes him realize the futility and emptiness of his past life. By accepting personal responsibility, he is able to convert paralysis of will into initiative.

Individuals who are unable to initiate seem to have little energy for work. They lack the capacity to stand in the limelight, to make decisions in full view of others. They prefer anonymity and are often compliant toward the wishes of their superiors. For them, assertiveness and initiative mean aggression toward authority and exposure to the threat of retaliation.

Occasionally, the discontents of subordinacy spread like a contagious disease and there may be group-supported rebellion. The president of a small research-oriented consulting firm had great plans for expansion and diversification, which, he felt, would lead to greater stability of the firm and, consequently, to greater security for his employees. The search for new ventures began to occupy more of the president's time. Soon after two new ventures were added to the original organization, he discovered a marked change in attitude among the employees of the original company. He sensed that they were isolating themselves completely from the new ventures, and were uninterested and even hostile toward the activities. Moreover, the president himself gradually became aware of an isolation from the employees of the original consulting firm. However, he had no complaints about the operating results; the performance of his employees seemed more than adequate. But he began to feel ill at ease during his visits to the consulting unit.

Most of the work of the consulting firm was done on a project basis. The president had been the main supporter of this arrangement; his contributions in research and his enthusiasm had been the main force in establishing the company after an initially trying period. But after he turned his attention to new ventures, he found it difficult to reassert his leadership in the original consulting group. Deadlines were not met, field work was not adequately completed, and there was a certain reluctance on the part of his employees to have him join projects. Eventually, exasperated by the failure of his attempts to overcome their negative attitude, the president decided to restrict his influence over the consulting unit to a number of financial controls, to relinquish leadership to the informal leader of the group, and to devote most of his time to developing other ventures. The president reasoned that, since most of the employees of the consulting unit were highly qualified professionals, he could not risk an open confrontation, which might end in their leaving him and joining a competitor. He felt that leaving them alone was the best solution.

A number of subordinates entered into a collusion to express their disappointment with the president's behavior. What first appeared a way to procure greater security for a company operating in a very unstable industry was interpreted by his subordinates, who had been very close to him, as neglect and rejection. After having been extremely dependent on their president, they reversed attitudes and expressed their apparent independence by excellent performance in the absence of the president and in other forms of behavior that were hostile. In time, the group managed to isolate the president from the original company.

Patterns and Dimensions*

As the previous examples have indicated, a position of subordinacy may generate psychological conflict that can find expression through group-supported rebellion or through action by individuals. Subordinacy can reflect and symbolize the motives, wishes, and tensions of the individual. There are two facets of this grouping of motives that deserve special attention.

One is the problem of dominance and submission. The potential source of conflict here is the balance achieved in the individual between his wishes to control and overpower authority figures, and, at the other extreme, his equally strong wishes to be dominated and controlled by these same figures. The theme of dominance and submission achieves a unity because both extremes aim at a single outcome: to secure the sole possession of figures who regulate and dispense life-sustaining rewards and punishments. This aim accounts for the intensity of reactions in subordinates, since the game is real and the stakes are high. In the case of bureaucracy, the stakes are often related to chances for promotion and career success.

The second facet is the balance achieved between activity and

* The model presented is based upon an earlier article by Abraham Zaleznik entitled "The Dynamics of Subordinacy" (*Harvard Business Review*, May–June 1965).

passivity in the individual's characteristic patterns of behavior. At one extreme, the individual initiates and asserts. At the other, he characteristically waits for others to initiate action and then reacts. The active-passive modes are usually well-established character traits, having special significance in personal history, particularly in the tensions of reward and deprivation, of energy expended and gratifications realized, of rage coming from frustration and of the need to defend oneself against this rage.

The combination of these two aspects can be used to describe four patterns of subordinacy and to illustrate various types of inner conflict (see diagram on p. 154).

IMPULSIVE SUBORDINACY

Rebellion is the main feature of the pattern of subordinacy that aims to dominate relationships with authority figures through active means. Mythology has captured the pattern in the story of Prometheus. Prometheus has always been the symbol of the archetypal rebel, courageous enough to stand up to Zeus when the latter wanted to destroy mankind. As the son of Earth, it was only natural for Prometheus to be sympathetic to mankind. But saving man from ignorance incurred considerable sacrifice. Chained to a mountain rock, his constantly regenerating liver eaten over and over by a vulture, Prometheus was punished for stealing fire from heaven and giving it to man. Prometheus, a name that means "wise before the event," endured the suffering because he knew that Zeus would eventually free him in exchange for a secret given to him by his mother. And we can hear his stubbornness and defiance when he says, in Aeschylus' play:

> I swear to you that I, humiliated as I am,
> Bound hand and foot in these long straps,
> Shall yet be needed by the lord of immortals
> To disclose the new design, tell him who it is
> Shall rob him of his power and his glory.
> The honied spells of his persuasive tongue shall not enchant me,
> Nor shall I cower under his fierce threats or tell this secret,

Patterns of Subordinacy

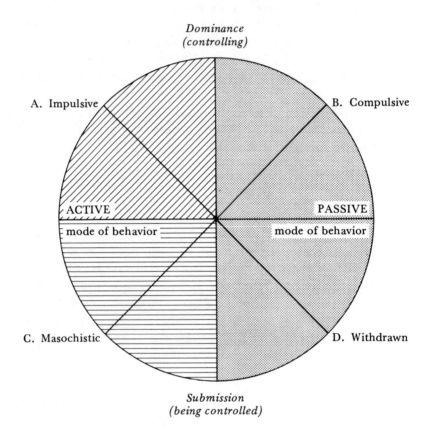

Submission
(being controlled)

Until he free me from these brutal bonds
And consent to compensate me for his outrage.[6]

Prometheus at last purchases release by revealing that Nereus' daughter would bear a son stronger than his father. Zeus, remembering how he had overthrown his own father, Cronus, was frightened by this message and immediately abandoned his pursuit of her.

Prometheus possessed the foresight, which made him secure in his defiance, a quality rare among rebels. What most rebels know, however, is that provocative behavior will rarely go unpunished; therefore, in a compelling, self-destructive way, rebels may have some control over their destinies. Their behavior can cause events that they themselves fear. The appeal of the myth of Prometheus is that it characterizes the universal themes of overthrowing authority and displacing the father. The way an individual incorporates parental images determines the balance between the desire to conform and to rebel. Rebellion as a means of asserting independence usually occurs during adolescence and becomes the confirmation of one's own existence. The need for the confirmation may continue beyond adolescence, and those who realize their need through rebellion can affect political movements by emphasizing the faults of the past while ignoring the visions of the future. In work situations, rebelliousness may provoke conflict with superiors and lead to one's inability to hold a job.

A highly gifted craftsman taunted his supervisor by placing notices on bulletin boards that demanded to know why certain kinds of tools were unavailable in the shop. The notices quoted authorities who recommended these tools, and each quotation was followed by a challenge to the supervisor and to the management as a whole.

The supervisor forbade the posting of notices, but the employee built a private bulletin board near his workbench on which he continued to post notices. One day, the supervisor called the employee in to talk to him. The employee became rude, told his supervisor to "go to hell," and found himself out of a job.

The employee's history showed a pattern of job-hopping. In

fact, the man expected to be fired, explaining that "it always happens." The mechanism of predicting dire events in the future stood as a self-fulfilling prophecy. The craftsman had, through his own behavior, made a reality out of a fantasy.[7]

The fantasy included a struggle with powerful authority figures in which losing became the only means of escaping from authority. The job-hopping was impulsive action that would break off contact when the fantasy of the struggle became too painful to endure. And the mixture of rebellion and submission became a demonstration of misery to elicit sympathy.

Rebellion is also a familiar theme in the personal history of entrepreneurs. They hate being controlled by authority, being dependent on others. The work history of entrepreneurs suggests periods of drifting because of their inability to function in subordinate positions. When they find ways to be on their own, they may settle into productive careers.

Individuals with an impulsive pattern of subordinacy try to dominate others and control events through activity. Paradoxically, rebels frequently have difficulty controlling and managing affairs once they assume power. Their fantasies about power contain a theme of the weak conquering the strong, the story of David and Goliath. In real life, however, the weak more often get hurt in power contentions; the impulse to act, despite its push from fantasy, provokes harmful consequences.

Much impulsive behavior is associated with painful loneliness. The rebel may very much want to be close to others but finds such closeness unbearable. To be close to someone means risking domination and control by that person. The craftsman who provoked his supervisor lived a lonely existence as a middle-aged bachelor with no friends. He enjoyed one activity — chess. He was a very talented player, which in itself was revealing because it indicated that his main human relationship took the form of a ritual of combat in which there had to be victor and vanquished. It was a relationship that was detached and abstract; it was without the danger of personal submission.

Impulsiveness and rebelliousness do not necessarily render a subordinate's behavior destructive. When the impulsive individual assumes control of his fantasies, he can become capable of highly constructive behavior. The spontaneous and courageous subordinate, for example, may rebel by speaking frankly, asserting his views constructively in discussions of work problems. He avoids compliance and conformity, not only out of impatience, but also out of the urge to create and achieve. It is attitudes of this sort that lead to constructive change. Such constructive use of dominance and activity makes it possible for individuals in subordinate positions to influence events. They are highly appreciated by authority figures who are secure in their sense of competence and weary of countless experiences with yes-men. However, to authority figures with doubts about their own competence and position, expressions of constructive rebelliousness may be very threatening.

The line between the constructive and destructive aspects of impulsiveness is difficult to draw. The dynamics underlying both is similar; the difference resides in the degree of individual self-control. The constructive rebel knows how to use his urge to dominate, and he acts in appropriate ways. The destructive rebel lacks the capacity for self-control; he becomes the marionette of his fantasies.

COMPULSIVE SUBORDINACY

Compulsive subordinacy attempts to secure dominance and control through passive means. It is represented by the B quadrant of the diagram. Where the impulsive type acts without thinking, the compulsive type acts with the weight of a powerful conscience and a strong sense of guilt. Ritualistic action that is devoid of any useful purpose reflects the endless inner debate over right and wrong decisions. Thinking takes the place of action and means dominate ends.

King Midas, granted a wish by the god Dionysus, was so eager for power, love, and admiration that he believed the means would satisfy his desires for the coveted end, that gold would bring him power and admiration. But the magic touch that was bestowed upon him became an implement of self-torture. Compulsive subordinates become obsessed, like Midas, with appearances, and never learn the difference between a real desire and an empty wish.

Compulsive subordinates often appear robotlike. They seem

drawn to ritualistic and repetitive activities and shun change and novelty. The emotional experience of these people is limited. The need to contain emotions goes hand in hand with the preference for what is routine and familiar. To experience emotions would result in opening the floodgates of aggression and the conflicts of a bad conscience.

Guilt plays a key role in compulsive subordinacy. The guilt is associated with the fear of aggression and unconscious hostility toward authority figures. Rather than confront their own potential aggression, compulsive individuals characteristically restrict freedom of ego. The restrictions satisfy a bad conscience, but at a terrible cost — the absence of flexibility of response and pleasure in experience.

Compulsive people also seem to be troubled by a sense of uncertainty; they keep asking themselves if their choices have been the right ones. They are indecisive, troubled by doubt, and hesitant about the right course of action. It is as if they are continually saying to themselves about their activities: "What I am doing is not *bad*, but is it good?" They live with the same fear as that of the soldier bringing bad news to Creon, king of Thebes.

> I'll not say that I'm out of breath from running, King, because every time I stopped to think about what I have to tell you, I felt like going back. And all the time a voice kept saying, "You fool, don't you know you're walking straight into trouble?"; and then another voice: "Yes, but if you let somebody else get the news to Creon first, it will be even worse than that for you!" But good sense won out, at least I hope it was good sense, and here I am with a story that makes no sense at all; but I'll tell it anyhow, because, as they say, what's going to happen's going to happen, and . . .[8]

The indecisiveness of compulsive subordinates frequently requires artificial deadlines. Deadlines impose an end to doubt and the resolution of conflicting paths of action; furthermore, a deadline serves as a constant reminder not to slacken one's pace. Individuals who require such deadlines seem to be excessively somber; they will even go so far as to force themselves to accept unpleasant tasks. Work may be drudgery, but it is a duty, a responsibility one cannot avoid. And since the compulsive subordinate feels that he has no control over his destiny, that there exists a higher authority that sets tasks and prescribes roles, he denies his right to live by his own choices. Relaxation becomes unpleasant because it negates his sense of purpose; worrying about problems and appearing burdened by endless amounts of work is part of the ritual.

Compulsiveness has a deadening quality about it. The compulsive person uses passive behavior to inhibit action and control people. Passivity makes itself known by indirect and manipulative attempts at influence, though the individual himself may be unaware of what he is trying to do. The clearest illustration of control through passivity is the hypochondriac. All indications point to illness and suffering as an experience that the victim endures passively. Yet the effect, as members of the hypochondriac's family know, controls the behavior of those close to the "sufferer." The entire family may be organized to meet his needs which, of course, is the unconscious wish underlying much of the suffering. The restrictions the hypochondriac lives by become the controls that dominate the lives of others. In short, the hypochondriac seeks to make others suffer, but by unconscious design rather than by conscious intent.

Compulsive subordinacy and passivity in character structure contain features that support a technologically oriented society. In such a society, the innovations come from a select portion of the population, usually well-educated people trained in the sciences and engineering. The technocrats design the system, which will work only if the people who man the machines and the assembly lines are willing to comply with the programs. If people try to innovate, to express their individuality, or to "malinger," they reduce rather than improve the effectiveness of technological systems. Consequently, their willingness to comply is more important than their active motivation to create, achieve, or express themselves. The complying person is often the compulsive individual, for whom repetitive work may be a release from the anxiety and doubt of thought, fantasy, and action.

There is an ironic history to the structure of technology and its demand for compliant and compulsive subordinates. One of the outstanding contributors to industrial management, Frederick Winslow Taylor, was himself a victim of a compulsive neurosis.[9] He invented a system to accommodate equally compulsive subordinates.

Taylor came from an aristocratic Philadelphia family. When he entered Phillips Exeter Academy, his family expected him to go on to Harvard and to become a lawyer, as his father had done. The young Taylor suffered an eye problem while at Exeter (he was a fine student and, if anything, he overworked), and the symptoms suggested an emotional rather than an organic cause. Before then, Taylor had suffered from insomnia and anxiety — his eye troubles were not isolated disturbances. The disorder permitted Taylor to thwart his family's plans; he returned to Philadelphia and apprenticed himself in a machine shop, an extraordinary choice for someone of Taylor's background. For Taylor, the choice provided structure for his hard work. He also turned a preoccupation with time and the control of activity into a careful study of men attending machines and the time it takes to perform the micromotions of work. He measured and experimented much the way he had kept records while traveling with his family in Europe as a boy, noting the exact time a train arrived in a station and the exact time it left. His experiments with tools recalled the ingenuity he had shown earlier, when he designed a contraption that harnessed him in bed in a certain posture he believed best for sleep. The contraption probably guarded against masturbation, which may have been one of the causes of Taylor's anxiety and insomnia.

Taylor's ability to manipulate time, machines, and materials provided him with comfort and respite from his fantasies as well as from his quarrels with other people. He continually fought with his superiors and with the workingmen whose time and motions he sought to control. Paradoxically, he seemed to make a better adjustment to superiors who were harsh and demanding than to the decent and amiable men who resembled his father.

Besides suppressing sexual fantasies, the repetitive activity in Taylor's own experience and in the system he developed was his solution to the problem of man's aggressive and competitive impulses. In the latter stages of his career, after many disappointments in his relations with superiors, Taylor turned into a prophet of "scientific management"; he urged adoption of his system to solve industrial conflicts between management and workers. Disputes about work expectations and compensation were to be stripped of human feeling and judgment and measured impersonally by work and its worth. But the system of social control could be successful only if participants accepted the principles of scientific management and were willing to conform to its prescribed behavior. It failed.

Compulsive subordinacy is fixed in doubt, attitude reversal, hidden aggression, and denial of responsibility. Compulsive doubt is the inability to make commitments. Every person launching a career is susceptible to hesitation and concern over lost opportunities. In work, lingering thoughts over the "other job" may interfere with effective performance, just as in marriage thoughts about the "other girl" may interfere with happiness. Where other individuals stake a claim on a career and then pursue their line of work, the compulsive individual continues to doubt.

Attitude reversal is a rapid oscillation between positive and negative feelings in human encounters. Ambivalence goes hand in hand with doubt, and together they maintain a steady level of tension in the individual's human relationships and work activity.

Hidden aggression is one of the tensions that remains a threat. The underlying object of the aggression is the parent and, later, other authority figures with whom one maintains an uneasy balance between dependent and independent attitudes. Anger about feeling dependent is offset by the fear of expressing the feeling and being detected.

The cause of much frustration among supervisors working with compulsive subordinates is the difficulty in making them accept responsibility. Compulsive people dislike taking positions and being held accountable. They may enjoy writing memos and clarifying options, but they do not often make recommendations and form conclusions.

MASOCHISTIC BEHAVIOR

Masochism is the quest for pleasure through pain. True masochism indicates a serious sexual disturbance, but also exists as a force in the organization of character. The masochist seeks submission at the hands of an aggressor. By irritating authority figures, masochistic subordinates invite punishment, which, in fantasy, equals sexual satisfaction.

Masochists appeal to the guilt feelings of others, particularly authority figures. A conflict exists between aggressive wishes against the feared (and desired) authority figure and complete surrender to this very authority figure. Whatever route is chosen, the goal is possession of the authority figure.

To guard against one's own aggression and the possibility that it will get out of control, the subordinate tries to turn the authority figure into the aggressor. Instead of hurting others, the person hurts himself by provoking others. Suffering becomes a demonstration of endurance, which may placate the feared authority figure who may then forgive the subordinate's aggressive thoughts. Freud described "criminals out of a sense of guilt" as individuals who provoke punishment to obtain relief from feelings of anxiety and guilt. These people hope to ingratiate themselves with the feared authority figure through regular sacrifice and so prevent the unbearable punishment of being abandoned.

Dostoevski described masochistic behavior in *Crime and Punishment*.[10] Raskolnikov, desperate about his poverty and misery, decides to kill an old woman — a pawnbroker — and steal her money. This would enable him to finish his studies and support his impoverished mother and sister. His rationalization is that the old woman is of no use to society; her death would be to everyone's advantage. Just before he commits the murder, he is tortured by a dream in which, during a country walk with his father, a miserable horse is beaten to death by drunken peasants. He wakes up, terrified at the orgastic thoughts evoked by the dream's aggression and cruelty.

After he accomplishes the crime, his torment increases, nearly driving him insane. He is plagued by guilt and the image of the murdered woman. It becomes evident that his aim is punishment. The beating dream suggests that his sexual tormentor is a father. Raskolnikov's masochism makes him betray himself to the authorities. When he is summoned to the police station for failing to pay his rent, his behavior suggests a more serious crime. He is compelled to return to the scene of his crime and, at last, unable to support self-torment any longer and plagued by his irresistible urge for confession, he turns himself in. There is deliverance in surrender and submission to authority.

In organizations, the accident-prone employee exemplifies masochistic subordinacy. He may want to be angry with his boss, a representative of authority, but he hurts only himself through inattention to potential dangers or by taking undue risks. A side-effect of self-punishing behavior is the evocation of sympathy and attention from others. At the same time, it asks for control by others and abdication of personal responsibility.

A more subtle form of masochism is the individual's inviting criticism and shame by turning in unacceptable work. Some aspects of the behavior of the advertising executive mentioned earlier in this chapter demonstrate the point. The explanation for the inadequacies does not lie in lack of ability, experience, or even laziness. All of the factors that make for good performance may be present, but they are not utilized and directed. Good performance means the ability to accept praise and responsibility; here, the underlying motivation is the endurance of persecution and shame at the hands of an imagined aggressor.

We observe, from time to time, persons in organizations who identify with the underdog; they are quick to see injustice in the actions of authority figures and to sense oppression in the lives of those who have little power and influence. There may be both oppression and an underdog, but identification with the helpless and the weak against the powerful and the strong frequently reflects a masochistic bent in personality. By identifying with the underdog, the subordinate wants to become a target of attack by powerful authority figures. Submission is the desired end; the active-aggressive behavior is the means.

A subordinate who reflects this tendency behaves like an older son who takes the side of younger siblings against the imagined oppression of the parents. The subordinate suffers vicariously, perhaps simultaneously finding an outlet for pent-up aggression. The target is the oppressor, standing in for the original authority figures, the parents. It can be useful to attack oppressors, but hazardous for those who see oppression where none exists. Where standards of performance are enforced in an equitable way, they may be mistakenly attacked as arbitrary discipline. The ability to discriminate between real and imagined inequity is often lacking in the person who organizes his experience around identification with the oppressed.

The masochistic pattern begins in the early years of the subordinate's experience. The hidden desire to endure suffering at the hands of a powerful aggressor recreates infantile wishes, which were used to solve, however poorly, the dilemmas encountered during early development. History repeats itself in the life of the individual. The repetition, however, does not occur because of impersonal forces or the whims of chance, but rather because of the person's inadequate mastery of inner conflicts. One way of responding intelligently to the provocations of the masochistic personality is to avoid the game being played. The masochistic subordinate seeks pleasure in being the target of aggression. Avoidance of aggressive response can break the cycle and return the issue to the place where it belongs: within the individual himself.

WITHDRAWAL

Withdrawal is a turning of interest and attention away from the outer world toward the person himself. This pattern of subordinacy is a form of submission; the individual no longer cares about the orientation and content of his work. The behavioral mode is passive — energy from within is released only sparingly. At first glance, withdrawn people appear to be self-contained and self-sufficient. Closer examination shows that the attitude covers a desperate yearning for love and affection. Alcoholism and drug addiction are common symptoms of withdrawal.

In organizations, changes in the distribution of power, authority, and responsibility, or situations of role conflict and role ambiguity, may contribute to withdrawal. A demotion and career stagnation, the sudden realization of the obsolescence of one's job, or the inability to perform as well as in the past, erode an individual's confidence, resulting in his gradual turning away from work and other people. Usually, a combination of personality disposition and sudden intensified life stresses causes this form of behavior.

The withdrawal from reality to fantasy is the route to the delusional state. Willy Loman, in Arthur Miller's *Death of a Salesman,* is disappointed with his elder son; he gradually withdraws into a fantasy world. But even here, he cannot escape completely the realities of life; eventually, he sees suicide as the only way out. He commits suicide when he realizes that there is no magic to insure success and that his illusions have destroyed his own sons.[11]

Withdrawal occurs when trust and belief disappear. The world then becomes malevolent and ungiving, and refuge lies in regression and fantasy. The subordinate's lack of trust, interest, and involvement render him immune to influence. He may acquiesce to directives, but without orientation and interest. He contributes little to the interchange of ideas necessary for innovative work. He may handle routine tasks well enough, but does little beyond the necessary demands of his job. He can be loyal and accepting of existing standards and, paradoxically, remain attached to his company beyond the point where a useful relationship can ever develop. A study of turnover rates among professional employees in a large research and development center showed the lowest quit rate among scientists who were emotionally withdrawn. The least valuable employee, from the point of view of management, may be the most reluctant to make a change.

The apathy of the scientists, evident in the absence of turnover, posed other contradictions. On the one hand, the withdrawn person expressed personal disappointment in his career, a feeling of fatigue, presumably neurotic in origin, some anxiety, and depression. On the other hand, he evaluated favorably the company, his supervisor, and colleagues. He expressed little desire to move elsewhere or to seek opportunities in other types of work.[12]

Withdrawal and apathy cannot be attributed simply to bureaucracy and inequalities in authority and power. Personal history and development prepare the way for detachment. Such a history typically includes a passive, withdrawn father and a cold, hostile mother. The net effect of parental identifications renders one unable to mobilize and use constructively his aggressive impulses. The withdrawal and apathy are themselves a consequence, along with depression, of turning aggression inward.

Developmental experiences in successive stages of the life cycle create the conditions for subordinacy. Direct and conscious confrontations with the problems of authority and subordinacy, however, usually take place during adolescence, a period of pain and anxiety for parents and their children alike. To a great extent, subordinacy conflicts in organizations represent the prolongation or continuation of the life crises particularly prominent during adolescence.

The essential task of the adolescent is to achieve independence from the family and to become a person in his own right. This task of identity is never fully completed, yet the recognition of identity depends on the capacity to work and to commit oneself in marriage and the family. The difficulty for the adolescent stems from the presence of opposite forces within the personality. There is both a "push" toward rapid maturation, for which the person may feel inadequately prepared, and a "pull" toward the securities of parental relationships. The concurrent push and pull account for much of the bizarre behavior of the adolescent. The person himself, as well as those who care for him, may not know whether to respond to the push of development or the pull of security and comfort in the family circle. One must be aware of both desires until they have been assimilated within the personality and a new equilibrium has been attained.

To make matters even more difficult for the developing adult, the crisis of adolescence reawakens conflicts from earlier stages of development, especially the conflicts of intimacy (the relationship between mother and child) and initiative (the triangle of mother, father, and child) .[13]

The pull felt by the adolescent is toward restoration of the primary love and dependency relationship with the mother.

During the earliest period of development, well before the child begins to acquire the capacity to use words and concepts, all of his life-giving needs are secured in the intimacy of the primary pairing with his mother or with a substitute figure. In many ways, the initial intimacy prepares the child for the experience of intimacy as an adult, but this process is not without dangers for mature functioning. Separation from the primary relationship usually generates considerable anger and rage, which must somehow be dissipated and channeled into constructive ends during development. Otherwise, it retains a destructive potential in the patterns of subordinacy. Furthermore, there exists always the desire to restore intimacy — a regressive pull that acts very strongly on the developing individual. If the pull becomes strong enough, and the individual gives in, he may remain markedly dependent all his life, unable to take the steps necessary for mature adulthood. Evidence of the strength of the pull toward restoration of the security of mother-child unity can be seen in such disturbances as alcoholism, depression, and gastrointestinal attacks. These symptoms reflect the desire for the primary intimacy relationship and also protect against, and substitute for, the rage and anger caused by separation.

Conflicts of initiative are also reawakened during adolescence because of the dangers imagined in the push toward maturation. Here again, the problem is not experienced for the first time during adolescence but is, instead, a reactivation of an earlier dilemma in development. The dilemma exists in the triangle of mother-father-child and the expression of rivalry. Oedipal strivings may be decisive in maintaining conflicts of subordinacy, and they may block the individual in his capacity to assume leadership and responsibility.

As with Icarus, who would not heed his father's warnings that it was dangerous to fly too near the sun or too close to the water, the person who aspires to leadership must negotiate the risky passage between dependency and assertiveness. The way in which one assumes command, the style of leadership, illuminates the individual's understanding of the risk.

CHAPTER 8

Superordinacy

"For man must strive and striving he must err."[1]

—*Goethe*

And I say to them there are many fine careers. This country needs good farmers, good businessmen, good plumbers, good carpenters. I remember my old man. I think that they would have called him sort of a — sort of a little man, common man. He didn't consider himself that way. You know what he was?

He was streetcar motorman first and then he was a farmer and then he had a lemon ranch — it was the poorest lemon ranch in California, I can assure you — he sold it before they found oil on it. And then he was a grocer. But he was a great man because he did his job and every job counts up to the hilt regardless of what happens.

Nobody will ever write a book probably about my mother. Well, I guess all of you would say this about your mother. My mother was a saint. And I think of her — two boys dying of tuberculosis — nursing four others in order that she could take care of my older brother for three years in Arizona and seeing each of them die and when they died it was like one of her own.

Yes, she will have no books written about her. But she was a saint.[2]

Richard M. Nixon's father was a failure and his mother was a saint, figures that allowed him little opportunity for identification in his development as a leader and as a user of power. Nixon's reflections on his past were made in the East Room of the White House during his waning moments as President of the United States, a time of great grief and personal disaster. But it is at such times, particularly for one who fought to control his actions as he sought to control the thoughts and actions of subordinates and constituents, that the truth about the self is likely to emerge. Mr. Nixon's tragedy lay in his fear of success, the certain knowledge that he would be tripped and thrown by some secret self-nursing grandiosity and resentment against an incompetent father and an ungiving mother. In her saintliness, suffering, and sacrifice, she withheld the warmth and nurture that can exist only in the close bond of mother and child. Deprived of warmth, Nixon learned to distrust; guilt-ridden because of his envy and resentment of the sick brothers who died, he tried to live outside himself. Yet he was always wary that his anger would erupt, as it did during the famous press conference of 1962 and the congressional campaign of 1972.

Reliving his grief, and still reminiscing about his saintly mother, Nixon read the words Theodore Roosevelt had written soon after the death of his wife:

> She was beautiful in face and form and lovelier still in spirit. As a flower she grew and as a fair young flower she died. Her life had been always in the sunshine. There had never come to her a single great sorrow. None ever knew her who did not love and revere her for her bright and sunny temper and her saintly unselfishness.
>
> Fair, pure and joyous to the maiden. Loving, tender and happy as a young wife when she had just become a mother, when her life seemed to be just begun and then the years seemed so bright before her. Then by a strange and terrible fate, death came to her.
>
> And when my heart's dearest died, the light went from my life forever.[3]

Nixon's mother died, symbolically, when he renounced her as a love object and developed a burning ambition for power. The consequences of the renunciation, and the inadequacy of the model his father offered him, lay at the root of his insecurity in spite of his seeming success. For Nixon, power came only in a struggle with the gods. Like Prometheus, who stole fire from the gods, he fought constantly with unseen, superhuman forces that sought to reclaim what he had stolen. Therefore, while holding power, he had to be defensive and cautious, and he never felt that his power was legitimate. He projected his fears and sense of illegitimacy on to the press, who, in his eyes, were out to get him, to expose and undermine him. But his distrust extended to intellectuals, the superior Easterners who had all the advantages he wanted, including fortunate birth and heritage. He envied people like John F. Kennedy. The "enemies" were ready to destroy him, but his real enemies were the projected self-images, which were suspicious, angry, and envious; the malevolent self, reflections of the saint and the common man, and the unconscious occupants of his psyche, who fed the well of mistrust and anxiety.

The fear of success and its counterpart, the fear of failure, tell us a great deal about the anxieties and conflicts of leaders. Richard Nixon is not an isolated case study of the man who seemed always to "snatch defeat from the jaws of victory." The fear of failure, of being incapable of exercising leadership, enables the individual to avoid command, like the enlisted man who refuses promotion to officer rank. The other anxiety, the fear of success, is far more damaging to leaders; it propels them to seek position. But once in power, their anxiety, mania, and depression lead them to defensive maneuvers and erratic behavior.

The Fear of Success and the Fear of Failure

It is easy to see that the fear of failure inhibits ambition and the willingness to lead. One may fear being uncovered as a pretender, like the emperor without clothes. One may feel inadequately equipped to meet the demands of responsibility or to make decisions that inevitably leave some people unhappy. The anticipatory guilt, that to take power is to displace the father, is an anxiety strong enough in some people to inhibit severely their capacity to lead. This inhibition also affects a person's ability to complete work. The artist or writer who cannot relinquish his masterpiece may harbor unconscious feelings that critics will attack and debase his work. Rather than suffer the defeats of public criticism, he keeps his work to himself so that, at least, he can claim the promise of a great book or painting, and live with the anticipation of success instead of the feared reality of failure.

Some people crave popularity; they enjoy the exclusive companionship of their peers. The distance that leadership imposes removes such a person from peer group warmth and support. He exaggerates the "loneliness of command" and inhibits his ambition, fearing isolation and loneliness. Finally, there is the person who identifies with those who have failed, usually his father, and assumes that a combination of fate and ineptitude that accounted for his father's failure will inevitably cause his own downfall. Therefore, he represses ambition.

Children need ideals, heroes who can provide them with direction and models of what is possible. In early stages of life, the need for the hero, "the great man," is so important that the image of the parent is unrealistic because it allows for no human weakness. Later in life, one begins to see the blemishes, which become so exaggerated that the image of the parent is grotesque and unrecognizable. This is the cycle of fantasy from the great man to the worthless man, which is incorporated both as a memory and as a part of the personality structure. To avoid the fate of one's father, the decline from hero to bum, one hides talent and restrains the possibilities of achievement because of impending failure.

> I'm not a leader of men, Willy, and neither are you. You were never anything but a hard-working drummer who landed in the ash can like all the rest of them! I'm one dollar an hour, Willy! I tried seven states and couldn't raise it. A buck an hour! Do you gather my meaning? I'm not bringing home any prizes any more, and you're going to stop waiting for me to bring them home![4]

Paradoxically, as with Willy Loman's son, the acceptance of the sense of failure and defeat sometimes promotes the rebuilding of identity and security. The pretensions of models and exemplars are cast off, and one begins to sense innate talents and dispositions that are the bedrock of competence. Although one may not necessarily become a leader of men, the chances of being true to oneself increase, along with the capacity to take risks with other people.

When Marcus Aurelius Arnheiter assumed command of the destroyer escort radar ship *Vance* in December 1965, he started a series of events that resulted in a heated debate in the national press about whether he was a patriotic victim of mutinous junior officers or a whimsical tyrant. The debate also led to two official inquiries, one by the navy and one by the House of Representatives.[5] Arnheiter wanted the hearings to clear him of charges that he was incompetent; he believed that he was a victim of a conspiracy to have him relieved of command. The hearings produced no evidence to clear him of the charges that he had destroyed the morale of his crew. Newspaper articles at that time compared Arnheiter's behavior during his ninety-nine days of command of the *Vance* with that of Captain Queeg, the protagonist of Herman Wouk's novel *The Caine Mutiny*. But whatever Arnheiter's behavior might have been, he succeeded — if only temporarily — in shaking off anonymity and gaining the recognition of the world at large; he thereby underlined his sense of importance — as well as his pretentiousness.

Before he took command of the *Vance*, Arnheiter's career forecast boom or bust. His enthusiasm and willingness to act on his own initiative were reflected in fitness reports that contained either condemnation or praise. Some superiors were impressed by his energetic style, his imagination, and his writing and speaking talents; others questioned his common sense.

When the officers of the various departments briefed Arnheiter as the new commanding officer of the *Vance,* the tone of the meetings was dismal. Arnheiter showed little interest in the technicalities of operations and engineering. Instead, he immediately tightened the dress rules, issued memoranda dealing with matters of military and social etiquette, bought a speedboat with the crew's recreation money and equipped it with a machine gun and an American flag (he planned to use it as a potential bait to trap the Viet Cong), and forced attendance at Protestant church meetings. Hints of Arnheiter's pretensions appeared in his first speech to the crew; he promised that he would take them "where there is lots of action" and "vowed that the enemy would feel the presence of the *Vance* in Viet Nam and that the ship would make a major contribution to the war effort."[6] But the rules of engagement allowed the *Vance* to use its firepower only in case of emergency. His assignment was to patrol the coast of Vietnam for contraband arms and ammunition.

Reports from the crew show that immediately after his arrival in Vietnam Arnheiter actively looked for a war to fight. Arnheiter saw porters carrying arms and supplies where others saw villagers fleeing from a bombed-out fishing hamlet. Although the *Vance* had a specifically assigned patrol zone, Arnheiter habitually ignored orders and went into prohibited areas, looking for action. He sent false reports to place the ship outside the prohibited areas. The Navy Information Office received for release vivid accounts of shelling the enemy, accounts that had no resemblance to the crew's shooting at sand dunes, rocks, and chickens. In one instance, Arnheiter became so enthralled with the fighting action of other ships and airplanes that he forgot he had command of the *Vance,* which was on a collision course with the rocks of a peninsula. Just before it was too late, the executive officer took over. In the meantime, the ship's guns destroyed a deserted masonry structure, which became, in Arnheiter's press release, "a hot Viet Cong machine-gun fortified emplacement." He also conceived of a plot to destroy a Chinese submarine, which would have been an illegal act of war had he succeeded.

The crew nicknamed Arnheiter "Mad Marcus." Rifles were left loaded on the bridge, since Arnheiter had the habit, while searching junks and sampans, of shooting over fishermen's heads and arresting them as draft-dodgers, suspected guerrillas, or deserters. A normal daily schedule on the *Vance* became impossible to maintain, given Arnheiter's operating style. It was not uncommon for an officer or sailor to do two four-hour watches in a row on top of his normal duties; those who were supposed to be on watch were sent away on special missions.

Arnheiter's actions began to tell on the crew. The executive officer developed symptoms of stomach ulcer. A sailor took pills to overcome depression resulting from the stress of Arnheiter's constant ridicule. One member of the crew even threatened to kill the captain. And one nearly did.

Rumors about a morale problem aboard the *Vance* came to the attention of the squadron commander. Matters reached a crisis when the commander received a letter and citation recommending Arnheiter for the Silver Star. (Arnheiter had forced his executive officer to make this recommendation.) Arnheiter's prose style was easily recognized, and the commander decided to relieve him of command.

Arnheiter had a desperate need to be recognized, to be successful when he took the position of command. His search for heroic deeds, the constant press releases, and his final request for the Silver Star only reinforce this point. Command became his opportunity — after many years of anticipation — to relive the heroic acts of his ideals of childhood, figures such as C. S. Forester's Captain Horatio Hornblower, and Lord Nelson, who still dominated his fantasies. His attachment to grandiose fantasy enabled him to deny unacceptable images that were just as much a part of himself as the masculine, powerful figures that he acted out as captain of the *Vance*. His father, a poet, musician, and voice instructor, seemed far removed from the heroic ideal; his forceful, dominant mother (who liked to call herself Dr. Arnheiter) may have contributed to confusion in self-images. Arnheiter's invention of a grandfather named Baron von Arnheiter, a pioneer in manned flight (information contained in his biographical data), is another indication of grandiose pretensions. There was an exhibitionism connected with these images, the wish to be seen and heard, which the obscurity of a routine command would have frustrated. For Arnheiter, command in wartime was his chance to break out of a dreaded anonymity into a sense of superiority and fame, so avoiding the obscure destiny he feared. Ironically, Arnheiter's impulse to act out his fantasies led him into obscurity, to the realization of a negative self-image, just as Nixon's overestimation of his power assured him of history's judgment that he failed to understand the obligations of position.

The "destiny neuroses," ones in which individuals hover over fragmented images of themselves, lead people to sabotage their own lives and careers. Like patients in psychoanalysis who unconsciously do not want to cure their neuroses, individuals in leadership careers can undermine their success. The inclination is perverse, going contrary to the individual's own interests. It reflects masochism, the need to suffer and to gain sexual pleasure in the process.

There are two faces of masochism: the first is the inner attachment to pain, the deep compulsion to suffer; the second is the diffusion of self-punishment in work activity, human relationships, and in thought patterns.

The desire to suffer defies rational understanding. It violates the notion of man as a pleasure-seeking creature, for which there is far more direct evidence than for an attraction to pain and suffering. If one were attached to painful feelings and suffering, it would be impossible to tolerate success — the compliments people are more than willing to pay, and the gifts they offer in esteem and admiration. To be a sufferer, especially if one is unconsciously so, one must be willing to wallow in emotional reactions. For sufferers, there is more than willingness; there is dire necessity. Like the stranger in Camus's novel, the person seems to come alive in the face of an abject surrender to pain. Otherwise, there is an emotional vacuum — to feel anything requires that one come to terms with overwhelming anger, which threatens control.

The source of the anger, or, more accurately, the object of the anger, is some memory of a parent, usually the mother, who simultaneously appears seductive and also cold and ungiving. This dual image of the mother is, in part, the result of disappointments (she did not give enough) and the consequent development of hard attitudes, and, in part, the result of suppressed memories of a warm relationship. The dual image of the mother comes from reactive fantasies and from the unconscious perception of the ambivalence the mother may have felt about her femininity and motherhood.

Success may unconsciously carry with it ideas about reunion with the early love figure. But under the sway of aggressive, and even murderous, impulses, the idea of reunion becomes transformed into primitive notions of merger and loss of the self. It is a form of annihilation and of self-destruction. If fantasies of reunion and annihilation prevent direct sexual pleasure because of the fears of loss of the self in orgastic responses, the sexual impulses then become attached to pain and suffering. Once the pathways through impulses and ideas become firmly established, especially if the cycle of longing for the object and anger at her occurs in the early years, they are difficult to reverse. Even in psychoanalysis, it is difficult to bring about therapeutic results for chronic sufferers. They need to stay on the familiar paths of pain and suffering to avoid the emptiness that accompanies the recognition of longings.[7]

The desire to suffer and to seek pain permeates the person's character and relationships with others. Unlike an isolated perversion, which can often be contained, the need to suffer affects the totality of the individual's responses, from the inability to accept other people to a brooding sense of aloneness and pessimism. To undo his character organization, the sufferer would be required to form a new orientation to work and to human relationships; in his eyes, the risks are often too great. He may have to face rejection and humiliation, the sense of being cast out and unwanted, a repetition of traumatic experience in childhood. The acceptance of success means that one can be trustful — that one does not risk annihilation on the one hand or isolation on the other. Confidence exists in the integrity of the self.

The fate of chronic sufferers, who in character and disposition need to defeat themselves even as they stand at the very pinnacle of success, resembles the self-fulfilling prophecy. In this case, however, the prophecy is unconscious, just as the mechanisms for fulfilling it are unconscious.

Those who fear success are not uniformly fated to the disaster they fear in response to achievement and recognition. Some are able to organize their lives to create distance between themselves and other people. In the course of partial withdrawal, they are able to defend themselves against the dangers of success. One such case is the life and career of Andrew Carnegie, the steel magnate of the late nineteenth and early twentieth centuries.

Andrew Carnegie was a self-made man, the son of Scottish immigrant parents; his rise from poverty to power and riches is celebrated in American business history. Carnegie's career is especially intriguing because of his style of leadership. There is little question that he controlled the moves that shaped his industrial empire, but he could not deal with his authority and power directly. He used an indirect approach, through various groups and key individuals. Carnegie was, for the most part, an absent figure in the hierarchy he created.

Using the equity structure of the business — the Iron-Clad Agreement that blocked subordinates from full rights as stock owners — and using the personal arrangements he made for the delegation of responsibility, Andrew Carnegie could influence from a distance and, at the same time, protect himself from the vulnerability of visible command. He achieved success by creating a barrier between himself and the onslaughts he feared might follow success.

His upbringing provides us with some clues to the origin of this extraordinary fortress of defense in the service of success. Whatever ambition he knew flowed from his mother, a competent, take-charge woman, who managed the practical arrangements of his family. She provided Andrew with a model for shrewdness and pragmatic success, and insulated him from the ills of the world, including poverty. She engineered the move to America from Scotland and, though the Carnegies were poor, "There had always been for [Andrew] the bowl of porridge on the table, the clean collar in the dresser drawer, the plum duff with the sailors on Sundays."[8] Andrew remained close to his mother until her death. He was a fifty-one-year-old bachelor when his mother died; soon afterward, he married.

Carnegie revered his mother and tried to emulate her, but he probably felt ambivalent about his father. The elder Carnegie experienced reversals in his trade as a weaver, first in Scotland and later in America. He appeared helpless in the face of economic misfortunes and weak compared with his decisive wife. Andrew's father died when the son was twenty years old and Andrew succeeded his father in more than symbolic terms.

For some individuals, the oedipal struggle remains a fantasy. For others, like Andrew Carnegie, the wish to overpower the father and possess the mother becomes all too real. Reality stimulates fantasy and reinforces the search for success without guilt and for penance without undermined achievement. At first, Carnegie solved his problem of psychological defense by finding father substitutes. One man in particular, Thomas Scott, guided Andrew in his career and, in doing so, exemplified what a strong man can accomplish.

Later, in managing the affairs of his steel company, Carnegie sent directives and memoranda, from the highlands of Scotland or the beaches of Cannes or Florida, to his younger brother, Tom, and, when Henry Clay Frick became chief executive, to Frick and other top managers of the Carnegie Steel Company. Although Carnegie was involved in, and controlled, the Carnegie Steel Company (only one of his top executives managed to survive all his years of leadership), the magnate fostered the image of noninvolvement, playing the role of the interested outsider. Abdication of direct responsibility while in control became the pattern of his management style. The bloody Homestead strike — a number of people were killed when striking laborers fought Pinkerton guards — is a good example of the pattern. The strike was a bitter event for Carnegie, given his role of philanthropist and champion of the working class. At the time of the strike, Carnegie was somewhere in Scotland and could not be reached. He would later argue that he knew about the incident only after the fact, stating, on his return to the United States:

> I hope . . . that the public will understand that the officials of the Carnegie Steel Company, Limited, with Mr. Frick at their head, are not dependent upon me, or upon anyone in any way for their positions, and that I have neither power nor disposition to interfere with them in the management of the business.[9]

Carnegie's plea of innocence and powerlessness was gross distortion. He was majority stockholder and very much involved in the company's management, though from afar. What his remarks indicate is that Carnegie himself desperately needed to believe the fantasy of noninvolvement when dealing with the conflicts of leadership. Distance was necessary for protection; control, for the reaping of rewards.

Before Frick assumed formal command of Carnegie Steel, Tom Carnegie had carried the major burden of running Carnegie's business empire. Tom, basically an unadventurous and conservative business manager, became more and more exasperated by his brother's management style and by the reckless gambles he was regularly asked to undertake. He must have hinted at his feelings occasionally, to judge from the tone of one of Andrew's replies:

> You wonder if we ever think of one who has notes to meet, etc. Indeed, we often do, and the more I feel myself drinking in enjoyment, the deeper is my appreciation of your devoted self-denial and the oftener I resolve that you shall have every opportunity to enjoy what I am now doing. I'm sure you have had a trying time of it and often must have felt disposed to throw up the game and write me advising my return, but I trust the skies are brighter now . . . and I am happy to believe matters are hereafter to be easier upon you. It is a heavy load for a youngster to carry, but if you succeed, it will be a lasting benefit to you. Talk to Mother freely. I always found her ideas pretty near the right thing. She's a safe counsellor, safer than I, probably, who have made money too easily and gained distance by carrying full sail, to be much of an adviser when storms are about, or sail should be taken in . . .[10]

Matters did not become easier. It seemed that his absentee style eventually became too much for his younger brother, who took up drinking and showed symptoms of depression, both of which may have contributed to his early death.

Although Carnegie's way of handling leadership took a considerable toll among his subordinates, he himself did not seem to suffer, nor did his absentee style hurt the operations of the steel empire. But how much deliberate planning was really involved in Carnegie's style? Was he aware of his unusual manner of leadership? We can assume that, after a period of trial and error — and here unconscious motivation figures — Carnegie found a style that struck a balance between his need to assert and his need to defend himself against the conflicts and anxieties of success. To appear as the one responsible would be to expose himself as the father figure and to become vulnerable to attack from sons who would seek to overthrow him. When he had assumed initiative in the past — as in his dealings with Scott about the Pennsylvania Railroad — he had run into conflict. The internal pain and damage wrought by these troubles had stayed with him. Thus, he sought a way to avoid personal rancor and still direct his business ventures.

Despite differences in personality and accomplishment, Andrew Carnegie and Marcus Arnheiter experienced similar problems centered on conflicts in command. In Carnegie's case, effectiveness was far from impaired despite his conflicts. By contrast, Arnheiter's difficulties with his fantasy life led to failure in command. Both men had a sense of being special, a legacy of their family, and also, for very different reasons, they were both highly visible, colorful individuals.

The behavior of Carnegie and Arnheiter can be contrasted with that of other individuals, not infrequently met in modern industrial society, who find themselves caught in a labyrinth of power coalitions, positions, and levels of hierarchy, and who look to the bureaucracy to circumvent conflicts. The officeholder avoids responsibility for leadership by hiding inside the bureaucratic maze of policies and procedures to evade anxiety. Rules and regulations turn into means to depersonalize the consequences of leadership. They enable powerful people to deny responsibility for their actions, to blame "the rules" for their behavior, and to claim innocent intentions, all of which divert the "wrath" of the victimized.

Besides the bureaucratic defense found in many segments of organizational life, there are other ways to by-pass conflicts about superordinacy. Participative management and other democratic norms for the uses of power substitute ideals for personal solutions to the conflicts of assuming command. Involvement by superior and subordinate in decision-making processes, the existence of formal bargaining procedures, the planning of acceptable, reasonable tasks, budgets, and future goals are certainly sound management practices. The situation becomes quite different, however, when participative management degenerates into a ritualistic activity, devoid of realistic performance appraisal, task setting, and budget review. If an individual uses participative management to defend himself against anxiety about command, the dangers for the future of the organization can be considerable.

But the business tycoon, the flamboyant "hero" at war, the colorless organization man, and the advocate of participative management all have in common loneliness and vulnerability. Their actions are ways of defending themselves against these dangerous, dreaded emotions, and of minimizing anxiety and guilt associated with their position, power, and responsibility. The exercise of power without acceptance of responsibility may lead to very irresponsible actions. Truman used to say about the Oval Office, "The buck stops here," a statement that is still valid, remaining so even for the colorless organization man who, after a long career of avoiding risks, finds himself in a position of superordinacy. Truman's words capture exactly that feeling of loneliness. The leader suddenly has to cope with the risks of exposure. If he can successfully erect structures or mask his power with rules and procedure, he is less vulnerable to these risks. On the other hand, if the coping mechanisms fail, he will break down.

In some cases, the individual may not have the heart to use impersonal structures for personal defense. He may give way to his fears of success in one part of his life, while he tries to go beyond the limits of vocation (at least as it is defined conventionally) to use his talents in exceptional ways. George Bernard Shaw reflected back to the time when he was nineteen years old and on the verge of success in a business career: "I had made good in spite of myself, and found, to my dismay, that Business, instead of expelling me as the worthless imposter I was, was fastening upon me with no intention of letting me go. Behold me, therefore, in my twentieth year, with a business training, in an occupation which I detested as cordially as any sane person lets himself detest anything he cannot escape from. In March, 1876 I broke loose."[11]

Shaw was not anxious about failure. What he could not tolerate were the implications of a career in business. "It was fastening its hold" upon him. He was dealing not with just an inhibition, but with a demand, which he could only dimly perceive at age nineteen, but which had to be recognized and respected. Undoubtedly, there are many fantasies about this demand that might lead one to reject success and to court the unknowns of some new vocation. It is such fantasies, along with talents and discipline, that eventually determine the course of one's life.

Another example of the inability to accept the success of a well-defined career is Joseph Conrad. One major book and a more recent article deal with the neuroses underlying his decision to reject the career of a sea captain.[12] History, of course, shows that Conrad's decision to be a writer engaged his real talents. He left a legacy of brilliant novels that bared many sides of the unconscious, instead of living out the anonymity of a humdrum existence, drifting from port to port, suppressing a rich fantasy life to maintain security and self-control.

Conrad, born in Poland, had a tragic childhood. His father was exiled for political activity, forcing his mother to journey with their four-year-old son into miserable living circumstances. She died of tuberculosis when Conrad was still a young child, and his father died when the son was twelve years old. The circumstances of his early life created in him a very strong attachment to his mother and to his father after her death. It was difficult, if not impossible, for him to effect the transitions from these early attachments to the more emotionally diverse and relatively safe ties characteristic of the peer relations of childhood, adolescence, and early adulthood. As so often occurs with gifted people, strong attachment followed by abrupt loss made it hard for him to direct his energies toward other people. Instead, he turned inward to find security and pleasure, as well as to face conflict and anxiety in his fantasy world.

Conrad left Poland when he was fifteen years old to take up the life of a merchant seaman, working his way up the ranks until he became a master and was eligible for command. Following an accident, he was laid up in a hospital; the nature of his disability casts some doubt upon whether it was really a physical problem. He had been in charge of the ship on which the accident occurred before a captain was appointed, and had been considered for command of this vessel, a prospect that produced personal anxiety and may have aggravated the effects of the injury. After leaving the hospital, Conrad signed on to steamship service, but he left to take command of a sailing vessel, *The Otago,* of which he was captain for one year. He then resigned abruptly and went to England. There he started a writing career in a language that he had to master as a young adult in unfamiliar surroundings.

Conrad's departure from a reasonably secure life and his rejection of the prospects of success as a sea captain indicated an inner restlessness and discontent. When his life was about to take the form of an established career, he bolted. He seemed irrevocably drawn to a cyclical existence, "which was destined to become the fixed pattern of his life: a positive thrust of aggressive energy suddenly interrupted by a condition of collapse, inertia, and defeat."[13] In his writings, Conrad used this cyclical mode and the conflicts between loyalty and responsibility on the one hand and the need for flight followed by passivity on the other. In novels like *Lord Jim,* the psychological conflicts found expression, enabling him to draw from the personal experience of abandoning his homeland, an act tantamount to flight from his father.

From what was Conrad escaping? What accounted for the cycles of attachment and withdrawal, the need to establish ties and then break away, as though to escape a horrible fate? For Conrad, attachment meant a rendezvous with death (there is some evidence that he made a suicide attempt in Marseilles after some real or fantasied relationship with a noblewoman). In death, one is reunited with the mother once loved and then lost, but at the price of annihilation. The reunion also involves fantasies of patricide, of supplanting and destroying the father. Command, for Conrad, implied all of these conflicts and many more, consistent with his tragic personal history and with the many symptoms of depression and anxiety he experienced throughout his life.

But creative writing allowed him to reveal and use his conflicts, rather than merely repressing and repeating them. One can, therefore, examine from two sides the significance of success and failure, and the psychological issues of what authority is and means to gifted individuals like Joseph Conrad. To assume command and to use power requires a measure of distance from psychological conflict. But in acquiring the distance it takes to hold a position of authority, the ego may become restricted. For some, those with creative gifts, the rewards of command are never sufficient to overcome the pull of fantasies. The fear of success in the highly organized fields of command, arenas that have become institutional in character, may lead to even greater accomplishment in the relatively form-free activities of the arts and sciences.

People take different career paths in life, depending on their talents, the latent dispositions emerging from the conflicts experienced during childhood, and also on the paths they are pushed to follow in cultivating their talents and dispositions. Socialization is another word for the preparation individuals undergo for a life plan. If the preparation for institutional leadership takes hold, the individual gains a great deal of personal protection from the ordeals of neurotic conflict. It is society's way of assuring continuity of leadership in which the individual assumes responsibility but gains the security of tradition, of comradeship, and of the dedication of the self to an external reality. The trade-off is the most enduring form of the control of narcissism, one of the implicit tasks of socialization. With narcissism controlled, the dangers of flagrant abuses of power become less probable. The striking contrast of narcissism controlled or unleashed in power is evident in the lives and careers of Dwight David Eisenhower and Richard Milhous Nixon.

Socialization and the Readiness to Lead

It is ironic that two men so different should have crossed paths and become dependent on each other. Their preparation for leadership followed such strikingly dissimilar paths that in many ways they were strangers, although in others they seemed bound in a father-son relationship. When, toward the conclusion of the first term, President Eisenhower suggested that his vice president make his own way, the impression given others was that Eisenhower had meant that Nixon should take himself off the ticket. Nixon chose to interpret the message differently; he was to assert himself and decide what was best for his career, rather than follow what the President really meant but did not say directly. In the code of the officer and gentleman, one need only give a hint; the subordinate should be able to read the message accurately and conform to the superior's implied directive. But Nixon, a self-made man, was not bound by the traditions of superior-subordinate relationships, and was able to exercise options not available to those schooled in the belief that one places personal desires behind the good of the organization.

But there were more important differences in Eisenhower's and Nixon's leadership than the extent to which they accepted codes of conduct. Nixon had had some experience with the rules and codes of conduct of institutions when he was a member of the House and of the Senate. His readiness to absorb these rules and to make them an integral part of his psychological make-up differed greatly from Eisenhower's. Eisenhower belonged; he had been trained for membership. Nixon was an outsider, a loner, who sought isolation, probably as a reaction to an isolated and traumatic childhood. Nixon's mother had been away from the family during his later childhood, nursing his sick brother, who eventually died of tuberculosis. Before that, a younger brother had died of meningitis. Nixon had had illnesses during childhood, including a serious accident when he was four. The illnesses, injury, separations from brothers, and deaths of two brothers must have been significant in the development of Nixon's personality, especially in his emotional capacity to relate to people and to the codes of human relations.

There were no such traumas in President Eisenhower's life, although his father had experienced economic reverses and financial hardships. When faced with difficulties, Eisenhower found people available to him, from his parents to his brothers and peers outside the family.

Dwight David Eisenhower was born in a small town in Texas. His father had come to Texas after the failure in a small business, one that cost him the money and land his father had given him. His departure, penniless, from Abilene, Kansas, was harsh enough. It was compounded by an inability to uphold the heritage of hard work, thrift, and self-reliance characteristic of his fundamentalist family, a disgrace that added to the injury to his self-esteem. Not long after Eisenhower's birth, his father returned to Abilene to work in a creamery owned by the church to which his family belonged. The evidence available indicates that the family was relieved to be back among kin. Dwight Eisenhower's family was financially pressed, but the cohesion of the family did not suffer. In fact, there was good cause for all to work hard and contribute to the family's well-being. But hard work was not a solitary or isolated activity. For example, Dwight and a brother grew vegetables in a small section of the family plot. They sold their output door to door, enduring humiliations together. Eisenhower wrote in his memoirs, *At Ease,* "He [his brother and business partner] thought his prospective customers always acted superior when he offered his wares for sale. They would search through his whole pack of vegetables to find the best, meanwhile disparaging the quality of the lot to beat down his price."[14] Eisenhower seemed ready to meet the hardships of everyday life. He competed on the football and baseball fields and had his share of fist fights with other boys. He remembered one fight well. Abilene was divided into one well-to-do section and one poor section. A boy from the wealthy section, Wes Merrifield, and Dwight Eisenhower, both good athletes, fought for over an hour without a decision. When the two boys quit, Eisenhower had a black eye but had won considerable respect from his peers.[15]

While being toughened under the cohesive conditions of family and friendship, Dwight Eisenhower, along with his brothers, cultivated ambitions. Their situation was like the one their father faced when David Eisenhower decided to go to college instead of staying on the farm, awaiting his inheritance of land and a small amount of money to start him on the way of life of a farmer. A circumscribed future did not sit well with the elder Eisenhower, and this, it appears, affected the sons.[16]

Harboring ambitions, however, was not relegated solely to

individual fantasy, particularly the kinds of fantasy that are filled with revenge or the reparation of damaged self-esteem. Ambition was to be shared; advancement came by helping and being helped.

Dwight Eisenhower recalled the words of the commencement speaker at his high-school graduation: "I would sooner begin life over again with one arm cut off than attempt to struggle without a college education." In recalling the speaker, Eisenhower said, "For me . . . such an emphatic pronouncement was iron in the spine of purpose."[17] Because the family had very little money, Dwight and his brother Edgar planned to finance their education by alternating periods of study and work. They shared this pursuit; while one studied, the other worked. Dwight worked the first year and Edgar studied.

After his year of work, Dwight became interested in the military academies as a way of completing his education. A close friend, Everett "Swede" Hazlett, convinced him of the value of going to West Point. Eisenhower wrote, "It was not difficult to persuade me that this was a good move, first, because of my long interest in military history and second, because I realized that my own college education would not be achieved without considerable delay while I tried to accumulate money."[18] Here, the formulation of personal goals and the influence of friends went together.

At West Point, Eisenhower was anything but a model cadet. He rapidly received demerits, but never enough to warrant expulsion. The rebelliousness, however, had a playful quality to it; again, it involved relationships with peers and was not an isolated defiance of rules. As Eisenhower told the story:

One day, having been found guilty — by a corporal — of a minor infraction of regulations, we were ordered to report to his room after tattoo in "full-dress coats." This expression signified a complete uniform. Tommy suggested that we obey the literal language of the order. The full-dress coat is a cutaway with long tails in back, and tailored straight across the waist in front. At the appointed time, each of us donned a full-dress coat, and with no other stitch of clothing, marched into the Corporal's room. We saluted and said solemnly, "Sir, Cadets Eisenhower and Atkins report as ordered." The sound that Corporal Adler let out was the cry of the cougar.[19]

An indifferent student, playfully rebellious, Eisenhower was deadly serious about sports. He was a successful football player until a knee injury forced him to stop playing. Then, instead of losing interest in sports, he shifted his activity to become a successful coach of junior varsity football teams.

The knee injury and his involuntary retirement from football was a major disappointment to Eisenhower. In his usual way, he turned toward his peers: "The end of my career as an active football player had a profound effect on me. I was most despondent and several times had to be prevented from resigning *by the persuasive efforts of classmates*. Life seemed to have little meaning; a need to excel was almost gone."[20]

Excelling meant doing well those things that involved other people, for which one gained the admiration of peers with similar ideas about life. Studies, books, and abstract ideas held no attraction for Eisenhower or for the friends at West Point with whom he identified. When he graduated from the academy, he ranked 61 out of a class of 164, a respectable but hardly distinguished standing. Thus, Eisenhower reinforced a view of himself and acquired associates with whom he would share a lifetime of service in the military. As Morris Janowitz, the military sociologist, said, "Once the potential officer gains admittance and survives the ordeals of initiation, the purpose of an academy education is to transform him into a member of a professional 'fraternity' . . . Since graduation from an academy means entrance into a group which disperses very gradually . . . academy education means acquiring lifetime colleagues and the necessity of accommodating to them."[21] Associates and friends, such as George Patton and Omar Bradley, would be with Eisenhower during the days of learning subordinacy and, finally, of command during World War II.

Eisenhower had to have a great deal of loyalty to the service and to his associates to overcome the boredom and frustration of his early career in active service. He could not get the assignments he wanted (his reputation as a football coach haunted him) and, most disappointing of all, he could not get assigned to combat duty either in Mexico or in Europe during World War I. He wrote, ". . . all the West Point traditions that nourished the élan and ésprit centered on battlefield performance . . . My mastery of military paper work, even of rudimentary training methods, hardly seemed a shining achievement for one who had spent seven years preparing himself to lead fighting men. Some of my class were already in France. Others were ready to depart. I seemed embedded in the monotony and unsought safety of the Zone of the Interior . . . that was intolerable punishment."[22]

We described in Chapter 5 the importance to Eisenhower of his assignment to General Fox Connor after the loss of his first-born son. He was psychologically vulnerable and, at the same time, amenable to influence because of his characteristic turning toward others in times of disappointment. As Eisenhower wrote later about Connor, "Life with General Connor was a sort of graduate school in military affairs and the humanities, leavened by a man who was experienced in his knowledge of men and their conduct. I can never adequately express my gratitude to this one gentleman . . . in a lifetime of association with great and good men, he is the one more or less invisible figure to whom I owe an incalculable debt."[23]

General Connor offered a piece of advice to Eisenhower, saying, in effect, that in a bureaucracy, one has to go along to get along. He told Eisenhower, "No matter what orders you receive from the War Department, make no protest. Accept them without question."[24] But going along alone does not insure that one will move from subordinacy to command. There has to be someone to provide the opportunities and give help behind the scenes. As though to test Eisenhower's commitment and endurance, the War Department assigned him to coach football after his tour of duty with General Connor. Eisenhower went along, and, true to General Connor's implied prophecy, the breakthrough occurred when Eisenhower received orders for the Command and General Staff School at Fort Leavenworth, one of the most competitive schools in the army. It had the reputation of providing the passport to greater responsibility and promotion. It was a coveted appointment, and Eisenhower took advantage of the opportunity. Unlike his academic performance in high school and West Point, his work at the Command School was excellent; he graduated first in his class.[25]

Eisenhower had launched his career. He worked on General John J. Pershing's staff and served in the Philippines under General Douglas MacArthur. He became a trusted advisor to President Quezon of the Philippines and learned how to negotiate differences between the temperamental MacArthur and the leader of the Philippine government. Although he had a great deal of difficulty working under MacArthur, he never let his relationship deteriorate to the point where the strains became known in Washington. Undoubtedly, President Quezon's admiration and support did much to help Eisenhower tolerate MacArthur's foibles and to keep a good record with his superiors back home.

Eisenhower had been schooled for command slowly, carefully, and always inside a matrix of friendship, commitment, and responsibility. Whether his socialization in the army prepared him for the presidency is debatable. He learned the ways of consensus leadership and adapted his personality to the intricacies of military bureaucracy. But above all, he accepted the code and lived with the loyalty and dedication to responsibility implied by the code. Command, therefore, was hardly a lonely experience for the general and, later, President. He functioned in a system where he had learned the ropes and could count on knowing how other people would react to the pressures of events and the demands for decision. The problems he faced in the presidency were new to him, but he could remain basically trustful because of his sense of being home, an insider. His character was inherently a product of the American tradition. The tradition does not insure greatness, originality, and creativity in its leaders; it does insure, to those who believe in the system, a sense of openness, trust, and fair play. This is why America said, "I like Ike," and was willing to confer the presidency upon him.

Richard Nixon was an openly ambitious man. Wanting to

excel, he worked hard and diligently for his successes. We described earlier the traumas in his early life — illnesses, separation from his mother, and deaths of two brothers. Perhaps these traumatic experiences are enough to account for the character of a man who acutely perceived the environment and increased his attention to things outside himself, while he maintained an avoidance of people, especially when he suffered stress and disappointment. He became a loner who pretended to heed others. The record shows that his talents lay in role-playing, in which the understanding of codes was hardly the product of deep internalization and acculturation, as it was in the case of Eisenhower.

After graduating from high school in Whittier, California, Nixon went to Whittier College. There he developed a reputation as a first-rate student and a campus leader. Although he was a highly visible student, there is little indication that his associations involved intimacy or the quiet give-and-take of peer relations. He was a poor athlete, yet still went out for the Whittier football team. The coach and team valued his enthusiasm — he cheered and encouraged others to hustle — but not his talents as an athlete. The biographical evidence suggests that Richard Nixon used his ambition to do the things that would insure his being well known and successful at the college.[26] The pattern of finding out what to do and then doing it quite visibly remained with Nixon. He managed a political comeback later in life, following this pattern after the Goldwater debacle of 1964. Aware that grass-roots Republican organizations needed a figure around whom local leadership could rally support, Nixon proved himself by his willingness to appear at meetings all over the country; he also managed to put local Republican politicians in his debt.

Richard Nixon's college record made it possible for him to win a rare scholarship to Duke University Law School. At Duke, the number of people who received scholarships dwindled as the class moved through law school, but Nixon kept his scholarship for all three years.[27] One classmate, William Alderson, recalled that he reassured Nixon about his scholarship: "Listen, Nixon, you needn't worry. The fact that you are studying so late yourself shows you don't mind hard work. You've got an iron butt. And that's a secret of becoming a lawyer."[28] The iron butt, the capacity to sustain hard work, enabled Nixon to finish third in his graduating class at law school, but the success hardly helped him to launch a career. Nixon wanted very much to join a prestigious New York law firm. He and two friends traveled to New York for interviews. The friends landed jobs, but Nixon got nothing more than polite attention.[29] He applied to the Federal Bureau of Investigation, but here again he failed. So he returned to Whittier and entered a small-town law practice.

Although his practice did moderately well, it did not satisfy Nixon's ambitions. He tried his hand as an entrepreneur. He and others formed the Citra-Frost Company to produce and market frozen orange juice. The venture, though ill-fated, was not unreasonable or totally unrealistic, but the company could not develop the proper container for the frozen juice and it failed.

With the outbreak of World War II, Nixon, impatient with the draft, wanted to contribute to the war effort. For the months preceding his induction, he returned to the East Coast and worked in Washington for the Office of Price Administration. As Milton Viorst stated, "To hear Nixon tell it, the OPA was a nightmare, a personal calamity and a traumatic experience that made a cynic of a nice Quaker boy, leaving his body personally wrecked and his soul forever scarred."[30] Though outwardly uneventful, Nixon's experience with the OPA, coming after past disappointments in his career, seemed to provide a target for his anger. His mildly liberal views became antibureaucratic and later turned conservative.

From all accounts, Nixon was an outsider at the OPA. Because of the war and their dedication to its purpose, employees at the agency enjoyed high morale; they believed they were making an important contribution. There was considerable idealism behind their work, a sense of esprit de corps that carried over to postwar reunions. Nixon did not share the group feeling either during or after his brief tour at the OPA. "Nixon was uncomfortable among the liberals, the eastern law graduates, the Jews he rubbed shoulders with on the job. Because he lacked sophistication and big city graces, he never quite fit in."[31] As one agency member put it, "He was a faceless guy. I think we'd have forgotten him completely except that he became famous soon afterward and whatever memories we had became fixed in our minds."[32]

In his public comments, Nixon kept returning to his OPA days, always with a degree of anger and frustration. As he stated to his biographer, "When I was in OPA, I also saw that there were people in government who were not satisfied with interpreting the regulations, enforcing the law that Congress passed, but who actually had a passion to get business and use government jobs to that end. These were, of course, some of the remnants of the old, violent New Deal crowd."[33] Despite Nixon's harsh and angry criticism of the OPA, the agency, in fact, never had had a serious scandal despite the opportunities present by the nature of its work.

It seems, instead that Nixon was frustrated by the sense of inertia of his career and embittered by his inability to become part of a group of intellectuals. The rejection by the New York law firm, his return to a law practice in Whittier, undoubtedly left him feeling that he was outside the mainstream, so he focused his anger on the OPA. He accused the staff of "feathering their nests."[34] He called them empire builders, and his accusations indicate a kind of projection in which he was attributing certain unconscious ambitions of his own to the people in the OPA whom he hated. The members of the OPA had never accepted Nixon as a peer. Later, Nixon tried to hide the fact that he had been employed by the OPA. In his official biography, he listed his employment in the Office of Emergency Management. Milton Viorst said, "It would be like an FBI agent saying he worked for the Justice Department or a Forest Ranger saying he worked for the Interior Department."[35]

Richard Nixon left the OPA in 1942 to join the navy. There is little indication of the significance of Nixon's war experience to his development. The main recollection of others seems to be that Nixon was a cautious and successful poker player. He returned to Whittier after the war and his big break came in

1946, when the local Republican organization was casting around for a candidate to oppose Representative Jerry Voorhis for a congressional seat. During this campaign, Nixon met Murray Chotiner, who taught him a formula for electoral success. The method, evidently well suited to Nixon's temperament and personality, was, in Garry Wills's terms, the "denigrative method"; that is, simply attack and mutilate the opponent.[36] For example, Nixon accused Voorhis of being a Communist, sympathetic to the labor unions. Later, in his senatorial race, he called Helen Gahagan Douglas, his opponent, the "pink lady." Still later, Adlai Stevenson was the man "who got a Ph.D. from Dean Acheson's college of cowardly communist containment."[37] In effect, Nixon's rise to power was through simulation of anger, attacking and tearing down seemingly respectable people by stating or implying that their pasts were tainted or that they had participated in conspiracies.

But this rise to power, based as it was upon attack and humiliation of opponents, did not provide a standard of conduct, a coherent set of ideas, or a group of associates whom one supported and from whom one derived the security that is a part of mutual relationships. Unlike Eisenhower, Nixon found command very lonely indeed; he constantly feared enemies, people who only wanted to get back at him.

In Emmet John Hughes's opinion, formed after he had observed Nixon as vice president, "Nixon's mastery of tactic and technique at its best never seemed quite to compensate for his uncertainty in strategy or substance. He was always the pupil who 'heard the music, but yet missed the tune.' He was the most obsessed with the setting of his table, but with no taste for food. And for the President [Eisenhower] who was his most powerful supporter, he had to remain the candidate who was 'just not Presidential timber.' To the many who tried to seek out the true identity of the man one conclusion seemed inescapable: this identity remained elusive because *he* was deeply engaged in the same quest as *they*."[38]

The formation of a sense of identity and the capacity to lead often depend on the systematic training according to a code and system that educates in subordinacy before superordinacy.

Eisenhower became the true soldier, with a code of honor to uphold and with traditions of leadership to respect. On the other hand, Nixon had only a past of frustration and bitterness to draw upon, which left him with a sense of isolation and loneliness in leadership. Eisenhower was the general, the army hero; Nixon was the Red-baiter and the outsider. Eisenhower commanded respect; Nixon aroused mistrust and even contempt. The difference between these two men lies not only in the fact that Eisenhower met Fox Connor and Nixon met Murray Chotiner; it is, rather, the contrast in ideas about service in institutions that affected their capacity to lead.

CHAPTER 9

Disappointment

> The spiritual haughtiness and nausea of every man who has suffered profoundly — it almost determines the order of rank *how* profoundly human beings can suffer — his shuddering certainty, which permeates and colors him through and through, that by virtue of his suffering he *knows more* than the cleverest and wisest could possibly know, and that he knows his way and has once been "at home" in many distant, terrifying worlds of which *"you* know nothing" — this spiritual and silent haughtiness of the sufferer, this pride of the elect of knowledge, of the "initiated," of the almost sacrificed, finds all kinds of disguises necessary to protect itself against everything that is not its equal in suffering. Profound suffering makes noble; it separates . . .[1]
>
> *—Nietzsche*

A FEW YEARS AGO, *Life* magazine printed some unusually astute reflections on the leadership of President Johnson. The editors of the magazine began with the comment that President Johnson was not equally at ease with each of the problems facing him. He would rather deal with domestic problems than international issues, and, if events forced him to look beyond borders, he would much prefer to work with the new nations, the "have nots" in Asia, Africa, and Latin America, rather than with the "haves" of the established industrial societies of Europe. This type of behavior is sometimes characterized as identification with the underdog. Apparently, President Johnson, left to his own devices, would attack the problems of poverty, disease, education — concerns at the core of human suffering. He invariably preferred to attend to those for whom he felt strong compassion.

These observations involve some oversimplification, but they appear justified by the record of his presidency. The editors of *Life* concluded with these comments:

It can be argued — and is by many presidential scholars — that the man in the White House does not have a great deal of choice about the problems he gets or even how to deal with them. Perhaps that is so, but the Presidency still is a highly personal office. What pleases and placates, what intrigues and gratifies, what stimulates and flatters the man in the Oval Office subtly regulates the push and the priorities in the affairs of state that in the long run shape the era.[2]

Two points strike the reader of the observations. The first is the rather tragic aspect of leadership implied in the notion that events outside one's control may not allow a man to do those things that he dearly wishes to do and for which his dispositions make him eminently suited. The second is the suggestion, if only by inference, that this tragedy of leadership is more than a special situation and more than the idiosyncrasies of one man at one time and in one place.

We are not dealing only with the problems of political leaders, although many of the examples we shall use are public figures, since their careers are well documented. The same problems beset the chief executive in business. For him, particularly, there may be some important generalizations about leadership in the idea that a man's inclinations, unknown to himself, direct his energies to a certain end. A chief executive may, therefore, count himself lucky if he can utilize those tendencies with which he feels most comfortable, and over which, in the end, he may have the least conscious control. Although, from a purely rational standpoint, a chief executive should be able to adjust the style and substance of his actions to the problems that press for solution, he is, after all, a human being. The strategies and policies offered in his name, and the rationalistic terms in which they are advanced, often obscure the personal commitment behind formal programs.

And, in fact, without the convictions drawn from personal commitment, the chief executive's attempts to persuade and influence are not compelling. On the other hand, the conviction may be apparent, but the direction of policy may appear inconsistent and unreal, indicating displacement of personal conflicts on to the business of the organization. In effect, then, a corporate executive may face a paradoxical situation: he must live with himself and be himself while attempting to formulate realistic goals and means for implementing institutional goals.

Personal Equation

Twenty-five years ago, the fate of a young businessman demonstrated some of the hazards involved in the paradox. Charles Luckman came to the presidency of Lever Brothers evidently intent on making a personal impact on the company and the business community in general. His career with the firm ended abruptly when it became clear that his concern for personal image dominated the development of sound business strategy and structure.[3]

In more recent times, the career of John Connor, former president of Merck & Company, Incorporated, and subsequently secretary of commerce in President Johnson's administration, illustrated another aspect of the paradox: the gap between personal initiatives and the practical opportunities offered by the power structure for expressing these initiatives. As *Fortune* commented, in "The Paradoxical Predicament of John Connor":

> Jack Connor took office with an ebullience he has been hard put to maintain. Within the Commerce Department, Connor is something less than the complete boss: his chief lieutenants are answerable less to him than to the President, who appointed them, has the power to promote, and holds their political loyalties. And despite his resounding Cabinet title, Connor finds he has a lot less influence on policy than he was once accustomed to.[4]

The gap between the expectations of a leader and the practical possibilities of action within the realities of power relationships poses a severe test for the individual. In Connor's case, according to *Fortune,* he endured the frustrations by acting the stoic: "Putting the best possible face on what could have only been a severe disappointment, Connor made no complaint."[5] But there is a limit to any man's endurance, as shown in

Connor's subsequent decision to resign and return to private enterprise.

For some executives, leadership is the conscious effort to suppress or subordinate their personal expression while meeting the standards and expectations set by others. Such executives do not usually provide remarkable case histories of business failure, but neither do they stand out as achievers. More significantly, they bear a burden of unrealized hopes.

When an individual expects, because of his ability, position, or wealth, to exert influence over events, he cannot escape the personal commitment to action. And when such commitment is great, the potential for loss and disappointment is equally great. Consider this example: In the spring of 1966, Howard Hughes sold his holdings in Trans World Airlines. He realized an enormous profit in the transaction, but incurred high personal costs, because he gave up his intention to influence, if not to control outright, a major international airline. The decision to terminate a fight for corporate control implied a personal reappraisal of the potential gains and losses involved. That it was no simple outcome of the logics of investment was reflected in the comments of Charles Tillinghast, president of TWA, who explained Hughes's actions this way: "Perhaps he is a proud personality and wanted to divest voluntarily."[6]

As the examples suggest, the executive's career turns on the subtle capacity to take personal risks, to make decisions, and to implement them. Psychological studies of creative people, including leaders, suggest that preoccupation with success may be less important than the effects of disappointment in the evolution of a career.[7] Great strengths or weaknesses often come to the fore when leaders must confront the disappointments that are inevitable in life.

The experience of disappointment is a catalytic psychological event; it can foster or retard development. When the individual faces disappointment, he usually has to pull back his emotional investments in people and activities, re-examining them before reinvesting them in a new direction. The key idea, however, is to face disappointment. If disappointment and the pains attendant on it are denied or otherwise hidden, the

chances are great that the individual will founder on the unresolved conflicts at the center of his experience.

Role of Conflict

To weigh ideas on the management of disappointment in the
development of the executive career, we return to the study of
the relationship between personality and leadership. This relationship involves the evolution of the individual's style of leading. To achieve psychological understanding of the motives
underlying a leadership style, we must be prepared to deal with
the unexpected. In human affairs, relationships seldom persist
for the simple reasons that appear on the surface; one must
grasp the meanings of behavior and the multiple causes of
action.

The concepts of meaning and cause, when applied to human
activities, have at least two points of reference. The first is the
relation of the leader's acts to some problem or tension in his
environment. For example, Sloan's actions in establishing a
rational formal organization for General Motors can be analyzed in relation to the problems of constructing a balance
between centralized and decentralized functions within a company made up of complex marketing, engineering, and production strategies. The second point of reference for behavior is
the inner world of the actor. Here, the concern is not only with
the goals the individual seeks to achieve, but also with the
nature of the stimuli that constantly threaten the individual's
capacity to tolerate painful sensations and experiences.

One of the major contributions of psychoanalytic psychology
has been to demonstrate the place of conflict in the development of the individual. We have observed that each stage in the
life cycle involves personal conflict because the individual must
give up one set of gratifications and search for alternatives that
take account, at one time, of biological, psychological, and social
challenges. Failure to relinquish gratifications impedes development, and overly rapid learning establishes a gap between
emotional processes on the one hand, and cognitive-rational

capacities on the other. This gap may mean that the individual will have a low tolerance for drives and emotions and a highly rigid set of conditions for the exercise of his competence.

As we have seen, the life and tragic death of James Forrestal was a case in point.[8] Throughout his life, Forrestal developed his capacity for work, but at the expense of achieving intimacy with his family. Forrestal broke with his parental family after completing college; in effect, he renounced his past. Such breaks with the past do not usually occur unless the individual has experienced basic disappointments with his development and his position in the family.

Although the data in Forrestal's case permit only reasoned speculations, they suggest the kind of disappointment one finds in a harsh mother-child relationship. Because of a complex psychological process, the individual renounces nurture and other tender emotional exchanges, and substitutes a burning ambition and drive to achieve. If the individual has ability, as Forrestal clearly had in abundance, he may achieve leadership and success by many standards used to evaluate performance. But the individual is vulnerable to continuing disappointment, which may lead to breakdown. For Forrestal, the major disappointment in his career in government was probably his failure to achieve a power base independent of the President of the United States. He may even have harbored strong ambitions for the presidency — a position beyond his reach, under the political conditions of the time. Forrestal's relationship with Truman, therefore, became competitive, which led to his replacement following the 1948 election. He fell ill immediately upon the acceptance of his resignation and upon Louis Johnson's appointment as secretary of defense. An active, ambitious man stripped of his power, he suffered a major deprivation, a severance of the lines formerly used to guide his energies. Unfortunately, he had no alternative modes and no human relationship to help him heal his wounds and rebuild his life.

The end need not have been tragic. Many great men work through their disappointments and emerge with greater strength and a heightened capacity for leadership. Winston Churchill must have suffered a similar disappointment during

World War I. The disastrous campaign at Gallipoli was Churchill's responsibility and interrupted the career of this ambitious and powerful man. But he mastered the disappointment and became a leader during the supreme crisis of World War II.

The process of mastery must have demanded the kind of psychological work that takes place in psychoanalysis. Here, the individual withdraws, refocusing energy and attention from the outer world to himself. The outcome, if successful, is a reorganization of personality based on insight, followed by the renewal of active concern for what lies outside oneself and the use of one's energy in work.

We know all too little about the self-curative processes undergone by "great men" in their struggles with disappointment.[9] But Churchill must have been aided immeasurably by his many talents, not the least of which was writing. He also found strength in his relationship with his wife. In short, he did not have all his eggs in one basket.

Similar processes must have been at work in the emergence of Franklin D. Roosevelt as a great leader. The injury he suffered (the psychological injury resulting from an attack of polio) was the critical episode in his career. But again unlike Forrestal, he had the psychological resources, and the help of others, for performing the curative work necessary to overcome a personal crisis.

Two final examples might clarify the complex way disappointment affects adults in career development crises. Disappointment is not simply a condition in which the visible evidences of success are absent or a failure to realize ambitions is critical. In his autobiography, John Stuart Mill described the onset of his late adolescent depression. He was reflecting on life and his ambitions, and asked himself the question: "Suppose that all your objects in life were realized; that all the changes in institutions and opinions which you were looking forward to could be completely effected at this very instant: would this be a great joy and happiness to you?"[10] His answer was no, and the outcome of his personal honesty was an intense depression, which lifted only after he was able to mourn and express the grief underlying the psychological loss that occurred when he questioned his ideals.

Henry Ford experienced a disappointment on the success of the Model T. That great achievement marked a turning point in his career. Previously, he could channel energies and direct others; afterward, he became increasingly rigid and unrealistic. He entertained notions of omnipotence and somewhat paranoid ideas, as evidenced by the ill-fated venture on the Peace Ship and by his support of the anti-Semitic campaigns of the newspaper, the Dearborn *Independent*.[11]

There are men who are spoiled by success and, as Freud pointed out, develop symptoms only after major accomplishment.[12] As explained in Chapter 8, the fear of success can haunt great achievers because fantasy affects their emotional stability. To produce a car, become president of a company, or make a great scientific discovery is not a simple dream.[13] Such dreams may contain the hopes for restoring the individual to some state of happiness that he may have once felt and then lost. Or he may be enveloped by a sense of privilege through which he sees other persons as barriers to the possession of what he feels he justly deserves. Actions informed by such infantile ideas are the most dangerous. "Hell hath no fury like a woman scorned" or a man whose ambitions are frustrated because his dreams are impossible to realize no matter how hard he works or how tangible his achievements. Ambitions that contain hopes for changing the past and reversing the psychological disappointments encountered in development are self-defeating. The best that one can do is to understand the past. One cannot change it.

Attachment to Self

All human beings experience disappointment, which is one reason that all of us are attracted to myth and legend. Here, we temporarily heal the wounds of disappointment and find ourselves cherishing again wishes once held but reluctantly abandoned so that we might preserve our grasp of reality and the objects we love. So the psychology of the leader is not different from that of other human beings; it shares the initial fate of injury and disappointment. But leaders may feel the effects of disappointment more acutely, and experience feelings of injury and rage.

Most people accept disappointment with a shared sense of the difficulties of life and the satisfactions that work and human relationships provide; the attitude of "we're in it together" makes it possible to bear pain and loss. For creative people and leaders endowed with special abilities, a sense of estrangement follows early developmental conflicts. It is not surprising that, like Narcissus, leaders often direct their emotional investments inward during childhood. The dreams and fantasies of child-hood, translated into ambition by the adult, help him to main-tain his sense of being special. Very often these fantasies assume a place in destiny; they have a role in a great deed, like that of Oedipus, who solved the riddle of the Sphinx, or of the biblical Joseph, who interpreted the Pharaoh's dreams.

The attachment to self leads to achievement, but only in conjunction with sharply developed talents. Without other qualities, such as the power to reason, to perceive the interplay of events in the environment, or to invent new solutions to old problems, the heightened sense of self would lead to heightened frustration and, in the extreme, to madness. But the sense of self enters strongly into the personality of the leader, the ties others establish with him, and his actions.

The nature of policy and strategy in business organizations is a direct outcome of the actions of leaders. Decisions are made by men who think and act in relation to the influence of author-ity figures, who themselves are bound to a general process of human development.

To reach decisions and to chart a course for an organization, a leader needs considerable clarity of vision and accuracy in per-ception. The heightened sense of self that has been identified as a major factor in the psychology of leaders is both a resource and a hazard in corporate management and the fate of the individual. It is a resource because it preserves the indepen-dence one must have if one is to weigh carefully the opinions and advice of others. It is good common sense to encourage subordinates to offer recommendations, but, in the final analysis, major policy cannot be advanced without the conviction of the chief executive. How does he achieve the conviction necessary to seal a decision? If he is dependent on others because of a lack of self-confidence, it will be very difficult for him to lead an organization.

The amount of investment in self as a component of leadership can create problems. Too little causes overdependence and diffusion of purpose. Too much investment in self poses problems even more complex than overdependence. The leader who loves no one but himself is an autocrat, who keeps subordinates at a distance, deprived of independent action. Such a man is not as idealized now as he was in the late nineteenth and early twentieth centuries; nevertheless, he still persists in many organizations with all his strengths and weaknesses. The autocrat provides direction, and if he selects a correct path, he usually leads successfully. As a leader, he tends to select subordinates in his own image, ones who reflect all his virtues and vices. Subordinates tell the leader only what he wants to hear, and the opportunities for communication are limited by his distance. If an incorrect or outdated strategy continues to guide the organization, trouble will probably follow. The extent of the trouble often can be assessed, as in the case of the Ford Motor Company. From the nineteen twenties until World War II, Henry Ford's refusal to examine a rigid product policy caused loss of some of his share of the market and serious financial problems.

At a more personal level, the leader must maintain balance and perspective through the inevitable disappointments — and especially those that he may experience at the height of his career. These may range from policy failures to family problems — including, for example, the discovery that his sons and heirs have their own personalities and problems. The experience with these disappointments may produce a psychic injury that reopens old wounds. The response may be rage and regressive thought patterns, which result in a sense of omnipotence, the denial of human frailty, and other hazards of disappointment.

Harry Truman evidently had some insight into the hazards of

disappointment, particularly those of the leader whose power to control events and the actions of others is limited. Neustadt describes Truman's sympathetic anticipation of Eisenhower's problems; the outgoing President said, "He'll sit here and he'll say, 'Do this! Do that!' And nothing will happen. Poor Ike — it won't be a bit like the Army. He'll find it very frustrating."[14] What Truman recognized is that, no matter how powerful the leader's position, his influence is still problematic. Power is not affected by the magical thinking that equates authority with influence.

The Narcissus-like leader, who invests only in himself, does not necessarily behave overtly like an autocrat, nor does he necessarily detach himself from others; we frequently observe leaders who have close relationships with subordinates. But we cannot conclude from superficial observation that the presence of such relationships indicates balance between investment in self and that in others. Closer observation often shows that the ties are not really between two individuals cooperating in a rational and purposive endeavor. Instead, individuals are placed around the leader in such a way as to reflect the self-images from the leader's infantile past. Such executive structures become dramatic re-enactments of fantasies that restored the self-esteem of the individual during his early disappointments.

The structure and dynamics of these relationships have a variety of unconscious meanings, which are carried forward into major episodes of corporate life. The relationships may help to alleviate anxiety; they may also become central to pathological processes within the leader and other key executives in the organization. Again, we suggest that the pathologies involve the re-experience of disappointment and loss when the relationships shift or, under the influence of reality, fail as restitutive episodes.

When the relation of subordinates to leader involves the enactment of archaic self-images, there is a great need for honesty and candor to protect the individuals involved. In *King Lear,* the king had to drive away those who loved him most because he could not tolerate the intensity of his love for his youngest daughter, Cordelia. The only figure who remained close to Lear and who would tell him the truth was his fool. But the only way the fool could exist and speak the truth was to become the castrated one, who himself posed no threat to the power of the leader.

Now the problem shifts. Why would anyone give up self-esteem to serve another, even though, paradoxically, he performs noble work in helping the narcissistic leader maintain his fragile hold on reality? To be the king's fool is to pay an excessive price for another man's contributions to society. Yet in subordinate-leader relations, integrity can be maintained, and the truth can be spoken, only by subordinates who do not use their relationship with narcissistic leaders to fulfill their own infantile fantasies.

Self-Scrutiny

Leaders, whether they know it or not, commit themselves to a career in which they have to work on themselves before they can effectively work with other people. This fact of leadership is so often neglected that it is important to re-examine the implications of the need to work on oneself as a license to collect and use power.

The analysis presented here suggests that a significant area for the personal and inner work on oneself is the experience of disappointment. In many cases, disappointment can be prevented by a careful examination of personal goals behind the decision to assume responsibility in a position. If the goals are themselves unrealistic, major disappointment is inevitable.

A glance at the theories of the late Douglas McGregor, a management theorist, is appropriate, since they indirectly offer some clue to how the clash between personal ideology and reality may obscure insight.[15] McGregor distinguished between what he called Theory X and Theory Y. Many managers of complex organizations act on the basis of an outmoded conception of human nature and institutions. This conception, Theory X, sees man as a stubborn, recalcitrant being who has to be motivated to work in directions consonant with organizational goals. Such a belief results in a self-fulfilling prophecy. The type of leadership fostered by the "mechanical" man is apt to produce stubborn, recalcitrant people who sabotage the organization rather than contribute to its well-being.

Advocating the opposite view, Theory Y, McGregor asked leaders to change their ideas about human nature. McGregor based his alternative on the findings of behavioral science, particularly psychology. McGregor appealed to managers to adopt a philosophy of leadership based on the assumption that individuals want to grow and want to live cooperatively. In this view, the leader is an agronomist who cultivates the organizational environment so that people can conform to this positive image of man.

The plea is responsible for McGregor's considerable stature as a management theorist. Its appeal lies in its humaneness and in the subtle way it addresses itself to the underlying guilt that plagues men who strive for power in modern organizations. All too often, leaders are uneasy about the influence they have over men and decisions, an influence accompanied by a sense of guilt and a desire for reassurance, love, and approval from associates. It is as though leaders listen for the voices outside themselves that will testify to their humanity and quiet the nagging inner voices that disapprove, depreciate, and accuse. McGregor's message was designed to deal as much with a bad conscience as with the realities of work, authority, power, and decisions in organizations.

But how lasting and relevant are these external cures for a bad conscience? Whether in the name of religion or science, the cure is temporary, compared with the more arduous route of self-knowledge and mastery. The Greeks' advice to "know thyself" is very relevant today for men of responsibility. Unfortunately, McGregor's theories avoid the inner conflicts and resolutions of the problems of leaders in their almost singular dedication to creating an ideal organization climate.

McGregor was keen on talking to managers, but he failed in a basic sense to identify with them. He was largely concerned with subordinates, and, in talking to managers, McGregor communicated the wish in all of us for benign and benevolent power figures. But to love and be loved is not enough to make a successful leader.

McGregor did change his views during a period of intense stress. In his essay "On Leadership," written as he was about to leave the presidency of Antioch College, a position he had held for six years, McGregor said:

> Before coming to Antioch, I had observed and worked with top executives as an advisor in a number of organizations. I thought I knew how they felt about their responsibilities and what led them to behave as they did. I even thought I could create a role for myself that would enable me to avoid some of the difficulties they encountered. I was wrong! . . . I believed, for example, that a leader could operate successfully as a kind of advisor to his organization. I thought I could avoid being a "boss." Unconsciously, I suspect, I hoped to duck the unpleasant necessity of making difficult decisions, of taking responsibility for one course of action among many uncertain alternatives, of making mistakes and taking the consequences. I thought that maybe I could operate so that everyone would like me — that "good human relations" would eliminate all discord and disappointment. I could not have been more wrong . . .[16]

The essay from which the quotation was taken appeared in May 1954. The subsequent essays, written while McGregor continued a distinguished career as professor at M.I.T., suggest he no longer had the insight that underlay his sense of disappointment. We may suspect that the insight was lost because McGregor was too hard on himself, as the brief quotation above suggests. In his book's later essays, McGregor returns to the message through which he appealed to authority figures on behalf of subordinates.

Had he retained the insight shown in the Antioch essay, he might have recognized that the essence of leadership is choice, a singularly individualistic act in which a man assumes responsibility for a commitment to direct an organization along a particular path. He might also have recognized that, as much as a leader wishes to trust others, he has to judge the soundness and validity of his subordinates' positions. Otherwise, the leader may become a prisoner of the emotional commitments of his subordinates, frequently at the expense of making correct judgments about policies and strategies.

McGregor's problem may have come from his noble purposes. But nobility of purpose is not paramount in establishing one's position as chief executive. In the personal assessment of one's intention to lead, it is far better to assign the highest priority to discovering those things that need to be done, and then to devote oneself to engaging the commitments of others toward these goals. Of course, this does not rule out the possibility that historians can later look at an executive's work and discover the nobility that surrounded his leadership. But no matter how hard an individual works to prevent their occurrence, sooner or later there will be disappointments, and the personal working through of these events must assume first importance.

It is difficult to face disappointment squarely. The psychology of individual response to disappointment avoids the pain of self-examination. If a pattern of avoidance is formed, the individual may pay dearly for it later. Usually, avoidance occurs because it has been the individual's habitual way of dealing with disappointment from childhood. It also seems clear that those people who are lucky enough to have learned from early years how to face loss are best equipped to deal with the personal crises caused by disappointments in the executive career.

For example, a line manager in a large corporation worked closely with a vice president, who, in the course of events, came out second best in a business rivalry. The vice president resigned, and his department was left in a vulnerable position, without a leader, and with great loss of status. The line manager, who was in his early forties, had spent his entire working career with the large corporation. He had an excellent reputation, and the senior executives genuinely hoped that he would remain with the company.

He thought the issue through and decided to resign, recognizing that his personal commitments to the former vice president were so strong that they would not permit him to re-establish ties with others and to work effectively without damaging his self-regard. He discovered that his experience and talents were in high demand, and he made a successful transition to another corporation where, after demonstrating his competence, he became a vice president and senior executive in his own right.

The decision to remain or to leave was not the significant test of whether the line manager was actually facing the disappointment he had endured. Rather, the significant test came in his silent work of self-examination, shared only with his wife, who matched his personal courage and willingness to take risks. The line manager learned to face events, to write off a loss, and to set forth on a new course.

The key factor in mastering disappointment lies in the capacity to experience and work through the emotions connected with personal career losses.[17] The flight from the kind of work that leads to mastery is usually connected with the individual's limited capacity to tolerate painful emotions.

An example of an attempt to face disappointment is poignantly described in the second volume of *The Diaries of Harold Nicolson*.[18] Nicolson, a member of Parliament, was parliamentary secretary in the Ministry of Information during the early years of World War II. Churchill asked for his resignation after a series of top-level changes in the ministry resulting from public criticism and charges of mismanagement. Nicolson resigned, and the following day (July 19, 1941) he noted this entry in his diary:

> I wake up feeling that something horrible has happened, and then remember that I have been sacked from the Government. Go to the Ministry and start clearing out some of my private possessions. Then attend the Duty Room, probably for the last time. I meet Gerald Campbell in the passage. "I hear," he says, "that you have been thurtled?" Everybody expresses dismay at my going. I have a final drink in the Press Bar with Osbert Lancaster, and then lunch at the Travellers with Robin Maugham. He is as charming as he could be.
>
> But I mind more than I thought I should mind. It is mainly, I suppose, a sense of failure. I quite see that if the Labour leaders have been pressing to have my post, there is good cause why they should have it. But if I had more power and drive, I should have been offered Rab Butler's job at the Foreign Office, which I should

dearly have loved. As it is, I come back to the bench below the gangway having had my chance and failed to profit by it. Ever since I have been in the House I have been looked on as a might-be. Now I shall be a might-have-been. Always up till now I have been buoyed up by the hope of writing some good book or achieving a position of influence in politics. I now know that I shall never write a book better than I have written already, and that my political career is at an end. I shall merely get balder and fatter and more deaf as the years go by. This is an irritating thing. Success should come late in life in order to compensate for the loss of youth; I had youth and success together, and now I have old age and failure. Apart from all this, I mind leaving the Ministry where I did good work and had friends.

This space indicates the end of my ambition in life. "Omnium consensu capax imperii nisis imperasset." [Tacitus on the Emperor Galba: "Had he never been placed in authority, nobody would ever have doubted his capacity for it."]

According to Nicolson's son, who edited the diaries, it took his father some time to assimilate the disappointment and plunge anew into lesser responsibilities. But Nicolson's apparent honesty and his gifts as an observer and recorder of events helped him during a difficult personal crisis.

Studies of those who get into trouble and present themselves for treatment to a psychoanalyst show that difficulties often lie in a limited capacity to tolerate emotions, especially those connected with loss and disappointment. Executives are especially vulnerable because they may have developed an unconscious strategy of forced activity or, more accurately, hyperactivity, to defend themselves against emotional awareness. The hyperactive executive is, of course, rewarded for his hyperactivity, since, in the conventional understanding of ideal executive behavior, busyness is generally considered a good thing.

However good it might be in some respects, it can be bad if it serves to build and maintain the wall between the inner worlds of thought and feeling. In the treatment of such people, the most positive indicator of progress is the appearance of sadness and depression. As the individual consciously assimilates the depression and relates it to his experiences with disappointment throughout his development, he becomes capable of undoing the ineffective patterns and substituting more effective ways to deal with the demands and stresses of responsibility.

No one is immune to disappointment. What is more significant is that individuals who want power and responsibility, or who seek creative expression, are especially vulnerable to suffering when reality does not conform to their wishes or intentions. But far from being an omen of continued failure in career, these periods of pain may actually stimulate growth and truly outstanding performance.

Much depends, however, on the quality of the psychological work the individual accomplishes under the stress of loss and bewilderment that frequently accompanies disappointment. As in all matters of personal development, the outcome will be determined by the quality of the man, the courage he can mobilize, the richness of his talents, and his ability for constructive introspection.

It is no easy task to examine our own motivations. In fact, the necessity seldom arises for many people until they meet an impasse in life. At this juncture, they are confronted with two sets of personal concerns: those connected directly with present disappointments and those related to experiences of disappointment in the past. Usually a crisis in the present reopens problems from the past, and the individual experiences a telescoping of time, in which the psychological past and present merge.

The degree of telescoping is critical in judging the intensity of stress involved in the management of disappointment. It is usually difficult enough to solve a current problem, with all its demands for accurate observation and realistic thought; the difficulty increases when the process of solving current problems involves examination of one's history of loss or deprivation. Then the most effective step the individual can take is to seek competent help.

In the course of examining reactions to disappointment, a subtle change may take place in the individual's perspectives and attitudes. He may come to recognize that it is not possible for him to achieve and fulfill certain goals and wishes, and he may then be willing to relinquish them, freeing himself of their demands on his behavior; at the same time, he may discover uncharted possibilities for productive work and pleasure. These possibilities usually remain obscure so long as the individual is intent on his quest for restitutive rewards to make up for his felt losses of the past.

There is irony in all of human experience, including the solutions to the problem of disappointment. The deepest irony of all is in discovering that we have been mourning losses that were never sustained and yearning for a past that never existed, while ignoring our real capabilities for shaping the present.

CHAPTER 10

Myth and Reality
of Entrepreneurship

> "But he hasn't anything on!" cried a little child.
> "Good heavens, hear the voice of innocence!" said the father;
> and one whispered to the other what the child had said.
> "There's a little child that says he's got nothing on!"
> "But it's true! He *hasn't* got anything on!" all the people
> shouted at last.
>
> —*Hans Christian Andersen*

INFANT ORGANIZATIONS reflect the strengths and weaknesses of dependency on a leader — the entrepreneur and founding father. Both the entrepreneur and his followers live by expectations that set the stage for severe disappointment later on. The entrepreneur, that peculiar combination of robber baron and conquistador, at some point faces the fact that the organization he created no longer needs him. Indeed, his continuing presence may jeopardize the organization's existence. For the subordinates, the recognition that, in certain respects, the emperor has no clothes produces an emotional vacuum, a loss of purpose, when they detach themselves from an involvement with the entrepreneur. Not infrequently, the same subordinates have to decide whether to break with the entrepreneur and, in some cases, to become instrumental in causing his departure.

Attitudes toward entrepreneurship have undergone major changes since the Industrial Revolution. Social awareness has replaced individualism as a virtue, and this has had an impact upon the development of entrepreneurship. The coveted individualism of the entrepreneur lost some of its glamour when it came to involve exploitation and irresponsibility. The shift paralleled the transformation of economic ideology from laissez-faire to welfare economics. The era of the Carnegies, the Krupps, and the Rockefellers has passed into history. But despite changes in social outlook, entrepreneurship remains a fascinating phenomenon. People are still curious about the personality and motivations of the entrepreneur.[1]

The Elusive Entrepreneur

Joseph Schumpeter, a pioneer in entrepreneurial theory, considered the entrepreneur an innovator, a catalyst, continuously interacting with a fluctuating environment.[2]

To implement his ideas, the entrepreneur must coordinate and manage. The personal requirements for management often conflict with those for innovation. As John Kenneth Galbraith states, "The great entrepreneur must, in fact, be compared in life with the male *Apis mellifera*. He accomplishes his act of conception at the price of his own extinction."[3]

Traditionally, entrepreneurs are risk-takers, though this has changed with the increasing division of ownership and management. In modern industrial societies, the capital needed for the formation and operation of an enterprise is often supplied by someone other than the entrepreneur himself. The financial uncertainty is now the burden of the capitalist, not the originator of ideas. But, although the entrepreneur does not necessarily bear the financial risk of an operation, he exposes himself to considerable social and psychological risk.

The "purgatory" before one becomes a recognized entrepreneur, that is, recognized by society at large, is often a period of emptiness, depression, and despair. The potential entrepreneur is at a loss about the direction of his career, and society often dubs him "misfit." Social comparisons make him aware of the psychological risks he runs.

The entrepreneur is the product of a delicate interplay of personality and environment. Environmental factors that are institutional — the protection of private property, the state of education and technology, and the availability of natural resources — conspire with a general acceptance of economic ideas as a frame of reference for society. Partly because of the writings of Adam Smith, his followers, and the Social Darwinists, economists in Western societies popularized the concept of economic man, in whom the characteristics of competitiveness, individualism, rationality, industriousness, and wealth accumulation were considered desirable. Not only were these values internalized by the participants, but legal and economic institutions were built around them. The new emphasis created an environment receptive to entrepreneurial activity, leading to the emergence of people, driven by psychological needs, who were willing and able to utilize available opportunities and to create new ones.

Everett Hagen's book, *On the Theory of Social Change*, develops a model, applicable to entrepreneurship, that attempts to explain the process of change in society at large. His model shows how the authoritarian personality in a traditional society (one who believes that power resides in position instead of achievement, who has a strong sense of righteousness and rigidity, and who adheres to conventional values) is subject to sociocultural influences that lead to changes in status and, eventually, to a loss of status. The rage and anxiety of the authoritarian person who has experienced a disruption of the status quo finds an outlet within the family. To use Hagen's words:

> In the first generation of withdrawal of status respect, the son perceived in his father a clear belief in the goodness of the traditional social position, and he perceived his father's pain and anxiety. *His* son will probably internalize the same social identity since he, too, has no alternative, but together with the expectation of pain he will see an aspect in his father's personality which was absent from his grandfather's, the suggestion that the road to safety lies in repressing one's values. It seems likely that this will be a convincing part of the model his father provides, and that the desire to avoid pain will propel him farther along that road than his father traveled. And *his* son still farther. Thus, over several generations, if the external withdrawal of status respect continues, the safety of not hoping for satisfaction in any role is apt to become more and more appealing and apathy to increase . . .[4]

The process of status withdrawal can result in the individual's becoming retreatist or ritualistic, evincing helplessness or

apathy toward outside reality. Unlike the authoritarian personality with a rigid conception of the world, the personality of the
retreatist or ritualistic individual is unstable. He cares little
about the boundaries between reality and fantasy. The retreatist does not have a reliable, secure identity image from his
parents. Fantasies gratify, taking over from reality, and the
individual tends to withdraw into himself, feeling that the outside world presents only disappointments and frustrations.

Over a period of generations, the conditions leading to re-
treatism and the dislocations of the individual from society
might produce the entrepreneurial personality. Rebelling
against the withdrawal and depression of father and grand-
fathers, entrepreneurs key themselves to action and change.

Several writers have described the origins of entrepreneurs in
ethnic and religious minority groups. Max Weber's thesis of
the Protestant ethic is a familiar example.[5] It is evident that
the belief in a value system different from that of society at
large may lead to frictions between the family and the outside
world. Members of a minority group can be subjected to dis-
crimination, which may be repeated within the family, causing
tension and stress.

Changes in the status of various social groups within a culture
may have the same effect. When colonizers move into a traditional society, there may be a rearrangement of the socioeconomic positions of various status groups within the society.
Internal, civil, or tribal wars are other common causes of disruption, as, of course, are international wars. We may speculate
that the total demolition of the social structure in Germany and
Japan during World War II, could have had some influence on
the process of change and on the rapid economic growth of
those nations in the postwar period. Although many other
countries were exposed to violent turmoil during World War
II, almost nowhere else was the psychological and material
devastation so enormous. The entrepreneurial climate and the
socioeconomic value systems in Japan and Germany that support hard work also contributed greatly to the growth of
enterprise.

During a period of change, the main "mover" is one who is
dissatisfied and frustrated with present conditions. He will try

to imitate and to adopt new means, whether political (such as a colonial administration), economic, psychological, or technological, to improve his situation. This signals the beginning of change. The reformer will introduce transformation on a grand scale; he will be the charismatic leader (religious or nationalistic) or the ideologist. On a more modest scale, the entrepreneur will also participate in this process of transformation.

An openness to other value systems has been found mainly among "reform" groups. These groups reject previous norms, causing a gap in an established value system. The Santri Moslems of Java, the Jains, Parsees, the Sikhs in India, Indians and Chinese in Southeast Asia, Lebanese in North Africa, and the Indians in South and East Africa exemplify this point.*

Ethnic and religious minorities, less hampered by a complicated, fully established social structure, tolerate a greater degree of turmoil than the majority. The turmoil can produce immediate results, as entrepreneurship in the United States has shown. Considerable time, however, may be necessary (perhaps measured in generations) to absorb values conducive to change before the first tendencies toward diffusion of values become apparent.

Nevertheless, a simple cause-and-effect analysis can be misleading. For example, membership in the black minority group in the United States has not led to the development of black entrepreneurs to any significant degree.

In addition to the fact that entrepreneurs have come from

---

* In Lebanon, although the Christians made up only 50 percent of the population, they provided 80.2 percent of the entrepreneurs around 1958. The Moslems, representing 44 percent of the population, provided only 16.4 percent of the entrepreneurial group.[6]

Japan provides a striking example of the role a minority can play. A study of fifty leading entrepreneurs in the early Meiji era in Japan showed that 46 percent came from the samurai class, which represented only 7 percent of the total population.[7]

Newly immigrated groups in a relatively established industrial society reflect the same process. In a sample of Michigan entrepreneurs in the study, *The Enterprising Man*, 19.8 percent of the sample were foreign-born, compared to a figure of 5.9 percent for the total population, and 35.0 percent were American-born with a foreign-born father, compared with 15.0 percent for the country as a whole.[8]

ethnic and religious minority groups, there is another prominent feature in the backgrounds of such men: in many cases,
their fathers were self-employed.* Self-employment was, perhaps, a necessity; they may have had no alternatives. Occupations were closed to them because of their "difference," which
put them under strain. Self-employment, with its uncertainties
and sociopsychological risks, will have an effect on the behavior
of the father, which will be perceived by his children. The
situation of stress can engender both frustration with a hostile
outer world and inner rage, which can be displaced on to other
members of the family. In the eyes of the children, the father as
an object of identification becomes a remote, unpredictable,
uncontrollable person over whom one desires to have power
and control.

The Entrepreneurial Personality

Since the father's social role is directed outside the family, he
will be the one most subject to frustrations, especially if he is a
member of a group whose status has been downgraded. His
feeling of rage may be transmitted to the family, causing retreatist or ritualistic attitudes on the part of the children.
These attitudes, because of their inherent instability, can be-

* In a study of fifty-eight technical entrepreneurs, 48.3 percent had fathers who
worked for themselves.[9] Of eighty entrepreneurs reporting in the study, *The
Enterprising Man,* 26 percent had fathers who worked for themselves, and an
additional 10 percent had fathers who were professional men; 19 percent of the
reporting group had fathers who were farmers. This brings the total of entrepreneurs who came from families in which the father was self-employed to
55 percent.[10]

In her discussion of small businessmen in Poughkeepsie, New York, an area
that can be considered representative enough to permit some generalizations,
Mable Newcomer arrives at a figure of 57.3 percent of entrepreneurs whose
fathers had been self-employed (including professionals and fathers who headed
the son's firm).[11] Yusif Sayigh, in his analysis of Lebanese entrepreneurs, found
that the most common occupations of the fathers were trade (31.3 percent),
industry (26.4 percent), and the professions (8.7 percent). He remarks that
industry in this context means workshops and home industries. These figures
indicate again that a large percentage of the entrepreneurs' fathers had been
self-employed.[12]

come the psychological material upon which creativity and innovation are based.

The turbulent childhood of potential entrepreneurs, socio-culturally and psychologically, is reflected in their words. In *The Enterprising Man,* a surprising number of themes relating to childhood emerged from interviews with entrepreneurs. Themes such as "the escape from poverty," "the escape from insecurity," "death and sudden death," "the parents who went away," and "the parents who were sent away" occurred repeatedly. They seemed part of the entrepreneurial "family romance."[13]

Sir Henry Deterding, the main figure behind Royal Dutch Shell, was six years old when his father died.[14] The father of Karl Benz, the entrepreneur who laid the foundation of the Mercedes-Benz concern, died when the son was one year old.[15] Jon Johnson, a black entrepreneur controlling the Johnson Publishing Company (which publishes magazines aimed at blacks), experienced the death of his father when he was six years old.[16] Carnegie and his family left their native Scotland for the United States when he was thirteen years old.[17] Deterding, Benz, and Johnson experienced poverty or near-poverty in their youth. Frawley, an entrepreneur whose empire consisted of Eversharp, Technicolor, and Schick Electric, among other companies, was sent to San Francisco from Nicaragua by his Irish father when he was five years old to attend school.[18] Emil Jellinek Mercédès, born in Vienna of a Moravian father and a Hungarian mother, was an entrepreneur who founded the Mercedes concern, which later merged with Benz's. He ran away from home when he was seventeen years old.[19] Bill Lear of the Lear Jet Company left home when he was sixteen.[20]

These are only a few examples from a far more comprehensive group. The themes of poverty, death, and loneliness recur, indicating how many entrepreneurs had disrupted childhoods, and emphasizing the influence of psychological deprivation. But, although death, poverty, emigration, and loneliness are important in the formation of the entrepreneurial personality, these factors do not explain everything in a complex picture.

In view of the importance of these various themes of rejection, desertion, and turmoil, we will offer some recollections of entrepreneurs:

> Well, I was born in Tacoma, Washington, or rather in a small town just outside of Tacoma. I actually grew up and went to school in Tacoma. As far as my family life is concerned, actually my father worked at a job until he went into the shingle business. My mother was against it terrifically. *She fought him.* She didn't want him to give up the security of a steady job and go into business. As a matter of fact, they fought for ten or twenty or thirty years afterwards. *So my father sort of retreated from us.* He would even be gone for two or three months at a time. We were a very poor family. We didn't starve, but we were very poor.[21]

Warner and Abegglen, two researchers of entrepreneurship who analyzed the successful, occupationally mobile man, reinforce the point about the unsettled childhood of such a man:

> My father was a plumber, and he was an invalid for I'd say the last twenty years of his life. My father was not a happy person when I knew him. I never knew him when he wasn't an invalid. He had arthritis. They called it something else then. Apparently he had a good disposition early in life. My father and mother didn't get along well. *His terrible disposition* was caused, I guess, to some extent by his pain and incapacity . . .[22]

Shell's Deterding, who, admittedly, fits the entrepreneur-manager type better, once made the following remarks about the consequences of his father's death:

> My father before his death had arranged that my two brothers, who were several years older than I, should be educated — one as an Army officer and the other as a doctor of medicine . . . Because I was so young when he died, no educational plans had been made for me, but this didn't trouble me . . .

After mentioning that all the available money was spent on the other two sons, Deterding continues, "nor was I myself, as the son who, in the family reckoning, had been left out in the cold, at all resentful."[23]

Deterding's denial gives insight into his defensive structure; the vividness of the memory after so many years is evidence of its psychological impact.

Family turmoil can produce conflicts of identification, conflicts that appear at the core of the personality disturbances of entrepreneurs, causing a splitting process of "good" and "bad" images in the unconscious. If there is reason in external reality for the fusion of these good and bad images, a healing process for these fragmentations of the self sets in, and a "reasonable," understanding father image, with whom the person can identify, may emerge and be incorporated by him. But the combination of a remote father image, regularly indulging in outbursts of rage, and a mother figure who occasionally appears threatening to the child can wield a powerful influence on the child's personality. So these undesired images may require excision, and this can lead to conflicts of identification.

A family in which the father played such an inconsistent, ambivalent, and threatening role would probably have a mother who would play not only a nurturing role but also a domineering one. Since there is no one else to take responsibility, the mother often has no choice. She will give the child his sense of direction. And in the case of the death of the father, there is no alternative. Examples of "directive" mothers can be found in *Big Business Leaders in America:*

> My mother was a very determined person, strictly disciplined. She was a person of the old school who believed in bringing up her children along a straight line. She had all the responsibility of bringing up the kids . . .[24]

We know from Carnegie's autobiography that his mother was a strong, decisive woman.

> My uncle soon gave up weaving and my father took his place and began making tablecloths, which he had not only to weave but afterwards, acting as his own merchant, to travel and sell, as no dealers could be found to take them in quantity. He was compelled to market them himself, selling from door to door. The returns were meager in the extreme. *As usual my mother came to the rescue.* There was no keeping her down . . . this wonderful woman, my mother, earned four dollars a week by binding shoes . . .[25]

One result of this kind of family can be ambivalence on the part of the children toward the mother who, after all, possesses the power of betraying their "secrets" and "misdoings" to that ambivalent, remote, and frightening individual, the father. If a father is not present in the family, powerful, unpredictable figures, existent or nonexistent, may be chosen by the mother as punitive images, which will — because of the impossibility of reality-testing — re-enforce feelings of anxiety and guilt.

The combination of a dominant, nurturing mother and a remote, ambivalent father can lead to confusion in roles and to defective identification, which, in turn, may have serious consequences for the development of an individual's sense of identity. A child may wish to identify with his father, but the unpredictability of his father's behavior might give him — unconsciously — doubts about the value of identification itself, which will influence later stages in the life cycle. In adolescence, there will be difficulty in making commitments and, later, confusion in that most crucial of decisions, the choice of a career. This is a period of trial and error, described in *The Enterprising Man* as "the school for entrepreneurs." The potential entrepreneur drifts from job to job, has difficulty conceptualizing his ideas, and is perceived by his associates as a "deviant," "eccentric," "irrational" individual.

Although he may have difficulties finding suitable models, the child who will become an entrepreneur can find an outlet for his wish to identify by indulging in fantasies; only in these will he be able to influence and control his remote, ambivalent, threatening father. The fantasies gratify. They are his way of fighting the "dangers in the environment." He can also resort to the defensive maneuver of reaction formation as a strategy for dealing with his failure to identify with his father (if I cannot be like my father, I do not want to be like him; I reject him). But even this solution will not be satisfactory in the end. There can be confusion about the actuality of rejection. Who was rejected and who the victim of rejection, father or son? Ambivalence, which we may view as an imitation of the father's unpredictable behavior, combined with fantasies about powerful figures, projections of the ideals of the potential entrepreneur, may lead to a split perception of the world: things are either good or bad; there is no middle.

To fuse feelings of love and hate, one must have a long period of ego development facilitated by an awareness of one's inner conflicts and a feeling of adequacy. The entrepreneur often is unable to resolve ambivalent feelings. Because of frustrations experienced in the early stages of his life, the entrepreneur often has persistent feelings of dissatisfaction, rejection, and powerlessness, which impair the ego processes. The feelings of rage experienced by the child because of the father's behavior, combined with the fear of loss of, and abandonment by, the mother (feelings that, undeniably, have a certain touch with reality if the all-demanding, possessive father is present) injure his self-esteem. Such injury induces tensions, which influence his future "deviant" behavior. But it is exactly this need for restitution, in a receptive environment, that can lead to creativity and innovation, though it may involve personal suffering.

The entrepreneur may be a folk hero, but he is continuously badgered by his past, which is experienced and re-experienced in his fantasies, daydreams, and dreams. The fantasies and dreams often have a threatening content — the recurrence of the early fear of separation, of injury, and of the anxiety and rage that stem from the lack of control over his environment. The results may be distrust and suspicion, and these could force the potential entrepreneur into a role in a nonstructured, less anxiety-provoking situation.

Lack of integration in the superego, the above-mentioned lack of "fusion," is reflected in the attitudes of the entrepreneur toward superior and subordinate. The entrepreneur is easily threatened, unable to work in a subordinate relationship, since authority carries the threat of repetition of the childhood frustrations he is still desperately trying to overcome.

The leadership style of the entrepreneur projects his persistent feeling of dissatisfaction. Even success does not produce satisfaction, since fears about illegitimate gains and undeserved rewards dominate unconscious thinking. In his search for legitimacy and mastery of his childhood frustrations, the entrepreneur will eventually find that accomplishments are insufficient. He needs social support, the esteem and the admiration that have been denied him for so long, in order to compensate for feelings of rejection centered on the father image. He is forced to realize his ideas, and the enterprise becomes a tangible means of acquiring the self-esteem he desires. However, the materialization of his ideas is also a risky proposition; success can induce guilt originating in ambivalent feelings about parental rejection.

The investment of the entrepreneur, his link to reality, is the enterprise itself. In a symbolic way, he unites with the enterprise. It can be his way of dealing with childhood frustrations, but it is an insufficient form of restitution for some entrepreneurs. Anxiety and guilt over their very success — along with unconscious imagery of jealousy and loss of love — will cause doubt about their right to such an enterprise. Tension can build up until it culminates in the destruction of the psychological peace of the entrepreneur and of the enterprise as well. One conclusion of the authors of *The Enterprising Man* was that "the observable career pattern, might for a number of men take on the aspects of a rather hair-raising roller coaster ride — a succession of ups and downs, dramatic reversals of success and failure, streaks of seemingly good and bad luck."[26] The entrepreneur is a kind of psychological gambler. And at the times of their greatest setbacks, many of these entrepreneurs seem to feel their best. Their unconscious belief is that, since they have finally been punished for their success, the worst is over. The resulting sense of relief from anxiety and guilt stirs them into fresh activities, starting anew the process of constructing an enterprise.

But there are problems associated with the self-destructive behavior of entrepreneurs. Because the entrepreneur undergoes role confusion, he depends on his enterprise for self-definition and a measure of security. The enterprise conveys to the outside world the entrepreneur's ability and, at the same time, it is his restitution in his private world. The enterprise becomes emotionally charged, and the entrepreneur has difficulty removing himself from it. Any influence that might threaten his total control over the enterprise could trigger irrational acts. Sharing power, authority, and responsibility becomes difficult. He will resist any intrusion into his autonomy and dominance because he fears the repetition of threatening childhood situations; this is a kind of paranoia. The entrepreneur tends to see acts by other individuals connected with the enterprise as attempts to remove him from control. Entrepreneurs, therefore, resist planning for management succession.

The ambivalent, paternalistic attitudes of the entrepreneur become a burden to the company as soon as the organization's structure demands sophistication. The need for greater systematization places new demands on the entrepreneur, demands he may be unable to meet. At this point, the situation is ripe for the professional manager and the bureaucratic style of leadership, and turns paradoxical: the successful entrepreneur, who has guided the enterprise through the formative period of growth and maturity, moves unconsciously on a collision course that leads to his own elimination. As Schumpeter observed, after the implementation stage, the entrepreneur will exchange his position with that of the manager. But this process is not automatic; many years of frustration — for the employees as well as for the entrepreneur — can elapse before it is completed. The entrepreneur is usually unwilling to give up his powerful position to provide for succession. If the entrepreneur is a majority stockholder, there is probably no means for deflecting the enterprise from its self-destructive course. If the entrepreneur is a minority stockholder, the other stockholders can band together to get control and redirect the enterprise.

Many companies have difficulties shifting to a more formally organized enterprise. Take, for example, the Head Ski Company. As the company continued to grow, it became apparent that Howard Head, the chief executive officer, was no longer suited to direct the enterprise, probably because of his inability to delegate authority and to relinquish control. He finally yielded his post to one of his subordinates, although he continued to function as chairman. He remarked that "This consolidation of the responsibility was in the interest of a more streamlined general management appropriate to the planned growth of the company and expanding diversity of its enterprises."[27] Head had mentioned earlier that "things were getting more and more disorganized. If something went wrong, my instincts told me to fix it myself, whether it meant rewriting ads or greasing machines. I was getting swallowed up."[28] But given the emotion-charged nature of the enterprise and the "all or nothing" attitude of the entrepreneur's lifestyle, the situation could not remain unchanged. Two months after the appointment of the executive officer, Howard Head announced that he was retiring from active management and selling most of his holdings in the company. One of his associates said:

> When Howard is involved in something, he has to be in it all the way . . . When he could no longer run the business, both he and the company felt it would be better if he got out, instead of just hanging along the sidelines.[29]

If the entrepreneur sells his company, personnel problems often arise. The enterprise under the direction of the entrepreneur is characterized by a chaotic organizational climate, which may be considerably different from the usually more structured, formalized environment of the acquiring company. In addition, the entrepreneur probably does not develop managerial talent; his inability to delegate authority weakens the quality of management.

In the case of acquisition, the acquiring company faces two main problems. Given the overpowering leadership style of the entrepreneur, good managers rarely stay, so the acquiring company can assume that the managers who have remained under the entrepreneur are of mediocre calibre and will have to be replaced.

The other problem area, often a painful one, concerns the question of the entrepreneur's future in the new company. If he is retained, there will be major conflicts; most entrepreneurs cannot operate in a subordinate position. Conflicting directions will create an atmosphere of disruption and distrust, culminating in the dismissal of the entrepreneur.

The entrepreneurial personality is a study in contradictions: imaginativeness and rigidity, the urge to take risks and the stubborn resistance to change. People often speculate about the possibility of changing the personality characteristics of innovators to eliminate the destructive qualities while preserving, if not enhancing, the constructive tendencies. These speculations are often based on wishful thinking — to have the best of the two possible worlds of innovation and maturation. Greater self-awareness and discipline would undoubtedly serve innovators well in making the transition from leading a new organization to conducting its operation during later stages of growth. But it is the rare individual who can develop this kind of awareness. Perhaps the more intelligent plan for an entrepreneur is to move away from his old venture while moving toward other areas of innovation. Instead of trying to change himself, he can continue to be a pioneer, but on new frontiers.

CHAPTER 11

Minimum Man and Maximum Man:
Changing Patterns in American Leadership

⌈Conceive something of this kind happening either on many ships or one. Though the shipowner surpasses everyone on board in height and strength, he is rather deaf and likewise somewhat shortsighted, and his knowledge of seamanship is pretty much on the same level. The sailors are quarreling with one another about the piloting, each supposing he ought to pilot, although he has never learned the art and can't produce his teacher or prove there was a time when he was learning it. Besides this, they claim it isn't even teachable and are ready to cut to pieces the man who says it is teachable./And they are always crowded around the shipowner himself, begging and doing everything so that he'll turn the rudder over to them.⌉ And sometimes, if they fail at persuasion and other men succeed at it, they either kill the others or throw them out of the ship. Enchaining the noble shipowner with mandrake, drink, or something else, they rule the ship, using what's in it; and drinking and feasting, they sail as such men would be thought likely to sail. Besides this, they praise and call "skilled sailor," "pilot" and "knower of the ship's business" the man who is clever at figuring out how they will get the rule, either by persuading or by forcing the shipowner, while the man who is not of this sort they blame as useless./They don't know that for the true pilot it is necessary to pay careful attention to year, seasons, heaven, stars, winds, and everything that's proper to the art, if he is really going to be skilled at ruling a ship.⌋ And they don't suppose it's possible to acquire the art and practice of how one can get hold of the helm whether the others wish it or not, and at the same time to acquire the pilot's skill./So with such things happening on the ships, don't you believe that the true pilot will really be called a stargazer, · a prater and useless to them by those who sail on ships run like this?[1]

— Plato

TODAY, the quality of American leadership faces severe crises. In politics, repeated miscalculations and undelivered promises have produced unprecedented public cynicism. The Watergate scandal perhaps represented the nadir of the credibility of American political leadership. In the business world, too, goals long accepted as sufficient, such as efficiency and return on investment, are challenged by those who insist on social gains as well. Leaders are being asked to respond to new and ambiguous principles: the quality of life, the rights of consumers, the principles of racial equality, and the importance of a clean environment. What has caused this crisis of leadership?

American organizations are dominated by consensus leadership, a form of decision-making that emphasizes the balance of power among interest groups and constituents. While this kind of leadership will work under ordinary circumstances, it may come up short in a search for solutions to new problems or the challenge of new opportunities. We plan, in this chapter, to examine consensus leadership and to trace its roots both in the soil of American political traditions and in the personality dynamics of individuals who are ambitious for power and position. The interpretation of consensus leadership depends on a comparison with its polar opposite: charismatic leadership. Unlike consensus, charisma (in its original sense of an inner light or a divine gift) implies a leader who follows his own visions rather than the compromises of the group.

The two antithetical styles, consensus and charismatic, have roots in different social and political traditions, which gave rise, according to David Riesman, to two types of national character: the other-directed and inner-directed.[2] We prefer to use the terms "minimum man" and "maximum man," to focus attention on the deeper layers of personality structure that nurture the consensus and charismatic leaders. Although minimum men and maximum men are opposites, one should not assume that "minimum" is used in a pejorative sense; nor is "maximum" an ideal. Rather, the sociopolitical context determines which leadership style is best suited for the times. The present crisis in American leadership has something to do with how minimum man and maximum man evolve psychologically and how they behave in bureaucratic organizations. By examining them closely, we hope to uncover the chronic diseases of bureaucracies: slowness in responding to crises, failure to innovate, and collective self-righteousness.

Leadership Styles: Consensus and Charismatic

Consensus leadership is a product of real and potential power conflicts in organizations. Organizations are made up of interest groups, some operating outside the formal structure — stockholders, bankers, government procurement agencies — others functioning as part of the bureaucracy, defined in terms of membership in sales, production, and research hierarchies. The interest groups together form constituencies that apply pressure for, and respond to, policy decisions; separately, they demand loyalty and conformity as the price for belonging.

The formation of the Tennessee Valley Authority in the nineteen thirties provides a nice example of consensus politics in decision-making. The tenure of David Lilienthal illustrates the consensus style of leadership.[3] The problem of the TVA was only in part that of the application of technology to generate electrical power. It was also a problem in rural development and the creation of a new quasi-public institution as an instrument of public policy. If Lilienthal and his associates had had conflictual and competitive relationships with the main constituent groups, the enterprise surely would have failed. As it was, it faced the overt hostility of the power-generating industry because it was a source of competition; it could ill afford hostile relations with consumers, landholders, and local politicians. Lilienthal mastered the arts of co-opting constituents — making them a part of the larger organization identified with the purposes of the TVA. This process required consensus in decisions, and participation, bargaining, and negotiation, in which all sides could feel themselves a part of the apparatus by which decisions were made.

The effective consensus leader is, above all, a good negotiator. He is able to listen to various points of view without distorting them. He will draw as many people as possible into the process of making decisions. He is also highly rational and pragmatic, understanding the nature of trade-offs, bargains, and the distribution of rewards. Decisions flowing through his management are, at their best, equitably balanced between the needs of the different constituents and the objective demands of production, technology, and hard economics.

Perhaps the extreme example of the consensus style of leadership can be found in the highly ritualized approach of Japanese organizations, the system of *ringi-sei*. Policies begin at the lower levels of management, which represent various groups in the bureaucracy. As consensus is reached (this is signaled by the initialing of appropriate documents), the policy moves upward through the hierarchy. Failure of consensus at one level forces the policy back down for review and new agreement. When the policy directives reach the chief executive, who, like a benign grandfather, symbolizes the unity of the organization, agreement is assured, awaiting only his final affirmation. He gives assent, but avoids new initiatives lest he upset a finely drawn balance among opposing forces. The problem of dependency in organizations stands on its head: there is so much faith in the wisdom of consultation and consensus that the leader is more dependent on his followers than they are on him.

American executives are often horrified when they hear a description of *ringi-sei*. But they are more horrified when they confront the reality in American business: these organizations, too, are built on consensus mechanisms, though they are not as formal as the Japanese. The truth is that owners and their representatives in business prefer to avoid heroic stances in decision-making. The risks are too great. They pay lip service to the charismatic heroes of business, rugged individualists and entrepreneurs like Henry Ford and Edwin Land, and they derive comfort from the consensus seekers.

The recent example of Robert B. Hansberger and the fate of the Boise Cascade Corporation is a case in point.[4] Hansberger tried to move Boise from a strong, yet traditional, position in forest products into land development and the housing industry, businesses that involve high risks but promise large returns. Boise could not control the sales force, and the company lost a fortune; in addition, its stock price dropped from $80 to $9 a share. Only closer reading of the Boise story would tell us if the fundamental problem lay in bad business judgments, undue reliance on unseasoned subordinates, or unwarranted dependence on a predominantly consensus organization. Whatever the reason for financial decline, the experiences of companies like Boise Cascade reinforce in investors, as well as managers, a conservative tendency to favor the slower moving but safer consensus organizations. For while the organization may move slowly, the mechanisms of checks and balances fostered by consensus leaders provide considerable security against impulsive actions and adventures on new roads that the organization is ill prepared to travel.

The search for security and the avoidance of high risks establish the climate for consensus leadership. The style itself, however, is not born of a rational, carefully thought out approach. It is reflexive, a product of tradition, an attachment to certain ideals that nourish belief in oneself, the group, the corporation. In this sense, the consensus style becomes part of the unconscious thought patterns of individuals, which, in turn, form the collective ideals of groups and institutions. Consequently, the style is self-perpetuating and resists change.

Organizations in the consensus mode are usually neat, clearly delineated structures that foster communication and participation in decisions. The organization under a charismatic leader is often drawn along competitive lines, encouraging power struggles in the effort to get at the man at the top. But the competition and aggressiveness frequently stimulate brilliant ideas and create an exciting work atmosphere, in contrast to the bland and often boring atmosphere of consensus organizations.

The comparisons of consensus and charismatic leadership structures go beyond the conventional terms of organization theory. Both kinds of structure can be either centralized or decentralized, subject to tight or loose controls, drawn on product-profit center cores or functional units, such as manufacturing, sales, and engineering. The comparisons are really concerned with dynamics. For example, before Nixon's difficulties with Watergate, his efforts to reorganize the office of the presidency appeared to be directed toward keeping initiatives and control in the White House and away from the bureaucracies and the cabinet departments. Was this a reflection of consensus or charismatic leadership? Commentators have observed that the new power elite in Washington were gray and invisible men, noted for their loyalty to President Richard Nixon and their total dependence on him for their power. None of the insiders had an independent constituency and none ever won office in elective politics (Kissinger, Shultz, Ash, Ehrlichman, Haldeman, all of whom, before the Watergate affair, with the exception of Kissinger, would go unrecognized on the street and possibly even in the Congress). Reorganizing to draw the controls to the top reflects, among other things, the distrust of initiatives in the hands of people who do not depend on the President for their power, and also on the bad working relationship between the executive and legislative branches of the government. But what does it tell us about the man? As chief executive, was President Nixon acting out, in his concept of organization, certain unconscious motives along with the conscious desires to control from the top?

Nixon was a consensus leader who built his power base by using a capacity to draw into the broad center diverse groups and their representatives. Applying the techniques of consensus and coalition politics, he had no difficulty dealing with Mao Tse-tung and Chou En-lai, despite his past record of militant anti-communism. For consensus leaders, tactics take precedence over principle, and the problems of consolidating and holding power bury more substantive policy questions. Because Nixon was a consensus leader, he was less persuasive about programs for which he professed concern (like the phased control of domestic inflation, the problems of the city, the environment, crime, and welfare); he concentrated more on structural change (including centralizing federal control in the White House and leaving domestic problems in the hands of the governors and mayors without providing them with the resources necessary to solve the problems).

It may be instructive to look at Franklin D. Roosevelt's tenure in office as a contrast to the organization and style of the Nixon administration. The times and the problems were different. But times and problems coexist with personalities and the limits any individual has over the control of his style of leadership. Franklin Roosevelt today would probably surround himself with strong, colorful, and controversial figures like Ickes, Perkins, Tugwell, Hopkins, Corcoran, and Farley. He would encourage others to develop initiatives and programs and expend little time constructing a symmetrical organization chart. In fact, the messier the chart, the more people compete, and through competition ideas emerge. Perhaps there is administrative waste and confusion (two groups of people can be working on the same problems at the same time without being aware of the other's assignment and approach), but the structure under the charismatic leader favors substance over procedure, aggressiveness over passivity, and competition over harmony. The outcome of the organizational disorder is new solutions, more innovative ideas, and powerful commitments to work and people.

One would like to have the benefits of both the consensus and charismatic styles and structures. One would want to know how to achieve an orderly administration with the stimulating atmosphere that exists when men pursue problems and feel personal commitments to the visions and new ideas personified in the charismatic leader.

These and other practical questions will be considered at the conclusion of this chapter. But first, we want to evaluate the differences in personality structure and dynamics that tell us how consensus and charismatic leaders grow, their strengths and weaknesses, their conflicts and modes of defense, and their need to perpetuate their particular style of leadership. In exploring questions of personality, we shall show that the best way to understand how a person functions is to determine where he is vulnerable. We have to weigh not only what a person wants, but also what he avoids; not only what image he seeks to portray, but also what voices and images from within command his drive for achievement.

Personality Dynamics

Most leaders are ambitious. But beyond this obvious similarity between consensus and charismatic leaders, there is little the two types have in common. On the one hand, consensus leaders, minimum men, are oriented outward, with a relatively diffuse inner personality structure. On the other hand, charismatic leaders are maximum men, struggling with dominant inner structures, and oriented inward.

There are excellent minimum men, gifted in bringing about consensus on difficult problems through diplomacy and negotiation. And there are genuinely evil maximum men, demagogues like Hitler. No organization could operate if it were led by maximum men alone. Usually, the maximum men start great businesses but leave their future in the hands of minimum men, who function until crises occur. There are problems connected with both kinds of leadership.

MINIMUM MAN

On a primary emotional level, the minimum man is concerned with the opinion of his peers. He would rather have egalitarian relations with men as brothers than be in the socially distant position of a father figure. He does not, therefore, lead public opinion, but follows it, searching for ideas and opinions from others.

The minimum man is essentially a "normal" person; he has the ability to adapt and to fit into his environment. He gains the safety and warmth denied to the maximum man. However, because he is so dependent on the opinions of others, he may lose his sense of self-esteem and, on the low end of the scale of effectiveness, be unable to make a decision.

Finally, the minimum man often appears bland and opaque. He does not reveal himself because there is a void and a fragmentation in his inner world. So he functions like radar, picking up opinions, ideas, and impressions. The scanning approach, a search for contact with people on the outside, is essential to one who calculates power equations. It results in adroit flexibility, but seldom in conviction. Intellectually and emotionally, it is like living out of a suitcase, allowing the person to avoid investments and, consequently, losses. The minimum man is a survivor, one who clutches power and holds on despite major shifts in goals and direction.

Two brief examples will help to illustrate the psychology of minimum men. The best example, perhaps, of the minimum man as bureaucratic survivor is Dean Rusk, secretary of state to Presidents Kennedy and Johnson. Rusk, according to David Halberstam, was chosen precisely because of his inoffensive qualities, what the general public saw as blandness. The journalist described the process by which Rusk was selected secretary of state:

> What it came down to was a search not for the most talent, the greatest brilliance, but for the fewest black marks, the fewest objections . . . So, quietly, the campaign for Rusk was put together and his qualifications tallied: not too young, not too old; a Democrat, but not too much of one; a Southerner but not too much so; an intellectual but not too much so; worked in China, but no problems on that — in fact . . . the acceptable man.[5]

Imagine how Rusk must have calculated and manipulated to create this aura of acceptibility. Indeed, the very genius of Dean Rusk as minimum man was his ability to cloak his ambitions and plans behind the image of Dean Rusk — bland, bumbling, not so smart, nice guy; in all, a person who seemed harmless and probably easy to control. His peers at the State Department, when Rusk was an assistant secretary, described Rusk's qualities in conflicting terms: one described Rusk as being open-minded. The attribute reflected, however, according to this colleague, uncertainty and only fair intellectual quality. Another noted that Rusk was too submissive to authority, never willing to contradict a superior; still another peer ascribed this characteristic to Rusk's intense loyalty. But they all agreed that his greatest asset was his intellectual flexibility and his ability to articulate clearly a given problem.[6]

These qualities are the characteristics of a minimum man fighting and winning the battles of political bureaucracies. One final example will give a glimpse of Rusk's skill in maneuvering and in utilizing resources in a bureaucratic power play.

In 1961, the Taylor-Rostow mission went to Vietnam to study, for President Kennedy, the nature of our commitment to South Vietnam. Rusk, instead of sending a State Department person of comparable rank on the mission (a decision criticized by Roger Hilsman and Arthur Schlesinger), sent a telegram warning Kennedy that, unless measures were taken to broaden the political base of the regime, the military measures might be in vain. When the necessary political measures were not implemented, the problem of South Vietnam fell almost completely under the jurisdiction of the Department of Defense. Daniel Ellsberg, describing the implications of the above, states:

> Rusk seems to have had an excellent sense of just what it was he was generously turning over to his Cabinet colleague [McNamara] . . . Rusk's sensitivity here to the perils of betting on a losing horse — and his dexterity in detaching his own prestige from the gamble — throws new light on the supposedly obtuse and simplistic quality of his thinking. In a bureaucratic endurance race, a man who had survived the test of being Assistant Secretary of State for the Far East during the loss of China and the outbreak of the Korean War was never one to bet against.[7]

Another dimension of the psychology of minimum men is provided by Pierre Du Pont.[8] Pierre Du Pont came to power with two cousins, Coleman and Alfred, in the collective succession from the preceding generation. Coleman eventually withdrew his interest, and Pierre and Alfred became contenders for leadership. Alfred had specialized in the manufacture of gunpowder and had isolated himself from others. Pierre, in his financial and strategic roles, had found it personally congenial to encourage initiatives from below and to solidify a coalition with subordinates. Pierre won the contest for power.

One of the personality attributes that made Pierre Du Pont a good consensus leader was a sense of attachment and responsibility to subordinates. Early in his life, his father had died, and Pierre became a surrogate to his younger siblings — in fact, they called him "Dad." Nonetheless, he remained a true older brother, avoiding the emotions and behavior of an autocratic father. The attachment to peers, both in his family and the Du Pont Corporation, probably had something to do with the fact that he did not marry until late in life. He remained childless.

The minimum man's relationship to peer and parent figures is the key to his style of leadership. The parents lurk in the background as the main source of reward. The consensus leader keeps his attention fixed on the parental authorities, toward whom he remains passive, but he actively manipulates his siblings or peers, over whom he seeks control. *Calculation* and *manipulation* are his tools. If he gains power by calculation, he does not take an autocratic role; he manipulates relationships so that rewards pass through him on their way to others.

Almost anybody can be a victim of at least transient mental illness, and we find the individual's character sharply defined by the form the illness takes. Angry paranoia suggests an isolated childhood, a world divided into friends and enemies long before this becomes a matter of survival within an organization. Depression suggests early and continual doubts about self-worth, arising from longings to be loved. In the same way, the forms of illness peculiar to minimum and maximum men highlight the outlines of their personalities.

If we follow the minimum man's quality of blandness down the road toward mental illness, we find the path turns at the point where the radar mechanism is overtaxed by too many impressions, too much communication, and diffusion. The result is a sense of depersonalization, the feeling of being unreal, among unreal people in an unreal world.

The childhood relationships of minimum man to his parents do not necessarily show any evidence of severe trauma, such as the death of a parent, to account for this inner impoverishment. Instead, we find a kind of emotional neutrality on the part of the parents, especially the father, who often appears weak and passive in comparison to the mother. This produces a confusion of the internal images — who am I? how does a man behave? — that are so vital later in defining an adult self. Instead of finding strength in his internal self-images, the child seeks it from attachments to persons and events outside himself.

The minimum man has many acquaintances but few friends, many sexual experiences but no deep attachment. At work, as he approaches a state of imbalance, he becomes a dilettante. What was adaptability in an effective consensus leader becomes, in this less successful extreme, a weird promiscuity in which friends and lovers, opinions and ideas are adopted and discarded with equal fervor.

The greatest difficulty of being selfless, enduring, and even suffering in order to fit in with the environment is the impoverishment of the ego. The minimum man seldom experiences the peace of mind that comes from security of purpose, the commitment of deeply held conviction, and the realization of mastery in his own house.

The minimum man devotes his energy to questions of procedure rather than substance. Questions of substance make clear all dimensions of a power struggle, requiring a man to take a firm stand. Procedure, on the other hand, tends to be neutral and to include everybody, so long as people believe the procedure is fair to all and to every point of view. This, again, is peculiar to the culture of peer relations.

Consensus leadership depends on delegation of authority from above and the flow of initiatives from below. If the procedure is fair, if it assures "equal time" to all initiatives, it gains commitment from subordinates, as we have already seen in the case of Pierre Du Pont. As he carries this notion of fair procedure further, the consensus leader will completely avoid any position of controversy, establishing his base in the center of opposing points of view, as Dean Rusk did. If he maneuvers the radar too long, subordinates may take a great deal of the power that the minimum man refuses to seize.

In sum, as a consensus leader becomes less effective, thanks to low self-esteem, he will have increasing difficulty making decisions or, finally, retaining his power.

MAXIMUM MAN

In contrast to the minimum man, the maximum man's relations with others is usually simple — he is their leader. At times he may be recognized practically on sight because of the glow of confidence his inner light gives him. He is charismatic; people are drawn to him by the power of his convictions and visions of reality. His presence inspires both dread and fascination; he evokes mystical reactions. The maximum man is a great innovator, but not always a good leader — he will have little use for subordinates who have different opinions — and his extremely high self-esteem may create problems.

Sigmund Freud said, "A man who has been the indisputable favorite of his mother keeps for life the feeling of a conqueror, that confidence of success that often induces real success."[9] Here we find a source for that charisma or inner light of the maximum man, the numinous individual. The maximum man is the chosen one in childhood, either because he is the only child, or because he has a special attachment to his parents, which is bedrock for his sense of self-esteem.

Franklin D. Roosevelt was a maximum man. His mother was a very strong, forceful person, and young Franklin was apparently the focus of her attention. We often expect that, if the mother is strong, the father is weak, but in the Roosevelt household this was not so; James Roosevelt seems to have been an equally strong personality, though he kept himself in the background. We have here one formula, at least, for producing great people: two strong parents who give attention and positive reinforcement to the child.

The maximum man may be said to carry within his psyche an *audience* for his actions. This audience criticizes or praises, but remains stable, a reference point for judgment and self-esteem. In the minimum man, we found these images of what is right or desirable to be weak and confused; in the maximum man, the images are strong. Images of strength and persistence from his childhood undoubtedly helped Roosevelt in his long battle with paralysis.

As the lack of these images produces the minimum man's dependence on others, so their strong presence in the maximum man diminishes his dependence, making him self-sufficient.

Two examples from the political world will show us how the images, the internal audience, function in the charismatic leader.

Charles de Gaulle was deeply attached to his parents; he successfully transformed this childhood attachment into inner strength and independence. He was guided by an inner light throughout his career, in school, as a junior staff officer, and, eventually, as a leader in exile. Because he behaved as if his power were real, he was an enigma to Churchill and Roosevelt. The images were even strong enough to allow him to wait for the liberation of France and for his second call to political power. He achieved a reunion with his childhood memories in his love affair with France; the translation of his love for his parents into ideals and commitments helped him to succeed.

Adolf Hitler never formed a close relationship with his father, doubted his father's legitimacy, saw him beat his mother, and came to hate him. He had a deep, incestuous, and double-imaged love of his mother, both as warm, earthy, and seductive, and as a powerful iron virgin (to use Erik Erikson's term).[10] This complex relationship with his parents lent elements of hatred, untransformed sexuality, aggression, and sadism to Hitler's intense and hysterical love affair with the German people. From the deepest insecurity sprang a seductive image, the dictator, omnipotent, permanent, unalterable, without limitations, one who will conquer death. This image brought down Hitler, Germany, and nearly the entire world.

The road to mental illness for the maximum man is clear, because this sort of personality always reveals itself, its weaknesses and pathological tendencies. If the minimum man comes to feel that he doesn't exist, because of a lack of inner images, the maximum man feels that *only* he exists, either because of estrangement from, and conflict with, his image-audience or because of such complete merging with it that he loses all contact with reality.

Mania, paranoia, and depression await the maximum man if he loses his balance. Short of these severe forms, we are certain to find narcissism — the individual's reserving of his most intense love for himself — in every maximum man. With the help of self-love, the maximum man achieves independence from people in the real world.

Such narcissistic independence can be very dangerous, as we saw in the case of Hitler, because there is nothing to guarantee a clear view of people and the world. In its benevolent form, it frees the maximum man to lead, rather than follow, the consensus. A love affair with his inner audience allows him, at his most fully realized, to act according to higher principles, ideologies, and causes.

The maximum man in an organization is full of contradiction. The charismatic leader may be worshiped by his subordinates, but he is also likely to be mistrusted, because he holds firm convictions about right and wrong courses of action while he is inconsistent with people. He may lead his organization to the height of prosperity through the power of his vision and persistence, but he is anathema in consensus situations because he can neither delegate nor be delegated to (except, perhaps by God) nor can he wait for initiatives to rise from below.

The successful maximum man is a great asset to society and its organizations. But though he may be in an organization, he is never of the organization. In other words, his identity and that of the organization must remain independent. The great business institutions, like the American Telephone and Telegraph Company, Exxon, and others, tend to choose their leaders from within. These leaders are both in and of the organization, which encourages the cultivation of minimum men, assuring very slow rates of change. The problem for large organizations is to accelerate change and to provide innovative leadership, despite their tendency to produce minimum men.

It is striking to note how the innovators in any generation tend to be the displaced people of the world. The generation of innovators we know best today are of two kinds: the financial wizards and the technologists. Both types are dogged in their pursuit of an idea. Unlike minimum men, they do not see problems from all points of view; instead, they relentlessly pursue a single viewpoint. Innovators can become displaced, feeling apart and different, removed from society and family. Such people often turn to science and technology, where they can be detached from people, turn inward, and identify with such great men as Copernicus, Newton, and Einstein as abstract and idealized images. These images serve as valid parental substitutes; that they are dead and distant serves to soften the ambivalent attitudes so painful and threatening in dealing with living people.

The story goes that Edwin Land, the genius behind the Polaroid Corporation, could not tolerate the constraints of academic institutions (M.I.T. and Harvard) and that he dropped out long before dropping out became a popular thing for young people to do. He was interested in light and color, and developed the Polaroid film and camera. It has also been said that Land was advised by academic consultants to sell his inventions to Eastman Kodak because it would be too difficult and risky to go it alone with his new still-photo method. But, again, displaced people learn to believe in themselves, maintaining a stubborn commitment to their ideas even in the face of the most well-meaning and rational advice. Land, of course, succeeded on his own.

Doggedness, narcissism, and the sense of being special or displaced — these characterize maximum men. The scanning of reactions, the desire to fit in, the capacity to adapt to environment and to live flexibly — these characterize the minimum man. Both sets of characteristics can be understood as outgrowths of personality structure erected early in life, and changed only slowly, if at all, during one's lifetime.

Personality Structure

The effectiveness or ineffectiveness of the minimum and maximum man will probably be determined by the quality of the superego, a legacy from relations with parents. If the superego is harsh, punitive, and absolute in its judgments of good and bad, cause and effect, crime and punishment, it can result in a minimum man who is a moralist. Acting without any awareness of his moral code or its derivatives, he makes concrete and manifest, in his relations with others, a sense of correctness and proper demeanor. He is our bureaucratic personality, who needs and manipulates external controls because he lacks firm recognition of inner control through his superego.

The maximum man with a harsh superego projects his primitive conscience on to the real world. He is a brooder and, at the extreme, a tyrant. Experience continually awakens the love and hate relations with parents, which are maintained in the superego. The internal love-hate images become real relationships with subordinates and family in alternating moods of seductiveness and sadism. The maximum man as brooder keeps the people he works with on edge. He maintains a climate of apprehensiveness within himself and for his subordinates.

The maximum man with the benign and benevolent superego is a creator, not a destroyer like the maximum man with a
harsh superego. The contrast between these two kinds of maximum man is evident in our earlier examples of de Gaulle and
Hitler. The existence of benevolent and loving relations with
the internal images that form the superego produces both self-
reliance and the capacity, the permission, to go beyond conventional ideas and forms. This capacity lies at the heart of
creativity, and the very fact that the maximum man gives himself permission to think and to go beyond conventional wisdom
conveys the same permission to subordinates, thereby stimulating the work atmosphere.

Leaders in organizations do take on personifications of the
superego. Given their real power over the lives of others, they
easily project their internalized conscience and ideals on to
others. This becomes a fact of life for subordinates and a harder
fact for subordinates who are themselves minimum men; minimum men as subordinates are dependent, though calculating
and rational. It is the maximum men, with their own strong
internal images, who are in the best position to maintain their
separate identities in organizations led by other maximum men.

The fourth type to be distinguished in comparing minimum
man and maximum man is the optimistic minimum man,
uncomplicated by emotion and somewhat simplistic in his
thinking. This type of minimum man is a good negotiator,
mediator, and seeker of the consensus. His tolerance and fairness are the bases of his leadership, since these qualities also
allow other people to exist and to work in their own right.

Organizational Dynamics

We saw that the "inner light" of the charismatic leader was a
kind of internal audience, a strong collection of internal images
with which the maximum man has a continuous dialogue. The
metaphor of an audience provides the key to the different ways
in which minimum and maximum men gain and hold power.

The dialogue of the charismatic leader is with himself, and

one has the feeling, observing him, of watching a dramatization. We are the viewers, fascinated by the unfolding of a personality, which occurs while the actor is unaware that his performance is being seen. It is as if the stage where he stands and the gallery where we sit are far apart.

This distance, as in the case of actual theater, gives both performer and spectator the safety to trust each other, and to suspend disbelief. Once they have made this leap of faith, their emotions surge up and join together; and when we have met the charismatic leader on this emotional level made possible by distance, the distance paradoxically disappears.

At this point, as we listen to the charismatic leader, we are on the inside, and have lost the separation between self and other that characterizes rational thought. Intellect and emotion are no longer distinct. Somewhere within us, the images of parents as protectors and love objects come to the surface in a collapse of time, a merging of past and present.

Now the charismatic leader exerts influence. If he is a demagogue, he can confuse past and mythology, seducing us into substituting our hatred for reality. If he is benevolent, he can try to go beyond narrow rationality and self-interest, projecting a vision through which intellect and emotion fuse into a creative force. The charismatic leader inspires his audience. His appeal depends on the maximum man's faith in his own internal audience, which provides the first step of the sequence we have just explored.

The minimum man, in contrast, is removed from his internal audience: the inner images are vague and illusory, though benign. They give him little warmth and support for his self-esteem, compared with the rewards he gets from activity and people. Depending as he does on others, he may become wary of his external audience of peers and subordinates. As a result, he by-passes emotional response in favor of the cool and distant form of *role-playing*.

Role-playing is a calculated method of communicating ideas. It has a structure with three parts: a stereotyped image, an audience of one, and the player. The audience of one and the player both accept the stereotype, but remain outside and distant from it: a fusion of player and stereotype, or of single and collective audience, must be prevented at all costs, because it leads to the arousal of emotion, which is typical of numinous actions and unacceptable to the minimum man's exercising power.

A good example of role-playing was Richard Nixon's famous "Checkers" speech, in which he presented the stereotype of the naive and honest son who is the oppressed victim of a powerful aggressor. The audience of one was the single eye of the television camera, a representation of the isolated viewer.

A further example of role-playing comes from Nixon's own description, in *Six Crises*,[11] of certain aspects of the "Great Debates" with Kennedy. In a discussion of Cuba, both candidates staked out roles to play. As Nixon tells it, Kennedy, defining his role, attacked Nixon and the Republican administration for letting Castro maintain his regime. Nixon was furious, for the CIA had briefed Kennedy on a design to overthrow Castro. What could Nixon do? He could say that Kennedy's proposal was being implemented, but such a statement would break security and jeopardize the whole operation. Garry Wills quotes Nixon on his eventual choice of roles: "What course was left for a man so hamstrung by virtuous reticence? 'I must not even suggest by implication that the United States was rendering aid to rebel forces in and out of Cuba. In fact, I must go to the other extreme: I must attack the Kennedy proposal to provide such aid as wrong and irresponsible because it would violate our treaty commitments.' Strange logic: because one is unable to do one thing, one must do the exact opposite. Prevented, say, from punishing a wife beater, one must punish the wife beater's wife."[12] Yet the logic is not strange within the concept of the minimum man. For, since the minimum man's commitment to principle is weak, Nixon selected the role that would have the greatest impact upon the audience. Again, the tactic and not the substance defines the role.

Television, a "cool medium," is ideally suited for role-playing: it maintains distance and keeps the audience from connecting with one another or with the player. The contemporary rise and dominance of cool, manipulative television over the currently declining form of hot, charismatic theater parallels, in another realm, the crisis of American leadership that we are discussing.

Innovation and Flexibility

These two qualities, innovation and flexibility, mirror and interact with each other: innovation must have flexibility so that it can react creatively, flexibility requires innovation so that it can be used, and organizations need both to grow.

Maximum men are, by nature, not flexible: they change and adapt to new circumstances with the greatest of difficulty, often at the expense of their own objectives. They are deeply committed to their internal standards, with all the strength of high self-esteem, and they resist adaptation on other people's terms.

This strength of conviction and sense of command is the basis for the maximum man's emotional appeal. It may also be the source of disaster for an organization when the maximum man refuses to bend or flex, and leads the organization to defy reality.

William Jennings Bryan was, by all accounts, a maximum man. Magnetic personality, rich voice, and inspiring oratory characterized the charismatic Bryan. But he had more. According to historian Paul W. Glad, "Voice, technique, rhetoric — all these are important, but not so important as a cause. Bryan . . . battled for a cause at Chicago, and the convention was exciting . . . because it climaxed a long campaign to win the party for silver."[13]

Yet this cause (or, more realistically, this panacea) was based on a Jeffersonian vision of America, a vision long outmoded. Furthermore, Bryan, not a calculating minimum man, excluded groups from his movement, making only feeble attempts to woo important interests like organized labor. The result, then, of Bryan's free-silver vision was electoral disaster. For forged in the election of 1896 was a party alignment that kept the Republicans in power until 1932. Bryan was faithful to his inner light; the results for the Democratic party, however, were calamitous.

The charismatic leader's lack of flexibility may also cause him personal damage. He will feel strong and secure so long as the group he leads is paternally oriented, with him as the father. However, if a counterreaction sets in, and his organization moves toward consensus, the charismatic leader is under severe stress: like de Gaulle, he must either retire or face a losing battle.

At this point we may encounter the mental illnesses common to maximum man: depression or mania, the emotional expression of conflict between the internal images, the ego and reality. The defensive reaction of paranoid delusion — that his inner light is the only truth in the world — is a further consequence when maximum man is struggling in a civil war.

Minimum man, of course, is flexible and fits in easily: this, in fact, is how he defines himself. Because of shallow inner conviction, he appears very normal, adapting himself quite well to whatever his radar tells him is the source of power. However, the lack of independence from others, based upon a rather empty inner life, prevents him from innovating.

The maximum man, with his capacity to move from rational to associative modes of thinking, can be highly innovative. Innovation is his greatest strength, and if his company can deal with the risks he presents, he can be instrumental in how a company does business.

The paradox is clear: organizations take risks if they follow the arrowlike flight of the maximum man toward his goal, but they immobilize themselves if they fall back into the uncommitted flexibility of the minimum man. Some way must be found for the organization to preserve the flexibility of a consensus style while it fosters innovative, maximum men — a difficult task.

Aggression and Survival

The world of business, like any other realm of human endeavor, conceals a good deal of the law of the jungle beneath its surface of cordial behavior. Men up and down the ladder of power are fighting for their lives; victories or defeats have lasting effects on personal income and self-esteem. Issues of aggression and survival are more than academic; they are vital and central.

Complex bureaucracies make survival possible for people who are not strong aggressors. It is in this environment, with its many crossing lines of influence and power, its preponderance of peer relations, and its clear, moderate standards of accountability and performance, that the minimum man makes his home. His adroitness and lack of conviction make him a survivor above all, one who can seize at least some power and hold on to it, despite major shifts in goals and direction.

In contrast, the maximum man is an aggressor. Aggression is his métier. When he encounters it in others, he meets it with more aggression. As he succeeds, he may even overplay it, because it makes his life exciting. It follows that maximum men have less chance of survival. A man who constantly uses aggression has a good chance of encountering somebody more aggressive than he. The charismatic leader may be shot down, but he may also fight his way to the top and be acclaimed a hero.

Here we discover why consensus-ridden organizations seem structurally unable to produce great men: they cannot develop or tolerate aggression. Their goal is to harmonize, to resolve and smooth over differences. The minimum men, who thrive in the consensus structure, find it difficult to tolerate the aggressive interplay and competition of ideas that encourage more innovative people.

Too much aggression, the kind of bloodthirstiness sometimes found in maximum men in highly competitive situations, will probably damage aggressor and organization alike. However, organizations that try to eliminate every trace of aggression from their operations will find themselves stalemated, stagnant, and barren of innovation.

Ethics of Charismatic and Consensus Leaders

It is in the realm of ethics that we find minimum and maximum man most sharply contrasted. Like mental illness, unethical behavior removes the screens that hide the man and reveal the underpinnings of personality.

Ethical questions are present but rarely acknowledged in the lives of minimum men. The central question for the minimum man is whether he is aware of ethical questions, granted his pragmatism, rationality, and urge to survive. Minimum man, constantly scanning with his radar for opinions and sources of power in others, tending by the very structure of his personality not to have an integrated set of commitments, may be led into a decision that is unethical. The consensus style, by its nature, would commit him to the pragmatic, self-serving choice, ethical or not.

For an example of the impact of pragmatism on ethics and ethical behavior, we can turn once again to the career of Richard Nixon. Daniel Ellsberg tells of an incident that happened when he was working in South Vietnam under General Lansdale, a man attempting to insure free and open elections. Ambassador Lodge, according to this account, was more concerned with programs like pacification, and felt that truly free and honest elections were too much to ask for under the current conditions in South Vietnam. The Lansdale team, including Ellsberg, was distressed by Lodge's attitude and hoped that the President, who was visiting South Vietnam at the time, could change his former running-mate's ideas. Ellsberg described the results of the meeting as follows: "After shaking hands with each of us, Nixon asked: 'Well, Ed, what are you up to?' Lansdale replied: 'We want to help General Thang make this the most honest election that's ever been held in Vietnam.'

'Oh, sure, honest, yes, honest, that's right' — Nixon was about to sit in an armchair next to Lansdale's — 'so long as you win!' With the last words he winked, drove his elbow hard into Lansdale's arm, and, in a return motion, slapped his own knee."[14] For Richard Nixon, a minimum man, the important consideration was success, not ethics.

Charismatic leaders, in contrast, constantly find opportunities to make large-scale ethical or unethical decisions. They are fortified by a deep trust and conviction in themselves, a sense of being favored or special people. But being special is perilous; the feeling produces devils as well as saints.

Much of the difference between the charismatic saint and devil lies in the quality of a man's internal images. As indicated earlier, these may be primarily benevolent or malevolent, giving or restricting, motivating or controlling — and they indicate the difference between creativity and destruction, and often between life and death. Some men need lovers, others need enemies, to dominate the structure of their lives. This personification reflects the quality of the internal images, rooted in the psyche from infancy and gaining form and substance as life progresses.

Adult life provides a further twist for the maximum man, the psychological hazards of narcissism, always present to some degree in such men. The narcissistic person loves himself enough to wish to shape reality rather than allow reality to shape him. In its benevolent form, this quality drives a man creatively to change things that do not sit well with him; his background acceptance gives him self-esteem, and he does not have to destroy his material or personal antagonist. Springing up from malevolent childhood images of hatred and fear, narcissism can cause the maximum man to ignore any aspect of reality — morals, integrity, justice — that gets in his way.

In the nonpolitical world, we rarely encounter ethical extremes as sharply defined as those personified by de Gaulle and Hitler. A few examples, however, will sketch the kinds of ethical problems that do arise. Billy Sol Estes was a Texas businessman who got money on collateral for grain elevators that simply did not exist. However, he had a strong strain of prudishness in his personal life; for example, he had separate swimming pools for men and women, and was a fundamentalist in his religious beliefs. This is a case of two sets of internal images — one righteous and moral, the other allowing him to take unethical actions — that do not communicate with each other, or do not communicate in the ordinary way.

In contrast to the unethical actions of maximum men, which are often gross and unambiguous, the ethics of the minimum man and consensus are subtle and difficult to pin down. The maximum man behaves unethically because he believes that *he* is right and justified; the minimum man performs unethical acts in the name of institutional narcissism: the corporation can do no wrong.

One of the past presidents of General Motors, Charles Wilson, asserted that what was right for General Motors was right for the country; so, by definition, the corporation could not act unethically. The same sort of thinking allowed for the power-transmission collusion among General Electric, Westinghouse, and other companies, which ended with a number of executives being sentenced to prison terms, and posed all sorts of ambiguous questions of responsibility and culpability. If an executive, because of his attachment to the corporate culture, acted in the best interests of his organization even though his actions were against the law, was he behaving unethically? To what extent was the chief executive officer responsible for perpetuating a corporate culture even if he had no information about, or had acquiesced in, the specific actions of subordinates?

The ethics of corporate activity, on the consensus model, depend on the capability of individuals to rid themselves of whatever satisfactions they derive from what can be described as institutional narcissism. The sense of self-esteem individuals secure from membership in large organizations can lure them into strange behavior, unless there is sufficient self-regard from within to outweigh the pride of belonging. Corporations that unwittingly foster such dependencies may be populated by loyal people but bereft of leadership capable of innovation and change.

The third law of thermodynamics deals with the concept of entropy. Entropy says a system cannot sustain itself if it is unable to find external energy sources. In consensus leadership, the minimum man brings no new energy to the organization. He tends to utilize the energy that exists. When an organization needs new sources of energy, in this case in the form of new ideas, new visions of some achievement, the consensus style fails.

If the consensus leader cannot provide the new input from himself, perhaps he can provide what is needed by devising structural innovations. Different relationships among people can draw untapped energy in the form of renewed commitments to the organization. Many structural innovations, however, lack substance and, at their worst, become ritualistic substitutes for creativity. But even if innovation in structure and authority is to overcome the tendency of consensus organizations to run out of energy, there must be someone with power to identify, and to act on, the weaknesses of leadership style. The consensus leader is hardly the one to criticize the system that brought him to power and helps him retain it. Perhaps this indicates the continuing need for maximum men who remain outside the dominant culture. Once they are identified and brought to light, they can make substantial contributions if they are properly supported.

How can one find such people? What do they look like before they arrive and are accepted as charismatic individuals? For one thing, they tend to be specialists rather than generalists in the early and middle stages of their career. As specialists, they are very good at something substantive, as in a technical-scientific field or other specialized training or expertise. They are productive and have no difficulty establishing the product by which they can be judged. They are more interested in ideas and concepts than in people and organizations, and they are very direct in saying what they think because they are not held in check by political considerations. They demonstrate a tenacity, seeing problems through to solutions, and have extraordinary powers of concentration. They are not troubled by forms of anxiety that inhibit thinking or the capacity to work. They not only tolerate, but enjoy, time alone, when reflection and associative thinking are best pursued.

They are easy to spot, provided one does not wear the blinders of the consensus mechanisms, which exclude from one's perceptual field people who may be very different from oneself. If this exclusion obtains, then we find operating, with respect to people, Gresham's law: just as cheap money drives out dear, consensus drives out charisma.

It is the nature of organizations to mold people into what is characteristic, if not idealized, in their culture. Unless there is conscious thought about the types of leaders organizations and society nurture, the sheer weight of consensus structures will dominate and, eventually, block gifted individuals. Americans are inherently optimistic people, who want to believe that institutions can function like great individuals. The evidence to substantiate the belief is yet to be sorted. Meanwhile, it may be wise to ponder what Emerson said: "There is properly no history; only biography."

CHAPTER 12

Philosophers and Kings

> Until philosophers are kings, or the kings and princes of this world have the spirit and power of philosophy, and political greatness and wisdom meet in one, and those commoner natures who pursue either to the exclusion of the other are compelled to stand aside, cities will never have rest from their evils — no, nor the human race, as I believe — and then only will this our State have a possibility of life and behold the light of day.[1]
>
> —*Plato*

INSTITUTIONAL LEADERS are usually active people, who often show a tendency to avoid reflection. So it is unlikely that philosophers will ever be kings. It may be argued that preoccupation with thought would limit the ability of leaders to decide and to act; after all, to view a problem in all its dimensions and complexity can lead to a paralysis of will, a surrender to outcomes that seem to be predetermined by forces outside one's control. An outlook like Hamlet's discourages action and assertive problem-solving. Despite the leader's fears of paralysis of will, his avoidance of reflection goes beyond a conscious preference for activity, which seems to be an integral part of the character structure of leaders, not a stance intentionally adopted because of the necessities of command. As there is the concept of loneliness of command, so there is the common image of a leader actively engaged in solving problems. In fact, activity reinforces propensities that already exist in personality structure, and there is no way to determine clearly whether the images are accurate reflections of the requirements of responsibility or are romantic projections of a burdensome role.

Quite apart from the objective requirement of the role, there are significant motives in the psychology of leaders for the avoidance of reflection and the turn toward activity. Those who seek executive positions appear to choose action over reflection and pragmatism over idealism. The consequences of these characteristics are especially interesting in view of the complexities of leadership and institutions in today's society.

There is a conflict inherent in the distribution of internal human energy and attention. This conflict is between objective reality, the world as it is, and the subjective experience and awareness of psychic reality. The turning of attention outward or inward, or the confusion between realities, differentiates the character and styles of individuals. What decides how attention will be distributed between inner and outer (subjective and objective) reality? What determines the confusion that so often occurs between fantasy and reality? The decisive causes lie in the developmental stages of childhood. In particular, the ways in which a life unfolds will be governed by the nature of painful experiences and the patterns of defense against the stresses of life. Traumatic experiences direct attention inward, toward the construction of fantasy. If the disruptions of childhood are not too severe, or if they befall those people who have creative talents and imagination, the turn inward can be developmentally positive. The individual builds fantasies that elaborate the nature and sources of pain at the same time as they attempt to overcome the pain and produce some sense of healing, if not of pleasure. On the other hand, in cases of severe trauma, or in individuals who lack imaginative gifts, painful events and their associative fantasies are linked so directly that they must be repressed and walled off in the psyche. There follows a precipitate turn outward, toward the environment, and the leaving behind of a divided and anxious self.

The conflict between reality and fantasy, the relation between the inner and outer world, is the substructure of character formation. When the turn outward is sudden, as it very often is in the case of institutional leaders, the attention to reality is accompanied by a lack of trust, the uncanny feeling of being observed. The hidden observer is nothing more or less than the unconscious fantasy and the divided self, which has been isolated and repressed. An illusion then takes hold: the thinking of such a person may strike one as being realistic, his attention seems to be well directed, and his problem-solving eminently rational. This illusion is dangerous because the leader is facing the real world with an attitude that, despite its assertiveness and aura of self-confidence, is defensive. Fact and fantasy intermingle and, sooner or later, reality gives way to egotism.

The chief executive of a large, beleaguered service organization will serve as an example. His institution faces a liquidity problem because it grew too rapidly, using bank credit, and, because of a recession, the debt is draining cash. His organization could be thrown into insolvency if the banks should decide to call the loans. What does he do under this stress? He constructs a mental scenario that will lead his institution out of its crises. The scenario has all the earmarks of a realistic plan, which includes gaining liquidity, reducing debt, and restructuring the organization to reduce its service commitments. But it goes beyond this. One suspects that the scenario is interwoven with fantasy: its sense of time is questionable; it fails to weigh the significance of other people and their power to act independently. The suspicion of the presence of fantasy grows because of the peculiar quality of the end of the scenario: it is not only happy (the institution is saved), but also grandiose (power is restored, images repaired, assets reacquired).

The difficulty with such scenarios and game plans is their lack of separation of fantasy from reality. This is the primary lesson of Vietnam, of the history of corporate failures, and of the rise and fall of public policy initiatives in economics and welfare. The initiatives that appear to be directed outward are rigid constructs warding off assaults against self-esteem. They resemble fantasies in their defensive function, but instead of being a private matter, a playful construct that aids intuition and imagination, the scenario becomes a public phenomenon, a cause of action and response from other people. In the nature of power relations, one cannot assume that the corrective effects of criticism and discussion will break through the layers of assumption that can flaw problem-solving. Power figures do not readily accept criticism or participate in the give-and-take of debate, particularly if their motive is defensive.

Fantasy-thinking by leaders is common, particularly in times of stress, but it is seldom recognized. People need to cling to the illusion of rationality. In the manifest content of problem-solving, the images of power and control, of deference and revenge, and, perhaps, of love and fulfillment appear remote, even though they feed mental activity. What gives away the motive and makes suspect the rituals of thought and action is the presence of manic expression and symbols of attack and defense.

Mania is the exaggerated sense of power and control. Manic thinking expresses itself emotionally in enthusiasm, elation, and a sense of anticipation. It is manifested as alertness, hyperactivity accompanied by extreme talkativeness, the inability to listen, and the excitement that goes with running a race. Mania is a reaction to depressive tendencies and melancholia, the sense of being divided and having lost a part of oneself. One feature of hyperactivity is the protection it offers against depressive reactions and their connection to emptiness, despair, to the feeling of arbitrariness and irrationality in life.

Joseph Conrad wrote about his vocation in a way that suggests how deeply this conflict between reality and fantasy, activity and thinking, commitment and being runs.

> A work that aspires, however humbly, to the condition of art should carry its justification in every line. And art itself may be defined as a single-minded attempt to render the highest kind of justice to the visible universe, by bringing to light the truth, manifold and one, underlying its every aspect. It is an attempt to find in its forms, in its very colors, in its light, in its shadows, in the aspects of matter and in the facts of life, what of each is fundamental, what is enduring and essential — their one illuminating and convincing quality — the very truth of their existence. The artist then, like the thinker or the scientist, seeks the truth and makes his appeal.[2]

Leaders, who orient themselves to power and action, are usually indifferent to the notions of psychic truth; instead, they care about practicality and feasibility. As we have suggested, this orientation is not simply a development based on trial and error and on the discovery of the paths that lead to rewards. It is a consequence of defense. For the truth, in Conrad's terms, can be sought only on the edges of depression, the potential for helplessness that must be acknowledged in the process of arriving at the understanding of goals and the manner of their pursuit. Depression is too painful for most people to endure, so they involve themselves in activity and, occasionally, in a preparanoid search for antagonists, danger, and obstacles that reality seems to be erecting for them to overcome. The consequence is insensitivity and lack of awareness, which diminish the capacity to perceive and communicate.

The recent popularity of sensitivity-training and encounter groups undoubtedly is an outgrowth of the dissatisfactions executives feel with themselves and their lack of fulfillment, resulting from their emotional isolation. What is wrong with sensitivity training is that it completely disregards the need to understand the origins and pressures of unconscious motivation. Also, it knows no theory of depression and uses one form of manic activity ("groupiness") for another. The group activity becomes ritualistic and sadistic as the members try to wrench emotional responses from one another.

Irving Kristol, writing in *Fortune,* addressed himself to the emotional isolation of leaders by contrasting the elitism of writers, who live at the extremes of emotional awareness, and the middle-class orientation to "decencies and amenities," which is the way of getting along by going along.

A vision of middle-class life as a kind of waking nightmare has been expressed by many of our most talented writers for close to two centuries now. Art has little use of humdrum decencies and amenities. Itself an inherently aristocratic enterprise — all artists see themselves as members of an elite, stretching back over the centuries — art is directed toward celebrating the extremes of human existence and is bored with the middling affairs of men. High nobility and low degradation, religious self-abnegation and diabolical self-aggrandizement, all the ways in which human beings transcend the ordinary and the average — this tends to be the stuff of art, and especially of literature. And since bourgeois society was the first in all history to establish the unexceptional man as its ideal human type, to scorn transcendence of the all too human in favor of a comfortable and widely shared tranquility, the artist has always been contemptuous of this society.[3]

Note the significance of what Kristol says: the artist will endure all kinds of emotional suffering, particularly depression, to transcend the ordinary and to evade the boredom that often accompanies such practical affairs as leading an organization. The justification of the artist, if he needs it, is that "Art induces greater sympathies (but also sterner judgments) than most of us are capable of in the daily conduct of our lives; it compels us to live less indifferently, and frees us from the irrelevant."[4]

To live less indifferently and to be free of the irrelevant implies a quality of self-esteem that is antithetical to conventional leadership and organization. Command today is a study in the psychology of coalitions and the conservation of power. The era of the narcissistic leader who loves no one but himself is obsolescent, reserved only for the severely disturbed or the rare charismatic figure. Yet by relinquishing his narcissism in the interest of power, the leader accepts emotional isolation and detachment from his fantasy world. Like the captain of a ship, he "[sails] over the surface of the oceans as some men go skimming over the years of existence to sink gently into a placid grave, ignorant of life to the last, without ever having been made to see all it may contain of perfidy, violence, and of terror. There are on sea and land such men thus fortunate — or thus disdained by destiny or by the sea."[5]

Men generally eschew the unknowns of emotional experience. Rather than suffer the effects of unforeseen response, people, in the course of development, adopt structures of isolation that wall off the interior regions of the psyche.

Comparing institutional leaders with artists should not be taken too strictly. One must not contaminate the pragmatism of one with the volatility of the other. But it is sometimes instructive to make such bizarre comparisons in order to reveal the ways in which individuals seek balance in self-organization through their vocations.

A. Alvarez was a friend of Sylvia Plath's; he was, perhaps, one of the last people to see the troubled poet alive. He devoted the first section of his book, *The Savage God: A Study of Suicide,* to a chronicle of the changes in Sylvia Plath that saw her become increasingly assertive and creative in her work as she moved steadily toward self-destruction. Sylvia Plath called Alvarez on Christmas Eve and asked him to come to her flat for a meal and listen to her read some of her current work. Alvarez agreed to come, but only for a drink; he had a prior engagement for dinner. As he listened to her poetry, he had a sense that all was finished, that "she was beyond the reach of anyone."

> I remember arguing inanely about the phrase "The nude/ Verdigris of the Condor." I said it was exaggerated, morbid. On the contrary, she replied, that was exactly how a condor's legs looked. She was right, of course. I was only trying, in a futile way, to reduce the tension and take her mind momentarily off her private horror — as though that could be done by argument and literary criticism! She must have felt I was stupid and insensitive. Which I was. But to have been otherwise would have meant accepting responsibilities I didn't want and couldn't, in my own depression, have coped with. When I left about eight o'clock to go on to my dinner party, I knew I had let her down in some final and unforgivable way. And I knew she knew. I never again saw her alive.[6]

The responsibility Alvarez feared was his own acceptance of Sylvia Plath's primitive fantasies to the point where he would be drawn into the experience, if only through her, of becoming aware of his own rage and depression. The type of sensitivity Alvarez had available, an artist's sensitivity, would become a tuning fork, which vibrates in response to the sound waves emanating from another source. Alvarez could not endure the resonance in him of Sylvia Plath's mania and depression. He had to leave her to drown in the well of her own love and hate.

Curiously, a less sensitive and less aware human being could, perhaps for a time, have stayed with her with only a moderate strain on his psyche. Over time, the strain would undoubtedly have made itself felt. But, for a while at least, a less sensitive man could have taken responsibility for her, although it would have been a kind of conventional responsibility, which differs from the emotional responsibility implied in Alvarez' understanding of a desperate person's needs.

Conventional responsibility means the adoption of fidelity to a role in the traditions of an institution. The role and the role-taker become detached, and the performance, therefore, impersonal. For those who respond and reciprocate through other roles, the performance must also be impersonal, to permit a low-key involvement and to isolate and subdue the feeling of attachment between leader and follower. When responsibility cannot be contained in reciprocal role relations, when emotions begin to stir and resonate, organizations are under considerable pressure to avoid the regressions and panic that follow the dissolution of collective defenses. Role relations support ego defenses, but only when organizations protect the self-esteem of their members. For economic organizations, self-esteem depends on reward and career satisfaction. But even in those cases where satisfactions are plentiful, the impersonality of role relations can eventually undermine the mutual support of individual and organization. Support may also fail when substantial numbers of members find themselves outside the mainstream of power and of belonging in work. Blue-collar workers, nonprofessionals, and even professionals in careers other than management often experience painful isolation. They do not necessarily gain the protection of self-esteem, and, in time, the satisfactions of economic security and intrinsic job rewards fail to sustain the motivation to work. The result is subtle sabotage and seething anger at authority.

The problem of leadership is that socialization, the institutional method of selecting and training leaders, perpetuates the isolated self. The former richness in the culture of institutions that provided material for deepening personal experience has been depleted in the programming of power. The conscious aim is to achieve goals; the implicit purpose is the conservation of power. The only protection for self-esteem under circumstances where the judgment of competence is so vague and obscure is detachment and depersonalization. If leaders in the new corporate culture succeed or fail, the end may be ascribed to a game in which one's fortune in acquiring, using, and even losing power can be considered apart from one's self-image. Without this detachment, which is defensive and not objective, the individual is too susceptible to injury and to the risk of depression, the condition he has learned to avoid through the cultivation of an optimistic front.

If power corrupts, it does so mainly by exaggerating a mental set whose origins in childhood predate the sophistications of corporate life. The corporate mind begins in a human situation where needs, while elementary, are imperative to growth. The part of oneself that remains behind, searching for a way to restore an idealized state, is the antagonist of that other part of the self, which bravely faces power contentions, acting as though it were the true representation of the individual. If kings are to become philosophers, perhaps they can do so by rediscovering childhood and the pleasures of intuition.

Notes & Index

Notes

Chapter 1

1. Emmet John Hughes, *Ordeal of Power* (New York: Dell Publishing Co., 1964) , p. 39.
2. *Ibid.,* pp. 40–41.
3. Barry Goldwater, Interview with Dan Rather, CBS News, June 19, 1973.

Chapter 2

1. Niccolò Machiavelli, *The Prince,* trans. Luigi Ricci, introd. Christian Gauss (New York: The American Library, 1952) , p. 84.
2. George Homans, "Bringing Man Back In," *Administrative Sociological Review,* vol. 29, no. 6, December 1964.
3. Max Weber, *The Theory of Social and Economic Organization,* ed. T. Parsons, trans. A. M. Henderson and T. Parsons (New York: Oxford University Press, 1947) .
4. Sigmund Freud, "Group Psychology and the Analysis of the Ego," *Standard Edition of the Complete Psychological Works,* vol. 28, James Strachey, ed. (London: Hogarth, 1962) .
5. Philip Selznick, *T.V.A. and the Grass Roots* (Berkeley and Los Angeles: University of California Press, 1949) .
6. *New York Times,* June 12, 1973.
7. M. Crozier, *The Bureaucratic Phenomenon* (Chicago: University of Chicago Press, 1964) .
8. Herbert A. Simon, *Administrative Behavior* (New York: The Free Press, 1965) .
9. Chester Barnard, *The Functions of the Executive* (Cambridge: Harvard University Press, 1948) .
10. Richard E. Neustadt, *Presidential Power: The Politics of Leadership* (New York: John Wiley and Sons, 1964) .

11. *Ibid.*, p. 6, italics ours.

12. *Ibid.*, p. 179.

13. *Ibid.*, pp. 165–166.

14. *Ibid.*, pp. 158–159.

15. R. A. Dahl, "The Concept of Power," *Behavioral Science,* vol. II, no. 3, July 1957.

16. *Ibid.*, p. 203.

17. A. M. Schlesinger, Jr., *The Age of Roosevelt,* vol. 2, *The Coming of the New Deal* (Boston: Houghton Mifflin Co., 1959), pp. 522–523. Quoted in Neustadt, *op. cit.*, p. 156.

18. Alexander L. and Juliette L. George, *Woodrow Wilson and Colonel House: A Personality Study* (New York: Dover Publications, 1964).

19. Perrin Stryker, *The Character of the Executive* (New York: Harper and Row, 1961).

20. Abraham Zaleznik, "Managerial Behavior and Interpersonal Competence," *Behavioral Science,* II, 1964, pp. 156–166.

21. D. Moment and A. Zaleznik, *Role Development and Interpersonal Competence* (Boston: Harvard University, Graduate School of Business Administration, Division of Research, 1963).

22. Neustadt, *op. cit.*, p. 165.

23. Schlesinger, *op. cit.*, p. 528. Quoted in Neustadt, *op. cit.*, p. 157.

24. Neustadt, *op. cit.*, p. 161.

25. R. C. Hodgson, D. J. Levinson, A. Zaleznik, *The Executive Role Constellation: An Analysis of Personality and Role Relations in Management* (Boston: Harvard University, Graduate School of Business Administration, Division of Research, 1965).

Chapter 3

1. Plato, *The Laws,* trans. Trevor G. Saunders (Harmondsworth: Penguin Books, 1970), p. 732.

2. *Ibid.*, p. 732.

3. Rollo May, *Power and Innocence* (New York: W. W. Norton and Company, 1972), p. 265.

4. Albert Camus, *Caligula and Three Other Plays,* trans. Stuart Gilbert (New York: Vintage Books, 1958), p. 72.

5. David Rapaport, "On the Psychoanalytic Theory of Motivation," *Nebraska Symposium of Motivation,* 1960, ed. Marshall R. Jones (Lincoln, Nebraska: University of Nebraska Press, 1960), particularly pp. 187–188.

6. William MacDougall, *Outline of Psychology* (New York: Charles Scribner's Sons, 1923), pp. 157–158.

7. Henry Murray, *Explorations in Personality* (Oxford: Oxford University Press, 1938).

8. David C. McClelland, *Studies in Motivation* (New York: Appleton-Century-Crofts, 1955).

9. Alfred Adler, *Superiority and Social Interest,* ed. Heinz and Rowena Ansbacher (New York: The Viking Press, 1973), p. 54.

10. William Shakespeare, Richard III (Boston: Houghton Mifflin Co., 1974), vol. I, pp. 712–713.

11. Alexander L. and Juliette L. George, *Woodrow Wilson and Colonel House: A Personality Study* (New York: Dover Publications, Inc., 1964), p. 320.

12. Surprisingly enough, in contrast to many subsequent studies this early psychohistorical study does not make a very reductionistic impression; many issues associated with character development are discussed in great detail. And if we consider the time pressure under which this book was written and the realism of the given prognosis — how Adolf Hitler would end — this study becomes an even more remarkable achievement. See Walter Langer, *The Mind of Adolf Hitler* (New York: Basic Books, 1972).

13. Plato, *The Republic,* trans. H. D. P. Lee (Harmondsworth: Penguin Books, 1972), pp. 354–355.

14. Thomas Hobbes, *Leviathan,* ed. C. B. MacPherson (Harmondsworth: Penguin Books, 1972), p. 161.

15. See Gordon W. Allport, Gardner Lindzey, *Assessment of Human Motives* (New York: Holt, Rinehart, and Winston, 1964).

16. Eduard Spranger, *Lebensformen* (Halle: Verlag Von Max Niemeyer, 1924), Chapter 5.

17. Harold Lasswell, *Psychopathology and Politics* (New York: The Viking Press, 1960).

18. *Ibid.,* p. 300.

19. Abraham Zaleznik, Gene W. Dalton, Louis B. Barnes, Pierre Laurin, *Orientation and Conflict in Career.* (Boston: Harvard University Graduate School of Business Administration, Division of Research, 1970).

20. See, for example, Louis Auchincloss, *The Rector of Justin* (Boston: Houghton Mifflin Co., 1964).

Chapter 4

1. Arthur Schopenhauer, *Essays and Aphorisms,* trans. R. J. Hollingsdale (Harmondsworth: Penguin Books, 1970), p. 176.

2. Sigmund Freud, *The Origins of Psychoanalysis: Letters to Wilhelm Fliess, Drafts and Notes, 1887–1902,* eds. Marie Bonaparte, Anna Freud, Ernst Kris (New York: Basic Books, 1954), pp. 216–217.

3. *Ibid.,* pp. 223–224.

4. Sigmund Freud, "Analysis of a Phobia in a Five-Year-Old Boy," *The*

Standard Edition of the Complete Psychological Works of Sigmund Freud, vol. 10, James Strachey, ed. (London: The Hogarth Press, 1955). All future references to Freud's works will be designated *Standard Edition.*

5. See T. W. Adorno, Else Frenkel-Brunswik, Daniel J. Levinson, R. Nevitt Sanford, *The Authoritarian Personality* (New York: W. W. Norton Co., 1969).
6. See Otto Friedrich, *Decline and Fall* (New York: Harper and Row, 1970).
7. Franz Kafka, *Letter to his Father* (New York: Schocken Books, 1971), p. 17.
8. Erik H. Erikson, *Gandhi's Truth: On the Origins of Militant Nonviolence* (New York: W. W. Norton and Co., 1966), p. 253.
9. *The Collected Works of Mahatma Gandhi* (Delhi: Government of India, Ministry of Information and Broadcasting, The Publication Division, 1956), pp. 209–210, quoted in Erikson, *Gandhi's Truth.*
10. William Manchester, *The Arms of Krupp* (New York: Bantam Books, 1970).
11. *Ibid.,* p. 172.
12. *Ibid.,* p. 170.
13. *Ibid.,* p. 550.
14. *Ibid.,* p. 546.

Chapter 5

1. Sören Kierkegaard, "Either/Or: A Fragment of Life," *A Kierkegaard Anthology,* ed. Robert Bretall (New York: Modern Library, 1946), p. 99.
2. See Sigmund Freud, "On Narcissism," *The Standard Edition,* vol. 14, and "Group Psychology and the Analysis of the Ego," *The Standard Edition,* vol. 18.
3. Erik H. Erikson, "Identity and the Life Cycle: Selected Papers," *Psychological Issues,* vol. 1 (New York: International University Press, 1959).
4. Heinz Kohut, *The Analysis of the Self,* Monograph Series of the Psychoanalytic Study of the Child (New York: International Universities Press, 1971).
5. Arnold A. Rogow, *James Forrestal: A Study of Personality, Politics and Policy* (New York: Macmillan Co., 1963), p. 17.
6. An excellent study of suicide is done by A. Alvarez, *The Savage God* (New York: Bantam Books, 1972).
7. Erik H. Erikson, *Young Man Luther* (New York: W. W. Norton and Co., 1962), p. 37.

8. Dwight David Eisenhower, *At Ease: Stories I Tell to Friends* (Garden City: Doubleday & Co., Inc., 1967).

9. Sigmund Freud, "The Case of Schreber," *Standard Edition,* vol. 12.

10. *Ibid.,* p. 71.

11. Anne Jardim, *The First Henry Ford: A Study in Personality and Business Leadership* (Cambridge: The M.I.T. Press, 1970).

12. See Arnold H. Modell, *Object Love and Reality* (New York: International Universities Press, 1968).

13. For an excellent analysis of transitional objects see D. W. Winnicott, *Playing and Reality* (New York: Basic Books, 1971).

14. See Edward Glover, *On the Early Development of the Mind,* Selected Papers on Psychoanalysis, vol. I (New York: International Universities Press, 1951), particularly Chapters 12 and 13.

15. Sigmund Freud, "Beyond the Pleasure Principle," *The Standard Edition,* vol. 18, pp. 14–17.

16. Abraham Zaleznik, C. Roland Christensen, Fritz J. Roethlisberger, *The Motivation, Productivity and Satisfaction of Workers: A Prediction Study* (Boston: Division of Research, Harvard Business School, 1958).

17. For background material about James Hoffa see Ralph James and Estelle James, *Hoffa and the Teamsters: A Study of Union Power* (Princeton: D. Van Nostrand and Co. Inc., 1965); or Clark Mollenhoff, *Tentacles of Power: The Story of Jimmy Hoffa* (New York: The World Publishing Co., 1965).

18. Kohut, *op. cit.,* p. 106.

19. See Ladislas Farago, *Patton: Ordeal and Triumph* (New York: Dell Publishing Co., 1970).

20. Boston *Globe,* February 19, 1973.

Chapter 6

1. Jean-Jacques Rousseau, *The Social Contract and Discourse on the Origin and Foundation of Inequality Among Mankind,* ed. Lester G. Crocker (New York: Washington Square Press, 1967), p. 231.

2. Abraham Zaleznik, "The Management of Disappointment," *Harvard Business Review,* November–December 1967.

3. *Fortune,* October 1966, "The Rocky Road to the Marketplace."

4. *Wall Street Journal,* September 17, 1969.

5. Gene Dalton, Louis B. Barnes, Abraham Zaleznik, *The Distribution of Authority in Formal Organizations* (Boston: Division of Research, Harvard Business School, 1968).

6. *Wall Street Journal, loc. cit.*

7. Norman Podhoretz, *Making It* (New York: Random House, 1968). pp. 58–61.

8. *Fortune,* February 1968.

9. "What Did Happen at Wards?" *Fortune,* May 1956.

10. Abraham Zaleznik, *Worker Satisfaction and Development* (Boston: Division of Research, Harvard Business School, 1956).
Abraham Zaleznik, C. Roland Christensen, Fritz J. Roethlisberger, *The Motivation, Productivity and Satisfaction of Workers: A Prediction Study* (Boston: Division of Research, Harvard Business School, 1958).

11. William T. Harry, *Huey P. Long* (Oxford: Oxford University Press, 1967).

12. Sudhir Kakar, *Frederick Winslow Taylor: A Study in Personality and Innovation* (Cambridge: The M.I.T. Press, 1970).

13. Anne Jardim, *The First Henry Ford: A Study in Personality and Business Leadership* (Cambridge: The M.I.T. Press, 1970).

Chapter 7

1. Albert Camus, *The Rebel* (New York: Vintage Books, 1957), p. 11.

2. Merle Miller, *Plain Speaking: An Oral Biography of Harry S. Truman* (New York: Berkley Publishing Corporation and G. P. Putnam's Sons, 1973), pp. 305–306.

3. Dean Acheson, *Present at the Creation: My Years in the State Department* (New York: W. W. Norton and Co., 1969), pp. 512–528.

4. Jeb Stuart Magruder, *An American Life: One Man's Road to Watergate* (New York: Atheneum Publishers, 1974).

5. Jaroslav Hašek, *The Good Soldier Švejk,* trans. Cecil Parrott (New York: Thomas Y. Crowell Co., 1973).

6. Aeschylus, *Prometheus Bound,* trans. Philip Vellacott (Harmondsworth: Penguin Books, 1961), p. 26.

7. See Abraham Zaleznik, *Worker Satisfaction and Development* (Boston: Division of Research, Harvard Business School, 1956).

8. Sophocles, *Antigone,* trans. Dudley Fitts and Robert Fitzgerald, *The Oedipus Cycle* (New York: Harcourt, Brace & World, 1939), p. 194.

9. See the study by Sudhir Kakar, *Frederick Taylor: A Study in Personality and Innovation* (Cambridge: The M.I.T. Press, 1970).

10. Feodor Dostoevski, *Crime and Punishment* (Baltimore: Penguin Books, 1951).

11. Arthur Miller, *Death of a Salesman* (New York: The Viking Press, 1958).

12. Abraham Zaleznik, Gene Dalton, Louis B. Barnes, *Orientation and Conflict in Career* (Boston: Division of Research, Harvard Business School, 1968).

13. For an interesting approach to human development, see Erik H. Erikson, "Identity and the Life Cycle: Selected Papers," *Psychological*

Issues, vol. 1 (New York: International Universities Press, 1959). In this monograph, he describes the life cycle as a series of eight overlapping stages.

Chapter 8

1. Johann von Goethe, *Faust,* part 1, trans. Philip Wayne (Harmondsworth: Penguin Books, 1949), p. 41.
2. *New York Times,* August 10, 1974.
3. *Ibid.*
4. Arthur Miller, *Death of a Salesman* (New York: Viking Press, 1958), p. 132
5. See Neil Sheehan, *The Arnheiter Affair* (New York: Random House, 1971).
6. *Ibid.,* p. 58.
7. Arthur F. Valenstein, M.D., "On Attachment to Painful Feelings and the Negative Therapeutic Reaction," *The Psychoanalytic Study of the Child,* vol. 28/1973.
8. Joseph Frazier Wall, *Andrew Carnegie* (New York: Oxford University Press, 1970), p. 83.
9. *Ibid.,* p. 577.
10. *Ibid.,* pp. 236–237.
11. Erik H. Erikson, "The Problem of Ego Identity," *Psychological Issues,* vol. 1, no. 1, p. 103.
12. This part of the chapter is influenced by Robert Armstrong, "Joseph Conrad: The Conflict of Command," *The Psychoanalytic Study of the Child,* vol. 26 (New York: Quadrangle Books, 1972), and the discussion paper presented as a reply to Armstrong's article by the main author (Zaleznik) to the Joint Meeting of the Western New England Psychoanalytic Society and the Boston Psychoanalytic Society at New Haven, October 23, 1971. See also Bernard C. Meyer, *Joseph Conrad: A Psychoanalytic Biography* (Princeton: Princeton University Press, 1967).
13. *Ibid.,* Meyer, p. 53.
14. Dwight D. Eisenhower, *At Ease: Stories I Tell to Friends* (New York: Doubleday & Co., Inc., 1967), p. 70.
15. *Ibid.,* p. 95.
16. *Ibid.,* p. 70.
17. *Ibid.,* p. 102.
18. *Ibid.,* p. 104.
19. *Ibid.,* p. 8.
20. *Ibid.* p. 16, italics ours.
21. Morris Janowitz, *The Professional Soldier* (New York: The Free Press, 1960), p. 127.

22. Eisenhower, *op. cit.,* p. 136.

23. *Ibid.,* p. 187.

24. *Ibid.,* p. 199.

25. *Ibid.,* p. 240.

26. Earl Mazo and Stephen Hess, *Nixon, A Political Portrait* (New York: Harper and Row, 1967). Additional sources are Richard Nixon, *Six Crises* (New York: Doubleday & Co., Inc., 1968), Garry Wills, *Nixon Agonistes* (Boston: Houghton Mifflin Co., 1969), Jules Witcover, *The Resurrection of Richard Nixon* (New York: G. P. Putnam's Sons, 1970), Bruce Mazlish, *In Search of Nixon: A Psychohistorical Inquiry* (New York: Basic Books, 1972).

27. Mazo and Hess, *op. cit.,* p. 21.

28. *Ibid.,* p. 21.

29. *Ibid.,* p. 22.

30. Milton Viorst, "Nixon and the OPA," *New York Times Magazine,* October 3, 1971, p. 70.

31. *Ibid.,* p. 72.

32. *Ibid.,* p. 74.

33. Mazo and Hess, *op. cit.,* p. 32.

34. *Ibid.,* p. 32.

35. Viorst, *op. cit.,* p. 76.

36. Wills, *op. cit.,* p. 78.

37. *Ibid.,* p. 87.

38. Emmet John Hughes, *The Ordeal of Power* (New York: Dell Publishing Company, 1964), pp. 276–277.

Chapter 9

1. Friedrich Nietzsche, *Beyond Good and Evil,* trans. Walter Kaufmann (New York: Vintage Books, 1966), p. 220.

2. *Life,* May 12, 1957, p. 46b.

3. See "The Case of Charles Luckman," *Fortune,* April 1950, p. 81.

4. *Fortune,* February 1966, p. 188.

5. *Ibid.,* p. 152.

6. "Howard Hughes' Biggest Surprise," *Fortune,* July 1966, p. 119.

7. See Gregory Rochlin, *Griefs and Discontents* (Boston: Little, Brown and Co., 1965).

8. Arnold A. Rogow, *James Forrestal: A Study of Personality, Politics and Policy* (New York: Macmillan Co., 1963).

9. See, for example, Erik Erikson, *Young Man Luther* (New York: W. W. Norton and Co., 1962).

10. See John Stuart Mill, *Autobiography* (New York: The New American Library of World Literature, Inc., 1964), p. 107.

11. See Anne Jardim, *The First Henry Ford: A Study in Personality and*

Business Leadership (Cambridge: The M.I.T. Press, 1970). See also Allan Nevins and F. F. Hill, *Ford: The Times, the Man, and the Company; Ford: Expansion and Challenge; and Ford: Decline and Rebirth* vol. 1, 1954, vol. 2, 1957, vol. 3, 1963 (New York: Charles Scribner's Sons).

12. See Sigmund Freud, "Those Wrecked by Success," *The Standard Edition,* vol. 14, pp. 316–331.

13. See Helen H. Tartakoff, "The Normal Personality in Our Culture and the Nobel Prize Complex," *Psychoanalysis — A General Psychology, Essays in Honor of Heinz Hartman,* ed. R. M. Loewenstein, I. M. Newman, M. Schur, and A. J. Solnit (New York: International Universities Press, Inc., 1966).

14. Richard E. Neustadt, *Presidential Power: The Politics of Leadership* (New York: John Wiley and Sons, 1964), p. 22.

15. Douglas McGregor, *Leadership and Motivation* (Cambridge: The M.I.T. Press, 1966).

16. *Ibid.,* p. 67.

17. See Elizabeth R. Zetzel, "Depression and the Incapacity to Bear It," in *Drives, Affects, Behavior,* ed. Rudolph M. Loewenstein vol. 2 (New York: International Universities Press, Inc., 1965).

18. Harold Nicolson, *The Diaries of Harold Nicolson: The War Years, 1939–1945,* ed. Nigel Nicolson (New York: Atheneum Publishers, 1967).

Chapter 10

1. For a more complete analysis of entrepreneurship and the process of change, see Manfred F. R. Kets de Vries, "The Entrepreneur as Catalyst of Economic and Cultural Change," unpublished doctoral dissertation, Harvard University, Graduate School of Business Administration, 1970.

2. Joseph A. Schumpeter, *The Theory of Economic Development* (Cambridge: Harvard University Press, 1934).

3. John Kenneth Galbraith, *The New Industrial State* (Boston: Houghton Mifflin Co., 1967), pp. 88–89.

4. Everett E. Hagen, *On the Theory of Social Change* (Homewood, Ill.: The Dorsey Press, 1962), p. 210, italics his.

5. Max Weber, *The Protestant Ethic and the Spirit of Capitalism,* trans. Talcott Parsons (New York: Charles Scribner & Sons, 1958).

6. Yusif A. Sayigh, *Entrepreneurs of Lebanon* (Cambridge: Harvard University Press, 1962), pp. 69–70.

7. Johannes Hirschmeier, *The Origins of Entrepreneurship in Meiji Japan* (Cambridge: Harvard University Press, 1964), pp. 248–254.

8. Orvis F. Collins, David G. Moore, Darab B. Unwalla, *The Enterprising*

Man (East Lansing, Mich.: Bureau of Business and Economics Research, Graduate School of Business Administration, Michigan State University, 1964), p. 234.

9. Edward B. Roberts and Herbert A. Wainer, *Some Characteristics of Technical Entrepreneurs*, Research Program on the Management of Science and Technology, Massachusetts Institute of Technology, no. 195–66, May 1966; percentage calculated from Table 1, p. 7 of this study.

10. Collins *et al., op. cit.*, p. 239.

11. Mabel Newcomer, "The Little Businessman: A Study of Business Proprietors in Poughkeepsie, New York," *Business History Review*, vol. 35, no. 4, Winter 1961, p. 516.

12. Sayigh, *op. cit.*, p. 75.

13. Collins, *et al., op. cit.*, p. 237.

14. Sir Henry Deterding, *An International Oilman* (London and New York: Harper and Brothers, 1924), p. 21.

15. Paul Liebertz, Karl Benz, *Ein Pionier der Motorisierung*, 2ᵉ Aufl., (Stuttgart: Reclam Verlag, 1950), p. 17.

16. A. James Reichley, "How Jon Johnson Made It," *Fortune*, January 1968, p. 183.

17. Andrew Carnegie, *Autobiography of Andrew Carnegie* (Boston: Houghton Mifflin Co., 1920).

18. Stanley H. Brown, "The Frawley Phenomenon," *Fortune*, February 1966, p. 138.

19. Guy Jellinek Mercédès, *My Father, Mr. Mercédès*, trans. Ruth Hassell (London: G. T. Foulis and Co., 1966), pp. 15–16.

20. "Is Bill Lear taking off again?", *Fortune*, July 1965, p. 140.

21. Collins, *et al., op. cit.*, pp. 46–47, italics ours.

22. W. Lloyd Warner and James C. Abegglen, *Big Business Leaders in America* (New York: Harper and Brothers, 1955), p. 67, italics ours.

23. Deterding, *An International Oilman*, pp. 22–23.

24. Warner and Abegglen, *op. cit.*, pp. 76–77.

25. Carnegie, *op. cit.*, p. 30–31, italics ours.

26. Collins, et al., *op. cit.*, p. 67.

27. *Wall Street Journal*, September 11, 1969.

28. *Wall Street Journal*, January 16, 1968.

29. *Wall Street Journal*, December 11, 1969.

Chapter 11

1. Plato, *The Republic*, trans. Allan Bloom (New York: Basic Books Inc., 1968), p. 168.

2. David Riesman, *The Lonely Crowd* (New Haven: Yale University Press, 1950).

3. David E. Lilienthal, *The Journals of David E. Lilienthal* (New York: Harper and Row, 1964–71).

4. See, for example, the *Wall Street Journal,* February 28, 1973.

5. David Halberstam, *The Best and the Brightest* (New York: Random House, 1972), pp. 31–32.

6. Milton Viorst, *Hustlers and Heroes: An American Political Panorama* (New York: Simon and Schuster, 1971), p. 170.

7. Daniel Ellsberg, *Papers on the War* (New York: Simon and Schuster, 1972), p. 66n.

8. Alfred D. Chandler, Jr., and Stephen Salisbury, *Pierre S. du Pont and the Making of a Modern Corporation* (New York: Harper and Row, 1971).

9. Ernest Jones, *The Life and Work of Sigmund Freud,* vol. 1 (New York: Basic Books, 1953), p. 5.

10. See Erik H. Erikson, *Childhood and Society* (New York: W. W. Norton and Co., 1963), Chapter 9.

11. Richard Nixon, *Six Crises* (New York: Doubleday & Co., Inc., 1960).

12. Garry Wills, *Nixon Agonistes* (Boston: Houghton Mifflin Co., 1969), p. 141.

13. Paul W. Glad, *McKinley, Bryan and the People* (New York: J. B. Lippincott & Co.), 1964, p. 115.

14. Ellsberg, *op. cit.,* p. 169.

Chapter 12

1. Plato, *The Republic,* New York: Modern Library, p. 431.

2. Joseph Conrad, *The Condition of Art* in *The Portable Conrad* (New York: The Viking Press, 1947), p. 705.

3. Irving Kristol, "The Young Are Trying to Tell Us Something About Scarsdale," *Fortune,* August 1971, p. 174.

4. Albert Guérard, *Conrad, the Novelist* (Cambridge: Harvard University Press, 1958), p. 129.

5. Joseph Conrad, *Typhoon, The Portable Conrad* (New York: The Viking Press, 1947), p. 208.

6. A. Alvarez, *The Savage God: A Study of Suicide* (New York: Bantam Books, 1972), p. 31, italics ours.

Index

Abegglen, James C., 222
Abuses of power, solutions aimed at controlling, 4–5
Acheson, Dean, 194
Activity, versus reflection, in leadership, 257–58
Adams, Sherman, 28
Addictive behavior, 98
Adler, Alfred, 47, 49, 51
Adolescence, crisis of, 166–67
Aeschylus, *Prometheus Bound,* 153–55
Aggression and survival, 250–251
Alderson, William, 191–92
Allport, Vernon, Lindzey Study of Values, 55
Alvarez, A., 263–64
American Foreign Service Association, 105
American Psychiatric Association, 5
American Telephone and Telegraph Company, 244
Andersen, Hans Christian, 215
Anxiety, and problem of mastery, 97–102
Arnheiter, Marcus Aurelius, 172–74, 180
Artists, comparison of institutional leaders and, 261–62

Ash, Roy L., 235
Auchincloss, Louis, 58
Authority: distribution of, 12–20; of position and of leadership, 26. *See also* Leadership
Autocrats, 205, 206
Autonomous motive, power as, 51–54
Avery, Sewell, 132–33

Barnard, Chester, 26
Bennett, Harry, 92–93, 96
Benz, Karl, 221
Boise Cascade Corporation, 233–34
Bradley, Omar, 188
Bryan, William Jennings, 249
Budgeting, capital, and allocation procedures: and management control, 21–24; for research and development, 115
Bureaucratic approach, to power, 141

Calculation, as tool of minimum man, 240
Camus, Albert, 40, 144, 175
Carnegie, Andrew, 176–80, 221, 223
Carnegie, Tom, 178, 179
Carnegie Steel Company, 178–79

Castro, Fidel, 248

Character trait, power as, distinguishing "political man" from other types of men, 54–59

Charismatic leadership (maximum man), 126, 231, 234, 235–36, 237; as solution to conflicts created by power, 4; Weber on, 13–14; ties between earliest infancy and, 79–80; psychology of, 241–45; effect of superego on, 245–46; organizational dynamics of, 246–49; and innovation and flexibility, 249–50; mental illnesses common to, 250; and aggression and survival, 250–51; ethics of, 251–56. *See also* Consensus leadership

Chotiner, Murray, 194, 195

Chou En-lai, 235

Churchill, Winston, 201–2, 211, 242

CIA, 248

Citra-Frost Company, 192

Coalitions: and consensus leadership, to safeguard against grandiosity, 7–8; and collusions, symbolic meaning of, 117–24

Cohesion, of the self, primary modes for achieving, 88–90

Cole, Edward N., 116

Commitment, confusion of compliance with, 113–14

Comparisons, by individuals, 109–10

Compensatory motive, power as, 46–51

Compliance: confusion of commitment with, 113–14; approach to power, 141–42

Compulsive subordinacy, 157–61

Conflict, role of, in managing disappointment, 200–203

Connor, Fox, 89–90, 189, 195

Connor, John, 198–99

Conrad, Joseph, 182–84, 260–61

Consensus leadership (minimum man), 231, 232–235, 236–37; coalitions and, to safeguard against grandiosity, 7–8; psychology of, 237–41; effect of superego on, 245–46; organizational dynamics of, 247–48; and flexibility and innovation, 250; and aggression and survival, 251; ethics of, 251–56. *See also* Charismatic leadership

Constellations, executive, 36–38; types of, 38

Conversion approach, to power, 141

Cooperation, and competition, 23–24

Copernicus, Nicolaus, 244

Corcoran, Thomas, 236

Coughlin, Father, 142

Crozier, Michel, 16

Cuba, 248

Curtis, Cyrus, 72–73, 100

Dahl, Robert, 29

de Gaulle, Charles, 242–243, 246, 250, 253

Dependency, need for, 14–15

"Destiny neuroses," 174–75

Detachment, need for, in leaders, 264–65

Deterding, Sir Henry, 221, 222

Dickens, Charles, 107

Disappointment, 196–98; effect of, in evolution of a career, 198–200; role of conflict in managing, 200–203; and attachment of self, 203–7; use of self-scrutiny to prevent, 207–14

Dostoevski, Fëdor, *Crime and Punishment*, 162–63

Douglas, Helen Gahagan, 194

Du Pont, Alfred, 239
Du Pont, Coleman, 239
Du Pont, Pierre, 239, 241
Du Pont Corporation, 239

Eastman Kodak, 245
Ehrlichman, John, 235
Einstein, Albert, 244
Eisenhower, David, 186
Eisenhower, Dwight D., 105, 107; and Joseph McCarthy's attack on George Marshall, 1–3; presidential style and use of power of, 28–29, 36; and Fox Connor, 89–90; and George Patton, 104; his rise to power, 184–90, 194–95; Truman on anticipation of presidential problems of, 206
Eisenhower, Edgar, 187
Ellsberg, Daniel, 239, 252
Emerson, Ralph Waldo, 256
Entrepreneurs, 215–16; elusiveness of, 216–20; personalities of, 220–29
Entropy, concept of, 254
Erikson, Erik, 79–80, 89, 243
Estes, Billy Sol, 253
Ethics, of charismatic and consensus leaders, 251–256
Excision and exclusion, as primary mode for achieving cohesion of the self, 88, 90, 91
Executive action, 25–30; psycho-political approach to, 31–38
Exploitation, 103–4
Exxon, 244

Failure, fear of, and fear of success, 170–84
Farley, James, 236
Flexibility, innovation and, 249–50
Fliess, Wilhelm, 61, 62

Ford, Edsel, 92–93, 96
Ford, Henry, 120, 205, 233; and the Model T, 91, 96–97, 142; his relationships with son Edsel and Harry Bennett, 92–93, 96; his experience with disappointment, 203
Ford Motor Company, 92, 96–97, 117, 120, 205
Forester, C. S., 174
Form, preference for substance over, as executive approach to power, 139, 140–41
Forrestal, James, 86, 201, 202
Fortune magazine, 114, 198, 261
Frawley, Patrick J., Jr., 221
Freud, Sigmund, 5, 9; on charisma, 14, 242; and relation of power to sexuality, 40; seduction theory of, 60–61; and the Oedipus complex, 62–63, 65–66, 73; his study of helplessness and self-destruction, 90–91; on anxieties and attempts at mastery, 99; on masochistic behavior, 162
Frick, Henry Clay, 178, 179
Friedrich, Otto, 72

Galbraith, John Kenneth, 216
Gandhi, Mahatma, 79–80
General Electric, 254
General Motors, 7, 96, 116–17, 200, 254
George, Alexander and Juliette, their study of Woodrow Wilson, 30, 48–49
Glad, Paul W., 249
Goethe, Johann von, 168
Goldwater, Barry, 8, 191
Grandiosity, 6–7, 91; and self, 102–8
Gresham's law, 18
Grief and mourning, 90

Guilt: as consequence of fusion of sex with power, 50–51; role of, in compulsive subordinacy, 158

Hagen, Everett, 217
Halberstam, David, 238
Haldeman, H. R., 235
Hansberger, Robert B., 233
Harper, Marion, Jr., 128–29
Harvard Business School, 57
Hašek, Jaroslav, *The Good Soldier Švejk*, 146
Hazlett, Everett "Swede," 187
Head, Howard, 227–28
Head Ski Company, 227–28
Healing, of splits in the ego, as primary mode for achieving cohesion of the self, 88–90
Helplessness, omnipotence and, 86–91
Hilsman, Roger, 239
Hitler, Adolf, 49, 141, 237, 243, 246, 253
Hobbes, Thomas, 52
Hoffa, Jimmy, 101–2
Homans, George, 11–12
Homeostatic leadership strategy, 31, 32, 33, 37
Homestead strike, 178
Hopkins, Harry, 236
House, Edward (Colonel), 30
Houser, Theodore, 32–33
Hubris, 6–7
Hughes, Emmet John, 2, 194
Hughes, Howard, 199
Humility, as reaction to self-doubts, 3
Hunger, as example of bodily tension, 44–45

Iacocca, Lee, 120
IBM, 114
Ickes, Harold, 236

Identification, 87
Ideology, as solution to conflict between power and purpose, 4
Impulsive subordinacy, 153–57
Individual assertion, need for balance between collective control and, 39
Individuals, orientations of, within organizations, 34–35
Inferiority complex, and theory of power as compensatory motive, 47–51
Informal groups, formation of, to counteract effects of hierarchy, 16
Innovation and flexibility, 249–50
Institutions, vesting power in, as solution to problem of control, 4–5
Interpublic Group, 128
Introjection, 87
Iron-Clad Agreement, 177
Isolation, emotional, of leaders, 261–62, 264

Janowitz, Morris, 188
Johnson, Jon, 221
Johnson, Louis, 201
Johnson, Lyndon B., 105, 196, 198, 238
Justice, essential to distribution of authority, 12–13, 14

Kafka, Franz, 77–78
Kennedy, John F., 105, 170, 238–39, 248
Kierkegaard, Sören, 85
Kissinger, Henry, 235
Knudsen, Semon, 116–17, 120
Kristol, Irving, 261–62
Krupp, Alfred, 82, 83
Krupp, Bertha, 83
Krupp family, 81–83

Krupp von Bohlen und Hallbach, Gustav, 83
Kurosawa, Akira, 150

Land, Edwin, 233, 244–45
Langer, Walter, 49
Lansdale, Ed, 252
Lasswell, Harold, 56–57, 58
Leadership: strategies, three types of, 31–33, 37; style, 35, 232–36; relationship between personality and, 200–203; crisis in American, 230–31; and personality dynamics, 236–37; by minimum men, 237–41; by maximum men, 241–45; and personality structure, 245–46; and organizational dynamics, 246–49; and innovation and flexibility, 249–50; and aggression and survival, 250–51; ethics of charismatic, and consensus, 251–256. *See also* Charismatic leadership; Consensus leadership
Lear, Bill, 221
Legal authority, 13
Life, 72, 196–97
Lilienthal, David, 232
Lodge, Henry Cabot, 49, 252
Long, Huey, 141
Luce, Henry R., 72
Luckman, Charles, 198
Luther, Martin, 89

MacArthur, Douglas, 144–45, 146, 190
McCann-Erickson agency, 129
McCarthy, Joseph, 1
McClelland, David, 45–46
MacDougall, William, 45
McGregor, Douglas, 207–10
Machiavelli, Niccolò, 11, 12
Management control, 20–25
Manchester, William, 81–83

Mania and depression, 250, 260, 263
Manipulation, as tool of minimum man, 240
Mao Tse-tung, 235
Marshall, George C., 1
Martin, Joseph, 144
Masochistic behavior, 162–64; two faces of, 175
Mastery, anxiety and problem of, 97–102
Maximum man, *see* Charismatic leadership
May, Rollo, 39
Mediative leadership strategy, 31, 32, 33, 37
Mercédès, Emil Jellinek, 221
Merck & Company, 198
Merrifield, Wes, 186
Mill, John Stuart, 202–3
Miller, Arthur, *Death of a Salesman,* 165, 171
Minimum man, *see* Consensus leadership
Montgomery, Bernard, 104
Montgomery Ward, 132
Motive (s), 43–46; power as compensatory, 46–51; power as autonomous, 51–54
Murray, Henry, 45, 46, 57

Narcissism: relationship of power to, 85–86; progression from, to object love in development of human relationships, 94–95; control of, 184; presence of, in maximum man, 253; institutional, 254; and emotional isolation of leaders, 262
Nasser, Gamel Abdel, 105
Navy Information Office, 173
Needs: differentiation between primary and secondary, 45; studies of, 45–46

Neustadt, Richard, 27–29, 35–36
Newton, Sir Isaac, 244
Nicolson, Harold, 211–12
Nicolson, Nigel, 212
Nietzsche, Friedrich, 196
Nixon, Richard M., 8, 174; and Watergate, 101, 145; and notion of grandiose self, 105; reflections of, on his past, 168–69; his fear of success, 169–70; his rise to power, 184–85, 190–95; consensus leadership of, 234–35; role-playing by, 248; ethics of, 252

Objects, relation of self to, 91–97
Oceanic power, 76, 78–81
Oedipus complex: discovery of, 62–67; and the orientation to power, 67–73; human development prior to stage of, 73–78
Office of Price Administration (OPA), Nixon's employment at, 192–93
Office of Strategic Services (OSS), U.S., 49
Omnipotence and helplessness, 86–91
Organizational politics, critical episodes in, 124–25; patricide, 125–30; paranoid thinking, 131–33; ritualism, 133–38
Organization(s): as political structures, 109; pyramidal structure of, 110; power relations in, 111–17; structure, problem solving approach to, 142–43
Otago, The, 183

Paranoid thinking, in organizations, 131–33
Partial, contrasted with total, executive approaches to power, 139–41

Patricide, in organizations, 125–30
Patton, George S., Jr., 104–5, 188
Pearson, Drew, 104
Performance (or "profit" and "cost") centers, 21, 23, 24
Perkins, Milo, 236
Pershing, John J., 190,
Personality dynamics, 236–37; of minimum men, 237–41; of maximum men, 241–45
Personality and leadership style, importance of, as evidenced by Nixon and Watergate, 8–9
Personality structure, 246–47
Persuasion, 20
Plath, Sylvia, 263
Plato, 4, 39, 51–52, 230, 257
Podhoretz, Norman, 126–28
Polaroid Corporation, 244–45
Political behavior, relationship between oceanic power and, 79–80
Political man: interpretation of character of, 54–59; types of, 58
Politics, and the grandiose self, 106–8
Presidents, U.S., comparison of, in their exercise of power, 26–30
Proactive leadership strategy, 31–32, 33, 35, 37
Problem-solving approach to organization structure, 142–43
Protestant ethic, 100, 218
Psychoanalysis, 5; and hubris, 6; and subtle distinction between sickness and health, 9–10; and relation of power to sexuality, 40–42; and power as compensatory motive, 46–47; and power as autonomous motive, 53–54
Psychosis, and anxiety and problem of mastery, 98

Quezon, Manuel, 190

Rapaport, David, 44, 45
Rasputin, Grigori, 14
Rather, Dan, 8
Rationality: essential to distribution of authority, 12–13, 14, 16, 19; levels of, 18
Reality and fantasy, conflict between, 258–60
Regression, 74
Rewards and compensation, 24–25
Ridgeway, Matthew B., 144
Riesman, David, 231
Ringisei, Japanese system of, 233
Ritualism, in organizations, 133–38
Rockwell, Norman, 72
Rogow, Arnold, 86
Role-playing, 34, 37, 38, 55, 247–48
Roosevelt, Franklin D., 105, 107; presidential style and use of power of, 28–30, 35–36; his handling of disappointment, 202; viewed as maximum man, 242; administrations of Nixon and, compared, 235–36
Roosevelt, James, 242
Roosevelt, Theodore, 169
Rosenwald, Julius, 32, 33
Roth, Philip, *Portnoy's Complaint,* 98
Rousseau, Jean Jacques, 109
Rusk, Dean, 238–39, 241

Sadistic power, 76, 77, 78, 81–84
Saturday Evening Post, decline and fall of, 72–73, 99–100
Satyagraha, 79
Scanlon Plan, 141
Scapegoats, use of, to draw controversy away from chief executives, 6
Schlesinger, Arthur, 239
Schopenhauer, Arthur, 60

Schreber, Paul, 91
Schumpeter, Joseph, 216, 227
Scott, Thomas, 178, 180
Sears, Richard W., 31–32
Sears, Roebuck, 132; correlation between management succession and changes in corporate strategy in, 31–33
Self: primary modes for achieving cohesion of, 88–90; relation of, to objects, 91–97; grandiosity and, 102–8; heightened sense of, 203–7
Self-made men, 7, 107–8
Self-scrutiny, use of, to prevent disappointment, 207–14
Selznick, Philip, 15
Sex: as example of bodily tension, 44–45; consequence of fusion of, with power, 50–51
Sexual behavior, sadistic, 81, 82
Sexual fantasies, 61
Sexual perversion, anxiety as cause of, 98
Sexual seductions, Freud's theory of, 60–61
Sexuality, relation of power to, 40–42
Shakespeare, William, *Richard III,* 47–48, 50
Shaw, George Bernard, 181–82
Shultz, George Pratt, 235
Simon, Herbert, 21
Sloan, Alfred, 200
Smith, Adam, 217
Smith, Gerald L. K., 141
Socialization and the readiness to lead, 184–95
Sophocles: *Oedipus Rex,* 62–63; *Ajax,* 86–87
Spranger, Eduard, *Types of Men,* 55–56
Stevenson, Adlai, 194
Stryker, Perrin, 31

Style, defined, 27

Subordinacy, 144–52; and dominance and submission, 152; and activity and passivity, 152–53; impulsive, 153–57; compulsive, 157–61; and masochistic behavior, 162–64; and withdrawal, 164–67

Substance, over form, preference for, as executive approach to power, 39, 140–41

Success, fear of, and fear of failure, 170–84, 203

Suicide, 88, 90

Superego, effect of, on minimum and maximum man, 245–46

Superordinacy, 168–70; and fear of success and fear of failure, 170–84; and Nixon's rise to power, 184–85, 190–95; and Eisenhower's rise to power, 184–90, 194–95

Survival, aggression and, 250–51

Taylor, Frederick Winslow, 142, 160–61

Taylor-Rostow mission, 238

Teamsters, International Brotherhood of, 101–2

Tennessee Valley Authority (TVA), 15, 232

Thang, Nguyen Duc, 252

Thematic Apperception Test, 57

Tillinghast, Charles, 199

Total, contrasted with partial, executive approaches to power, 139–42

Traditional authority, 13

Trans World Airlines, 199

Truman, Harry S., 105, 107, 146, 181; his firing of General MacArthur, 144–45; and James Forrestal, 201; his insight into disappointment, 205–6

Trust, extended to leaders, 5

Tuchman, Barbara, 105

Tugwell, Rexford Guy, 236

U. S. Gypsum Company, 132

Vance, 172–74

Viorst, Milton, 192, 193

Voorhis, Jerry, 194

Wall Street Journal, 120

Warner, W. Lloyd, 222

Watergate, 8, 101, 145, 230–31

Weber, Max, 13, 218

Westinghouse, 254

Wills, Garry, 194, 248

Wilson, Charles, 254

Wilson, Woodrow, 30, 36, 48–49

Withdrawal, 164–67

Wood, Robert E., 32, 33

Wouk, Herman, The Caine Mutiny, 172